The Snowflake Man
A Biography of Wilson A. Bentley

by

Duncan C. Blanchard

The McDonald & Woodward Publishing Company

Granville, Ohio

The McDonald & Woodward Publishing Company
Granville, Ohio

The Snowflake Man
A Biography of Wilson A. Bentley

20 19 18 17 16 15 14 13 12
10 9 8 7 6

Library of Congress Cataloging-in-Publication Data

Blanchard, Duncan C.
    The snowflake man: a biography of Wilson A. Bentley / by Duncan
C. Blanchard.
        p. cm.
    Includes bibliographical references and index.
    ISBN 0-939923-71-8 (alk. paper)
    1. Bentley, W. A. (Wilson Alwyn), 1865–1931. 2. Snowflakes. 3.
Nature photography. 4. Meteorologists—United States—Biography.
5. Photographers—United States—Biography. I. Title.
QC858.B46B55   1998
551.5'092—dc21
[B]   98–6561
                                                                      CIP

Contents

To Julie,

with love and gratitude for always being there

Prologue

Almost everyone has heard that no two snowflakes are alike. I don't remember when I first heard this, but it was a long time ago. Miss Parsons may have told me. In the 1930s, she was the teacher at the one-room schoolhouse in the small farming community of New Lenox in the Berkshire Hills of western Massachusetts, where about fifteen children were scattered among six grades. We children loved the snow. During stories told by Miss Parsons, she probably said that every snowflake is unique.

Miss Parsons may not have known that Wilson Bentley, a farmer from Jericho, Vermont, was the first to photograph and to popularize the uniqueness of each snowflake. He did this in his first published article in 1898 and continued to extoll the rare beauty and loveliness of each snowflake in numerous articles and lectures until his death in 1931. I first heard of Bentley about 1948 when, as a young and very inexperienced scientist, I was working at the Research Laboratory of the General Electric Company in Schenectady, New York. I was the newest member of a small team of scientists excitedly exploring new ideas made possible by the recent discoveries of cloud seeding by silver iodide particles and dry ice.

Curiously, my introduction to Bentley was not through his classic work with the snowflakes. Though we had projects to measure the sizes and types of snowflakes, we were equally interested in understanding how rain formed in clouds, and that meant trying to measure the sizes of raindrops, a project I was working on. One day Vincent Schaefer, a senior scientist and the discoverer of dry-ice cloud seeding, came by my desk, gave me an article, and said, "Dunc, I think you'll find this of interest." It had been published in 1904 by Wilson Bentley on how to measure raindrop size and on his ideas of how rain formed in clouds. Yes, I was interested but didn't yet know enough about the science of rain formation to realize how startlingly original Bentley's work was.

Nearly twenty years later, as an atmospheric scientist at the Woods Hole Oceanographic Institution on Cape Cod, Massachusetts, and very familiar with the frontiers of research on rain formation, I knew that Bentley was an American pioneer in the science now known as cloud physics, and that his work was about forty years ahead of its time. I also had seen and was enthralled by the exquisite beauty of the thousands of photographs in his great book *Snow Crystals*, his life's work published the year of his death. I had learned that by the 1920s, Bentley, at the height of his fame, was known to tens of thousands across the country simply as the Snowflake Man.

In 1967, Doubleday published my book *From Raindrops to Volcanoes*, an account of the scientific adventures my colleagues and I at Woods Hole shared over the years. Intended for a general audience, I wrote about the clouds over the rain forests of Hawaii, how the oceans influence the electrification of the atmosphere, and how the fury of volcanic eruptions in 1963 on the newly-formed island of Surtsey just south of Iceland was intensified when tons of seawater poured into the crater to crash into the hot upwelling lava in the throat of the volcano. Though I mentioned Bentley and his work with the raindrops and snowflakes only in the first chapter, I kept thinking about him during the next year or more while writing the rest of the book.

What sort of a man was this Bentley, who was so obsessed with the water wonders of the atmosphere — the raindrops, the dew, the clouds and the frost, but mostly the snow — that he spent a lifetime photographing snowflakes and talking about their haunting beauty to all who would listen? The week after giving the manuscript of my book to the publisher, I took several days vacation and drove up to Jericho, a small town in northern

Vermont snuggled up against the majestic Mount Mansfield, the Olympus of the Green Mountain range. I saw the state historical marker alongside the road in Jericho commemorating the genius of Bentley, the store on the village green in Jericho Center where Bentley bought his supplies, and on a remote dirt road winding through a small valley in eastern Jericho — the farmhouse where Bentley lived his entire life. But best of all I met the late Amy Bentley Hunt. During long animated, tape-recorded conversations, she told me about her Uncle Willie and life in Jericho during the early years of the century. When I left Jericho to return to Woods Hole, I was determined to write this biography.

But it would have to wait. Soon after *From Raindrops to Volcanoes* was published, I left Woods Hole to accept a position at the Atmospheric Sciences Research Center of the State University of New York at Albany. My research began to take new directions, and I became involved in teaching and in the supervision of graduate students. Research on the Bentley biography slowed to a crawl. I did, however, make several more trips to Jericho and other towns in Vermont over the next few years to record conversations about Bentley with nearly fifteen other people who knew him well. Becoming frustrated with not being able to find the time I knew would be needed for the extensive research preparatory to writing in detail about Bentley's life, I resorted to writing shorter articles about him.

I retired from the Atmospheric Sciences Research Center late in 1989, primarily to work nearly full-time on chasing down the ghost of Wilson Bentley. I obtained copies of his notebooks from the Buffalo Museum of Science, where they and all his photographic plates had been sent after his death. Though the best of his photographs had appeared in his book *Snow Crystals* in 1931, it has long been out of print. Fortunately, in 1962, Dover Publications reprinted it, and it is still in print today. The book is a classic still being used by the connoisseurs of the beautiful in nature. Hardly a Christmas season passes without my seeing a Bentley snow crystal on a Christmas card, and throughout the year my wife calls my attention to silver-plated Bentley crystals on necklaces and earrings in gift catalogs she receives.

After retirement I made more trips to Jericho, talked to more people, visited once again the old Bentley farmhouse, and slowly walked along the dirt road that passed by it. Standing on a bridge just down the road from the Bentley house, I saw what appeared to be an old swimming hole in Mill Brook just before it crossed the road to wind through a meadow behind what had been Bentley's barn. In my mind's eye I could see Bentley and his boyhood friends swimming there. It was an eerie yet comforting feeling, for as a young boy in New Lenox I, too, spent many a summer's day with my friends in a swimming hole in a brook that tumbled down the mountain to pass near our house. And my brook, like Bentley's, was named Mill Brook.

Putting together the pieces of the puzzle of the life and times of Wilson Bentley has been rewarding but difficult. The main difficulty by far has been the lack of his letters. I think I have unearthed all his published articles and have read them over and over again to find those little nuggets that reveal something about the inner man. But every biographer knows that it is our letters that reveal our true selves, our frustrations, our hopes, our dreams. It is not that Bentley didn't write letters. He did, by the hundreds, perhaps thousands. But all were burned a few months after his death by a member of his brother's family. When I asked this woman why she had burned them all indiscriminately, she said that "his personal letters were his business. I didn't think anyone had any right to read letters he got from his girlfriends ... so we burned them." *C'est la vie!* With help from various people, historical societies, and libraries, I have found over twenty letters to or from Bentley. All reveal touching aspects of his kind and gentle nature that did not always come through in his articles. Most of these letters have been woven into the fabric of this book.

Had Bentley lived long enough to read C. P. Snow's *The Two Cultures*, he would have wondered what the fuss was all about. To him, science and the humanities all blurred together into one grand tapestry of nature. For Bentley, the snow crystals were not just a cold sliver of ice to be scientifically analyzed. They were also a metaphor for all things beautiful on earth. He once wrote that "The snow crystals . . . come to us not only to reveal the wondrous beauty of the minute in Nature, but to teach us that all earthly beauty is transient and must soon fade away. But though the beauty of the snow is evanescent, like the beauties of the autumn, as of the evening sky, it fades but to come again."

Of all the reasons I had for writing this book, there is one that must be mentioned. While Bentley saw the snow crystals as a metaphor for beauty on earth, I saw Bentley himself as a metaphor for every person, be it ourselves or one of our neighbors down the street, who has been laughed at or ridiculed for wanting to pursue a new idea. Were it not for his mother, who recognized the sensitive artistic temperament in her youngest son and constantly encouraged him in his pursuit of the beautiful in nature, Bentley would never have accomplished what he did. His own father and brother until their dying days thought he was wasting his time "fussing with snowflakes," and for many years, until he became famous in the 1920s, most of his neighbors thought him "a little cracked."

Nothing worthwhile in life is ever accomplished unless one has the courage to pursue one's dreams in spite of daily frustrations and obstacles thrown in his or her path by others. Wilson Bentley is a shining example of one who had this courage.

Duncan C. Blanchard
Albany, NY

The Snowflake Man

Chapter 1

In The Beginning

Wilson Alwyn Bentley seldom strayed far from his hometown of Jericho, Vermont. He did not have to. The world eventually came to him to learn more about his love affair with the water wonders of the atmosphere. Bentley, more than any man before him or since, had a passionate desire to show the world the wondrous beauty in the endless variety of snow crystals that tumbled from the winter skies.

But he apparently had little passion to understand the origin of his Bentley ancestors in Vermont. At age fifty, in a brief family genealogy prepared for the *History of Jericho Vermont*, he went back no further than his grandfather, Shelly Bentley. He wrote that Shelly had come to Vermont from Wells, Connecticut. This is impossible. There is no town named Wells in Connecticut, but there is one in Vermont. Wilson apparently never questioned his grandfather about family origins. Had he done so, he would have found that his Bentley ancestors in Vermont go back two generations before Shelly, and that their story is full of the courage and hardship so typical of the early settlers of Vermont.[1]

William Bentley, five generations before Wilson, was born about 1680, possibly in Dorchester, Massachusetts. In 1703, he married Mary Eliot in Stonington, Connecticut. They settled down to raise a family, and in 1720, James, the sixth of nine children, was born in the nearby town of Lebanon. Years passed, and in the early 1770s, James, now married to a woman whom the records indicate only as Mary, was living in Salisbury, Connecticut. He and Mary had their own family, four boys and a girl. James was now over fifty, and his oldest son, Samuel, had a family of his own.

Meanwhile, up north in that forested and largely unexplored territory called Vermont, a state of nearly continuous turmoil had existed almost from 1609 when Samuel de Champlain, the first white man to gaze upon the verdant hills and mountains of Vermont, paddled with Algonquin Indians through the lake that now bears his name. In the century following Champlain's exploration, various claims were made by the French, English, and Dutch for having made the first settlement in Vermont. But many of these were not permanent. Most historians agree that the first permanent settlement was in 1724 in Brattleboro, in the southeastern corner of the territory on the Connecticut River, to protect the Massachusetts settlements from Indian raids.

In 1741, Benning Wentworth was appointed governor of New Hampshire by the King of England. He turned out to be an unscrupulous character who became rich by skimming off for his own pockets some of the money received from grants of land sold to settlers in the Vermont territory. The first of the New Hampshire grants was to establish the town of Bennington, far west of New Hampshire and nearly into the New York territory. Other grants followed, and settlers slowly moved into Vermont. But they were not to be there for long. During the French and Indian War, 1754-1760, the war between England and France, the Indian allies of the French made numerous raids into Vermont. The burning of the settlements and the scalping that followed soon drove most of the settlers back to where they had come from. They did not return until the French were finally defeated at Quebec and Montreal.

By the mid-1760s, charters to well over one hundred towns had been granted by New Hampshire. But the governor of New York claimed that New Hampshire had no right to the Vermont territory and that it really belonged to New York. He petitioned the King to stop Wentworth from making any more grants. The King sided with New York, declaring that New

Hampshire had no rights to any land west of the Connecticut River. New York now declared all of the Vermont territory as her own, and decreed that land owners who had received grants from Wentworth would now have to repurchase their land from New York. The settlers, caught in this political squabble between New York on their western flanks, and New Hampshire on the eastern, were not about to pay once again for land they were laboriously clearing for the planting of crops and the building of houses. Increasingly concerned about sheriffs' posses from New York that were ejecting settlers who refused to pay money to New York, a convention of towns at Bennington in 1770 decided that they would resist the demands of New York by whatever force necessary. A militia was formed. It came to be known as the Green Mountain Boys, a loosely-organized band of guerrilla fighters led by Ethan Allen.

Into this confusion over the governance of the Vermont territory came Samuel Bentley and his family. In 1773, he obtained a two-hundred-acre grant of land in Cornwall, about seventy-five miles north of Bennington and ten miles east of the lower part of Lake Champlain. Life must have been good for Samuel, for a year later his father, James, his brothers and sister, and many of his former neighbors in Salisbury made the trek north to join him. They were among the first settlers in Cornwall. Life, however, could not have been good for long. On April 19, 1775, the "shot heard 'round the world" at Lexington and the attack against the British Redcoats at the Concord bridge ushered in the American Revolution.

In May of 1777, James Bentley, now a Captain and quite possibly associated with the Green Mountain Boys, became actively involved in the war. A party of Tories who had openly declared allegiance to the British was spotted south of Cornwall, making its way north to join the British in Canada. Captain Bentley and several other men, including two of his sons, set out to capture the Tories. As Bentley's group made its way north, they recruited twenty-two other men from the towns through which it passed. Scouts informed Bentley that the Tories were camped in the woods outside Monkton, a town about twenty miles north of Cornwall. Late at night, when the Tories were asleep, Bentley and his men captured all thirteen of them without a shot being fired. A few days later, a special court decided that the prisoners should be taken to Fort Ticonderoga, which had been captured from the British by Ethan Allen and his Boys in May, 1775, in the first aggressive act of the war. Bentley and his men marched their captives to the fort, about a fifteen-mile trek from Cornwall. They delivered the prisoners barely a month before the fort was abandoned by the colonists in the face of General Burgoyne's massive British army of eight thousand men descending upon them from Canada. The British once again occupied Fort Ticonderoga in July, 1777.

Raids by the British into the upper regions of the Vermont territory now became more frequent, and the settlers were forced to abandon their homes. The record becomes hazy at this point, but it appears that the women and children moved to towns farther south in Vermont or perhaps returned to their home towns in Connecticut. Many of the men, however, stayed behind to join the Green Mountain Boys in keeping track of British troop movements. By 1781, when the Revolutionary War came to an end, Vermont had declared itself the Independent State of Vermont, but in 1791 adopted the Constitution and became the first state after the war to be admitted to the Union.

Just prior to and for a few years after the end of the war, the Bentleys and other settlers made several petitions for land to the Vermont State Legislature. One such petition read:

> Your petitioners are inhabitants of the frontiers of this state and have suffered much in the present war by reason of frequent incursions made by the common enemy, and have been obliged to quit our habitations for months together at sundry times. By which means we find ourselves greatly reduced. And very few are proprietors in any grants of land made by the Legislature of the State and are desirous to procure settlements for our sons

Acknowledgments

Many people were of immense help during the years of researching and writing this biography. Among those who wrote and talked to me about Bentley I am indebted to Betty Bandel, Randall Bentley, Duncan B. Blanchard, Katherine Brigham, Martha Caldwell, Nellie Canning, Mrs. Carl Clemens, Terry Bentley Conlon, John Conover, Kendall Crocker, Allene Davis, Robert Eather, Carl Francis, Roberta Goldstein, Keith Kidder, Hans P. Kraus, Jr., Alfred Lawton, Edna MacGibbon, Agnes Manson, Elinor Merle, Holland Smith, the late Levi Smith, Scott Vonnegut, and Mr. and Mrs. Ralph Whittemore.

I owe much to the late Ruth Amy Nash and her indomitable spirit for her lively and detailed accounts of Jericho and Wilson Bentley of nearly one hundred years ago. I thank Elizabeth Sansalone for her letters about her great aunt, Jean Thompson, as well as numerous pictures of Jean, three letters Bentley had written to her, and articles and snow crystal photographs he had sent to her over the years. Dianne Shullenburger, who with her family lives in the old Bentley farmhouse, graciously allowed me to wander through the house to see where Bentley lived and worked. Without Caroline Sparks, whose detailed genealogy of the Bentley family had been sent to me by Mr. and Mrs. Ralph Whittemore, I could not have traced the arrival of Wilson's ancestors in Vermont before the Revolutionary War.

I very much appreciate the gift from the late Ronald P. H. Winder of two boxes of Bentley's lantern slides of snow crystals, frost, and dew. This was the source of most of the photographs used in this book.

On many occasions over the years I went to Vermont to tape record conversations with people who had known Wilson Bentley. Their lively accounts form the basis for nearly all the quoted conversations in the book. These people who gave so freely of their time are Izetta Barrett, who also let me photocopy two letters Bentley sent to her, the late Anna Trieb Bentley, the late Mary Brunell Bentley, the late Mrs. Samuel Bentley, Homer Gile, Robert Hadley, the late Alice Bentley Hamalainen, the late Amy Bentley Hunt (who also gave me many pictures of Bentley and the family), the late Vrest Orton, Helen Shiner Poissant, the late Arthur Pratt, the late Levi Smith, Howard Wagner, and Mr. and Mrs. Ralph Whittemore.

Numerous people at libraries, historical societies, and research institutions aided me in my quest for Bentley materials. My thanks to those who helped me at the Houghton Library at Harvard University, The New York City Public Library, The New York State Library at Albany, and the Bailey/Howe Library at the University of Vermont. I appreciate the help of Sam Silverman and John Armstrong at the Phillips Laboratory, Hanscom Air Force Base, Massachusetts; they sent me copies of some of the Bentley notebooks. Paul Donovan at the Vermont Department of Libraries and Paul Carnahan at the Vermont Historical Society kindly sent me copies of rare Bentley articles, including a Bentley letter. My thanks go to National Life of Vermont, Montpelier, Vermont, for allowing me to use the artist's drawing of the young Wilson Bentley trying to draw a picture of a snow crystal. Librarians at the Atmospheric Sciences Library, National Oceanic and Atmospheric Administration, were of great help in supplying me with the Bentley materials they had on file. For technical advice on the structure of ice and snow crystals, I am indebted to Charles Knight at the National Center for Atmospheric Research and John Ricci, Jr., at the University of Southern Maine.

Virginia Cummings, the late retired director of the Buffalo Museum of Science, devoted several years to the Herculean task of cataloguing Bentley's many thousand photographic plates that are owned by the Museum. I appreciated her quick responses to questions I had about some of the Bentley photographs. While director, she made it possible for me to receive copies of several of Bentley's notebooks. All of his surviving notebooks, along with his original glass plate negatives, are at the Buffalo Museum of Science.

Bentley spent his entire life in Jericho, and it is the Jericho Historical Society that has the most diversified collection of Bentley materials. I have spent many happy hours visiting, talking, and writing to several members of the Society. Jean Smith, the former archivist, sent me copies of Bentley articles that otherwise would have been hard to get. I am equally grateful to Ray Miglionico, the present archivist, who sent me many photographs of Bentley, his relatives, and friends. But most of all, I am indebted to the indefatigable Blair Williams, who for more than twenty-five years has been building up the Bentley collection at the Jericho Historical Society and has not let the citizens of Jericho or the world beyond forget Wilson Bentley. I have treasured the exchange of many letters with Blair.

As each chapter of the Bentley story came off my word processor, I gave copies to three people and asked for their comments and criticism. My mother, Edna Blanchard, liked most of them and had only the mildest of criticism for sections of others. Like mothers everywhere, her children can do no wrong! My wife, Julie, however, was not about to let sloppy writing get by her. Though I sometimes grumbled, I appreciated her many suggestions on how to improve both grammar and syntax. With most of them incorporated in a clean copy, I gave it to the late Bernard Vonnegut, my good friend and scientific colleague for many years. Bernie swept up some things that escaped Julie, but most importantly his many comments helped me in the places where I discussed the technical aspects of Bentley's work.

I am grateful to Jerry McDonald, my editor and publisher, not only for teaching me some of the finer points of editing, but for accepting my book after some other publishers had turned it down.

within this state, but find ourselves unable to purchase lands [except] at very dear rates for them.

Apparently the Bentleys were successful with these petitions. In 1783, James Bentley built a home in Middlebury, a town next door to Cornwall, and remained there until his death in 1813 at age ninety-three. In 1785, we find his son Samuel, also in Middlebury, farming a two-hundred-acre parcel of land. But by 1790, he appears to have left town, since he does not show up in the United States census. It seems likely that his wife, Bethia Washburn, had died; his teen-aged children were living with his oldest son Abisha. Samuel married a woman named Polly as his second wife, but where he went to raise his second family remains a mystery. One may assume, however, that part of his travels took him to Wells, Vermont, a town about halfway between Middlebury and Bennington. His son Shelly, Wilson Bentley's grandfather, most likely was born there in 1795 and not, as Wilson thought, in the nonexistent town of Wells, Connecticut. Samuel had a total of ten children, five with Bethia and then five with Polly.

Exactly when Samuel and his family showed up in Jericho is not known, but it appears he was there by 1800, when the town had a population of over seven hundred. He acquired a farm; the last three of his children were born there. His traveling days most likely were over. The 1810 census found him in Jericho but he was missing from the census of 1820. Presumably by then he was dead.

Shelly Bentley at about age thirty married Abigail Stevens, a local girl whose father had served three years in the Revolutionary War. Initially, they lived in Richmond, a town just to the south of Jericho on the Winooski River, but eventually they returned to Jericho to remain there for the rest of their lives. Shelly and Abigail had six children, three boys and three girls. The third, born in Richmond in 1829, was Edwin Thomas Bentley. Edwin spent his entire adult life in Jericho, and while in his twenties married Fanny Eliza Colton, a school teacher from

Bolton, a small town southeast of Jericho and, like Richmond, on the Winooski River. Fanny and Edwin settled down to life in a farming community. They had only two children. Their first child, Charles Franklin, was born in 1863, and the second, Wilson Alwyn Bentley, arrived on February 7, 1865. Wilson was named for an uncle, Wilson Amos Bentley, who, for a bounty of sixty dollars, had enlisted for nine months in the Union Army near the beginning of the Civil War. Wilson Amos never saw Jericho again. He died in 1862 in Alexandria, Virginia.

In February, 1865, when Wilson Bentley was born, the long years of the Civil War were coming to an end. Lee's army was trapped in Richmond, Virginia, while Grant's army was preparing for the final assault of the war. But the folks up north in Jericho were still feeling the effects of the war. *The Daily Free Press*, a newspaper published in Burlington, then a large town about ten miles west of Jericho on the shores of Lake Champlain, announced that Burlington alone was going to draft ninety-four men to fill quotas not filled by volunteers. Most of the newspaper, however, was filled with dozens of advertisements placed by merchants, doctors, and con men, the latter praising the virtues of Cancer and Canker Syrup that "has cured cancers after the patients have been given up as incurable by many physicians," and The Peruvian Syrup "that can cure nervous affections, female complaints, liver complaints, chronic diarrhea, boils, and all diseases of the kidneys and bladder." Such were the times into which Wilson Bentley was born.

❅

Jericho, like many Vermont towns, came into being in the eighteenth century. In June, 1763, Benning Wentworth issued a charter to about sixty men "for the due encouragement of settling a new plantation within our said province." The "plantation" contained 23,040 acres. One of the conditions of the charter was "that all white and other pine trees within the said township, fit for masting our Royal Navy, be carefully preserved for that use." Another condition, perhaps to be expected, considering the character of Wentworth, was that he claimed five hundred acres for himself. For reasons unknown, none of the men to whom the charter was issued ever showed up to claim land in Jericho. The name of the town, incidentally, not only on the charter but for many years after, was spelled *Jerico*. The change of the spelling to *Jericho*, presumably to be in accordance with the biblical name, was not made until 1837.

The honor of being the first settlers in Jericho belongs to Joseph Brown, his wife Hannah, and their two young sons. They left their home in Connecticut in 1774, a year after Samuel Bentley left, to settle on three hundred acres of land they had purchased in Stowe, a town over the mountain to the east of Jericho. After a long and perilous journey they reached Vergennes, a town south of Burlington on Lake Champlain. From there, according to one story, they followed a line of marked trees that was to lead them to Stowe. But while stopping to rest alongside a river in Jericho, they were met by a land speculator from New York who had title to land in Jericho. He told them that the land in Stowe was rocky and of little worth and convinced them to swop their land for his two-hundred-fifty acres in Jericho, plus his horse, saddle, and bridle. One wonders who got the best of that deal! Another story has them going east from Vergennes, but not following the line of marked trees. Instead, they followed an Indian trail along the Winooski River that ran south of both Jericho and Stowe, and by mistake turned north too soon. Finding desirable land along a river, they decided to settle there. Later they purchased the land. The river, which now bears their name, is one of the three main streams in Jericho and runs through the northern part of the town.

The Brown's were not destined to live happily ever after, at least not for several years. After about a year of hard work clearing land from the Jericho wilderness, building a cabin, planting crops, and taking care of their livestock, the Revolutionary War began. Survival now became even more difficult. The British in Montreal offered to the Indians a bounty for each captive they could get from the rebellious colonies.

Accordingly, Indian raids into northern Vermont increased. The Brown family, isolated and living far within the wilderness, escaped detection for about a year. Eventually, however, Joseph and both sons were captured and delivered to the British. When released a few months later, they returned to Jericho. But they were not to enjoy their freedom for long. They were captured again, along with Hannah this time, and once more turned over to the British. They spent over three years in captivity, to be released only at war's end. After the long journey back to Jericho, they rebuilt their cabin and barns which had been burned by the Indians. Life now became easier and other settlers poured into the town.

On a map the borders of Jericho look like an alpine house with a high peaked roof that points north. From the peak to the bottom is about eight miles, and not quite seven from side to side. Over the early part of the nineteenth century, two separate sections or villages of Jericho evolved. One, Jericho Corners, is just inside the northwest border of the town, and Browns River and Lees River run through it. The other, Jericho Center, not quite three miles southeast of the Corners, is on a hill almost in the geographical center of the town. Because of its location remote from water power and, subsequently, railroads, Jericho Center, unlike Jericho Corners, never developed an extensive business interest. But by 1800, an attractive village green had been built in front of the town's meeting house. A church soon followed. A few small businesses moved in, and by 1820, with the population of Jericho just over twelve hundred, a country store was in operation. In 1884, the Jordan brothers bought the store, and it was here by the village green that Wilson Bentley bought many of the necessities for life on his farm.

Browns Trace, often called the Richmond Road, undulating both sideways and up and down over small hills, makes its way south from Jericho Center, finally dropping rapidly down into the town of Richmond some five miles away in the Winooski River valley. A mile south of the Center the Nashville Road, a narrow dirt road named after the numerous Nash families who lived there in the 1800s, takes off due east from the Richmond Road and winds its way past meadow and stream before ending nearly four miles later in West Bolton at the base of Bolton Mountain. Nourished by summer rains and winter snows, Mill Brook comes tumbling down from the mountain heights to flow alongside the Nashville Road, crossing it several times as if trying to make up its mind on which side to flow and finally leaving the road at its end to run on alone into the Winooski River.

At various times during the 1800s there were several small mills and other businesses along Mill Brook and within a mile of the Richmond Road, all taking advantage of the power supplied by the swift moving waters. There was a clothier mill, a grist mill for the grinding of corn and other grains produced by Jericho's farmers, a starch factory where the farmers could sell their potatoes at ten cents a bushel, and a saw mill. Perhaps of more importance to many of the hard-working farmers and lumbermen of the early 1800s, there was a distillery for the distillation of whisky and rum. Drinking was commonplace. Drunkenness, however, "was disgraceful but the limit was wide, for a man was not held to be drunk as long as he could keep upon his feet. When he fell, and clung to the grass to keep himself from rolling off the heaving earth, he became open to the charge of intoxication."[2] But this all changed about 1830 when the distillery closed down, probably because of the temperance movement that began to sweep through not only Jericho but the rest of Vermont and the country. In 1842, the Jericho Center Temperance Society was formed. It encouraged citizens to sign a pledge not to drink alcohol in any form except for "sacred or medicinal purposes." After passage of state and local laws, alcohol was not sold in Jericho for the rest of the century. As we will see later, Wilson Bentley attributed much of his success in snow crystal photography to his strict adherence to the principles of the temperance movement.

On the north side and just over two miles down the Nashville Road, Mill Brook winds its way through a meadow. The Bentley farmhouse was on the other side of the road. It was here that Wilson Bentley was born to Edwin and Fanny. They now had two sons. With the exception of an adopted daughter who was to come into the family some years later, there were to be no more children.

The view to the east from the Bentley homestead was nothing short of magnificent. Cradled in a small valley with low hills both north and south, the Bentleys could watch the sun rise each morning over the 3,680-foot-high Bolton Mountain. In the summer, the mountain wore its various shades of green, and in the winter the sun's rays sparkled like diamonds from the cloak of frost and snow thrown heavily over it. But this was just a prelude to what they could see immediately to the north of Bolton Mountain. Here was Mount Mansfield, the Olympus of all the mountains of Vermont. From the valleys below, the sky line of Mansfield's craggy peaks looked as though a person's profile had been stretched out like a rubber band. Increasingly higher in elevation, the Forehead, then the Nose, and finally the Chin thrust itself into the sky at an elevation of 4,393 feet. Just under the Chin in the Cave of the Winds, and nowhere else in Vermont, snow can always be found, even in mid summer. No wonder that Wilson Bentley grew up to appreciate and love in a near mystical way the water wonders of nature, and especially the snow crystals.

---

[1] Information regarding the Bentley family from 1680 onward was obtained from a detailed genealogy prepared by Caroline Sparks of Wilmington, Delaware. Details about the founding of Jericho and its early history were found in *The History of Jericho, Vermont,* first printed in 1916 by the Free Press Printing Co., Burlington, Vermont, and reprinted in 1989 by the Queen City Printers, Inc., Burlington, Vermont.

[2] Rowland E. Robinson, *Vermont: A Study of Independence*, Charles E. Tuttle Co., Rutland, Vermont, 1975, p. 320.

Chapter 2

Growing Up

From what little is known of Wilson Bentley's childhood, it appears to have been a happy one. His father, stern and business like, was the pragmatist who first paid attention to the proper running of his farm, and then, and only then, enjoyed engaging in political argument with his neighbors. His mother, an ex-schoolteacher with a love for learning and the fine arts, recognized early on and encouraged young Wilson's wonder and awe in contemplating the natural world around him, whether with the swirling waters and the moss-covered rocks in Mill Brook, or the ever-changing shapes of the clouds as they drifted overhead and disappeared beyond Bolton Mountain.

The Bentley farmhouse was shared by three generations of Bentleys, Wilson and his brother Charles, their parents, and their grandparents Shelly and Abigail. This was not uncommon in New England farm families of that time. Generation after generation lived and worked the same land, and the sons were expected to take care of the parents in their old age. Thus it was that, a few years before Wilson was born and probably not long after Edwin and Fanny were married, his grandparents gave up title to property that had been shared with Edwin and Fanny. In return, as the legal document read, Edwin promised to provide them "with food, clothing, drink, and medical aid . . . during their natural lives . . . and support them as children ought to treat and support their parents." And yes, Edwin had to agree to give Shelly five dollars every six months "for his own private use." It appears that Edwin lived up to this promise.

Precisely how long Wilson's grandparents lived in the farmhouse is not known. The census taker found them there in 1860 and 1870, but by 1880, when Wilson was fifteen, they had moved a few houses down the road. Shelly, now eighty-four, and Abigail, seventy-six, were living with and apparently being taken care of by a young married couple. Why had they left? Perhaps Fanny found that Shelly in his advancing years was a stubborn old cuss and just too difficult to put up with. Many years later, one of Wilson's nieces obtained some old letters that had been written by her grandmother Fanny about Shelly. The letters revealed that Fanny finally could no longer put up with what she considered was Shelly's strange and erratic behavior. She sent him to the Brattleboro Retreat, a hospital and home in Brattleboro, Vermont, for the mentally ill. The niece said, "You see, he was cussing and grandmother couldn't put up with that." But soon Shelly was back from the Retreat, saying there was nothing wrong with *his* mind; the rest of the family had better worry about their *own* minds! The doctor told the family that Shelly was an old man set in his ways. "If he wants to chop and haul wood, let him do it . . . and the cussing will stop."

The problems between Fanny and her father-in-law may have been brought to a head by something else that happened. In 1880, the census taker found not only had Shelly and Abigail moved out of the farmhouse, but, like a game of family musical chairs, two sisters, nieces of Edwin, had moved in. They weren't exactly nieces, but that's how Edwin described Mary Blood, age nine, and her six-year-old sister, Melissa. The parents of the two young girls were Alonzo and Emma Bentley Blood. Emma's grandfather, Samuel Bentley, Jr., was Shelly's half brother. Why the two young sisters moved in with the Bentleys one can only conjecture, but if we believe what a third sister, Charlotte, related later in life, it makes a bizarre story. Charlotte said she and her two sisters were orphaned, and that Edwin and Fanny brought Mary and Melissa into the household to be future brides for Charles and Wilson. She said that Mary was only fourteen when she was forced against her will to marry Charles, who was nineteen. A similar fate, according to Charlotte, was to befall Melissa in an arranged marriage to Wilson. But Melissa, she said, would have none of this and ran away.[1]

There may be some elements of truth in Charlotte's scenario, but on the whole it cannot be true. To begin with, the girls were not orphaned. Both parents were living at the time, although Charlotte, who was born in 1880, probably had little memory of her mother, who died a few years later. Accordingly, she may have felt orphaned when she, too, went to live with another family. But it seems more plausible that the breakup in the Blood family occurred because Emma Blood developed cancer. She did not die until January, 1886, but it's possible that the ravages of the disease were taking such a toll on Emma that in 1880 she and Alonzo arranged to have the daughters move in with relatives. As for Charles taking Mary as a child bride when she was only fourteen, it was even worse than that. Mary was only twelve! There is no evidence, however, that she was forced into the marriage, though one can reasonably wonder if such a young girl could easily resist subtle pressures toward a marriage she might wish to delay or avoid entirely. The early years of the marriage appeared on the surface to be happy ones, and by all accounts Mary got along very well with Fanny. The later years, however, were not happy ones, and after having eight children Mary left and Charles got a divorce.

It also appears that Charlotte's story of a planned marriage of Wilson to Melissa is not true. On February 3, 1886, Edwin Bentley made and signed his Last Will and Testament. In it he bequeathed several parcels of land, one in particular to his two sons "and to my daughter Melissa Bentley." Obviously, sometime between 1880 and 1886 Edwin had adopted Melissa. It is not likely he would have done so if he had plans to marry her to Wilson. It is more likely he adopted her because Emma's cancer had reached the point where she could no longer take care of her children. Melissa apparently grew up with the Bentley family on Nashville Road, and in January, 1893, at age nineteen, married

Edwin McGee, twenty-four, who came from Fanny's hometown of Bolton.

Fanny Bentley's previous experience as a schoolteacher was put to good use in the education of her two sons. Both were taught at home, although it's likely she spent more time with her younger son when she recognized his intense yearning and aptitude for knowledge. Wilson never set foot in a school until he was fourteen, and it's doubtful that he spent much time there, considering the intermittent sessions at the near-by one-room schoolhouse. Under Fanny's watchful eye, Wilson learned to read and write, to comprehend some of the principles of mathematics and science, and even to appreciate poetry and music. He must have shown a special aptitude for music. Before he was out of his teens he had learned to play the piano, the organ, the clarinet, the cornet, and the violin.[2] But he did not stop there; he composed music for the piano and for a local marching band. None of this music has survived, but written comments by those who knew him enthusiastically attest to Wilson's talent for it.

Growing up on a farm means work for young and old, especially before the age of electricity and the labor-saving machines that came with it. On many a cold winter morning Wilson probably was up long before the sun's rays peeked over Bolton Mountain to cast their warm glow on Mill Brook Valley. With a kerosene lamp swinging before him in the darkness, he made his way to the barn across the road. The cows had to be fed and milked, and the horses taken care of. In addition, during the long, hot days of summer, there was haying to be done and endless rows of potatoes to be dug. Sometimes the Bentleys worked their own farm, sometimes others. It was common practice in the valley, especially when it was a race against the weather to get the work done, for the farmers to help and work for one another. The digging of potatoes was something that the young Wilson became uncommonly adept at, probably because there were so many to dig. In the aftermath of the potato famine in Ireland in the late 1840s, many Irish families came and settled in Mill Brook Valley. And they brought their appetite for potatoes with them. Just down the road from the Bentleys were the farms of Irish immigrants, such as the Sweeneys, the Barretts, and the Learys.

After the chores were done, there was fun to be had. But it was not the kind of fun that young people in the late twentieth century enjoy. There was no radio for Wilson and Charles to listen to, no television to watch, or movies to attend. There was no automobile for the Bentley family to use for a Sunday afternoon drive through Jericho and the countryside. All of these inventions were yet to come. Most of the fun and enjoyment that came Wilson Bentley's way had to be initiated by himself. Slight of build, quiet and introverted by nature, he found that reading was a great source of joy. Fortunately, his mother had many books around the farmhouse, including a set of encyclopedia, and Wilson spent many an afternoon reading of the wonders of the world far beyond Mill Brook Valley.

Outdoors he may have played in a variety of games, but one thing he never did was to go hunting with the other boys, whether for squirrels, rabbits, or deer. He had no use for guns, but his dislike for hunting was more than balanced by his liking for fishing. This he greatly enjoyed, and took pride in his prowess in catching trout in Mill Brook. When not fishing, he might be found on a warm summer's day with a number of other boys at a swimming hole in the brook not far from the farmhouse. In the nearby meadows and hills numerous wild berries and nuts abounded, and Wilson could sometimes be found picking them.

Late in winter, Wilson and his friends looked forward to those early spring days when a warming sun rose higher in the sky and the nights were still cold. It was then that the first signs of life appeared in the thousands of sugar maples that dotted the valley. This was the signal for the time-honored ritual of tapping the trees and collecting their sweet-smelling sap. Every day, sap was collected in large buckets, and the bearer, wearing a neck-yoke and often on snowshoes, carried the sap through the woods to the sugar house. There it was poured into large kettles, to steam slowly night and day over crackling wood fires until enough evaporated to produce that wonderful aroma in the sugar house indicating the kettles contained pure maple syrup. When enough syrup had been produced, the children of the neighborhood were invited to the sugarin'-off party at the sugar house where they were treated to dishes of maple syrup that had been poured on pure white snow. What began in childhood stayed with Wilson Bentley for the rest of his life, for year after year he tapped his own sugar maples, made maple syrup, and invited his young nieces and nephews to his own sugarin'-off parties.

Wilson had a sense of humor, and practical jokes were part of the fun in growing up. His delight in watching and trying to understand the ways of the birds resulted in his learning how to imitate their calls. Sometimes when his mother was working in the house near an open window, Wilson would hide outside and loudly whistle the call of a particular bird. Eventually, his mother, curious to see this bird, would come out of the house only to find her young son grinning at her.[3] On other occasions, the jokes would be on visiting relatives and sometimes did not work the way Wilson hoped. A great aunt from Montana came to visit one time when Wilson had a red squirrel in a cage with a wheel for the squirrel to run on. One evening he let the squirrel out near her. The squirrel ran up the outside of her dress and bit her ear. For punishment, Wilson got no supper that night, and his great aunt returned to Montana, probably vowing never to return to Jericho again.

Many of the farming families in the valley attended Sunday church services either in Jericho Center or Bolton, but it is not known if the Bentleys did. If they did, the habit did not stay with Wilson. He did not go to church later in life nor did he embrace any formal religion. What religion, if any, he subscribed to, he kept to himself. One might infer, however, from his later writings that he believed in a form of pantheism; he saw God in the workings of the universe and in particular in the splendor and grandeur of the snow crystals. But he was familiar with the Bible, for in two or three of his articles on snow crystals he quoted some Scripture.

Chapter 3

The Magnificent Obsession

Life on the Bentley farm in the late 1870s followed the ebb and flow of the seasons in a regular rhythm. The winter snows gave way to the warm breath of spring, soon followed by the drowsy days of summer, which in turn drifted all too soon into autumn's blanket of color, until once again the snows of winter descended upon Mill Brook Valley. Though the chores on the farm changed from summer to winter, they were never-ending. Edwin and his sons took care of most of the outdoor work, but the house was Fanny's domain. She cooked, washed and mended clothes, and scrubbed the floors. Her home literally was her castle, and no king had more say in the running of his castle than did Fanny in the running of hers. When the men came in from the barn or the fields, Fanny wasn't about to let them track manure or mud through her house. She laid down the law that all shoes had to come off and be left in an outer room before the men came into the kitchen.[1] They could either walk around inside in stocking feet or change to another pair of shoes, but she made it abundantly clear that shoes that had been in the fields or barn were not to come into her house. And that was that! Could it have been this, in addition to the restrictions on the chopping and hauling of wood, that got Shelly to "cussing" so much that Fanny had him sent to the Brattleboro Retreat?

Changes in the Bentleys' way of life must have occurred when Mary and Melissa Blood moved in with them. But from Wilson's point of view, the greatest change probably took place on his fifteenth birthday on February 9, 1880, when he received the gift of an old microscope that had been used by his mother during her school-teaching days. From that time on he was not the same. He had found a focus in life. He became obsessed with the fragile beauty of common things from the world around him as seen through the microscope, especially the delicate beauty of the snow crystals. Years later, Bentley had this to say about the beginning of this life-long obsession.

> When the other boys of my age were playing with popguns and slingshots, I was absorbed in studying things under this microscope: drops of water, tiny fragments of stone, a feather dropped from a bird's wing, a delicately veined petal from some flower.
>
> But always, from the very beginning, it was the snowflakes that fascinated me most! The farm-folks up in this north country dread the winter; but I was supremely happy, from the day of the first snowfall — which usually came in November — until the last one, which sometimes came as late as May.
>
> Under the microscope I found that snowflakes were miracles of beauty; and it seemed a shame that this beauty should not be seen and appreciated by others. Every crystal was a masterpiece of design; and no one design was ever repeated. When a snowflake melted, that design was forever lost. Just that much beauty was gone, without leaving any record behind. I became possessed with a great desire to show people something of this wonderful loveliness, an ambition to become, in some measure, its preserver.[2]

It was one thing to see that "snowflakes [actually snow crystals] were miracles of beauty" under the microscope, but quite another to preserve this beauty and show it to others. But Wilson was determined to try. He took the microscope to an unheated woodshed attached to the back of the house. There he spent hours peering through his microscope at snow crystals captured on a microscope slide from the snow falling outside. He quickly learned that those elegant six-sided crystals, that were to be erroneously portrayed by artists in the twentieth century as snowflakes, were but the building blocks of the snowflakes. Born high within the clouds, snow crystals fall, collide, and adhere to other crystals. Often these tiny clumps of snow break up only to collide again with other clumps, so by the time the snowflakes reach the ground, they are composed of tens or hundreds of bits and pieces of snow crystals that did not survive intact the demolition-derby ride from cloud to ground. Sometimes when a snowflake hits the ground or a coat sleeve and breaks into many pieces, one can see an individual snow crystal that has escaped being broken and showing its six-fold symmetry. And sometimes in a snowstorm, especially when it's snowing lightly and the snowflakes are small, snow crystals can be seen falling alone among the more numerous snowflakes. It was these snow crystals that Wilson looked for amongst all those snowflakes he saw falling upon his collecting surface. Even here, however, he had to have the patience of Job, because all snow crystals do not have that elegance in form he was seeking.

In popular lore, there is no difference between snowflakes and snow crystals. This is hardly surprising. Dictionaries, in Bentley's day and even today, usually define a snowflake as a flake or crystal of snow. But atmospheric scientists have long recognized the difference between the two, and so did Bentley. Years later, in his technical articles, which he knew would be read primarily by scientists, he always used the correct term *snow crystal* to describe what he was working with. And even in his popular articles he usually mentioned snow crystals rather than snowflakes. It was only when newspaper reporters or magazine writers were interviewing him that he consistently spoke about snowflakes rather than snow crystals. He realized that most people, if shown a snow crystal, would call it a snowflake. Little harm was done and he let it go at that.

As if Wilson did not have enough difficulty finding a snow crystal and getting this tiny sliver of ice safely under the microscope in the back woodshed, he had to be extremely careful not to breathe out in the direction of the crystal; otherwise it would melt instantly before his eyes. Holding his breath while looking through the microscope, he tried to sketch on a piece of paper exactly what his eyes were seeing. When he could hold his breath no longer, he turned his head away, rapidly exhaled, gulped in another lungful of cold air, and returned to his drawing. This went on for snow crystal after snow crystal, all different, and for storm after storm, not for one but for three years. By this time, he had about four hundred drawings,[3] but he still had problems. Even though he avoided breathing on and melting his snow crystals, and even though he was willing to sit there in the bone-chilling temperatures of the woodshed and patiently continue to draw until he had an exact replica on paper of the crystal, nature placed a severe limit on the time he had to work. Snow crystals are made of ice, and water molecules evaporate or sublime from ice, even at temperatures far below thirty-two degrees Fahrenheit, in the same way, though at a much slower rate, as they do from liquid water at a far higher temperature. An added problem facing Bentley was that the evaporation does not occur at the same rate from all places on the crystal. It occurs much more rapidly from the tips or sharp edges to flatten or smooth them and thus distort the crystal as it shrinks in size. Depending on temperature, humidity, and the size of the crystal, Bentley probably had less than five minutes to get his drawings done. Anyone who has seen the beautiful but complex structure of snow crystals knows that even fifty minutes would not be enough time to draw them. Faced with this problem, Bentley knew he would never be able to capture these "miracles of beauty" in his drawings. Somehow, somewhere, he would have to find another way.

Not long after Wilson became involved in his passion with the snow crystals, another passion surfaced in the family. It was between Charles and Mary. There is little on record about it, but on September 27, 1882, they were married.[4] Charles was nineteen but Mary was only two months beyond her twelfth birthday! Why did Edwin and Fanny ever allow Charles to marry a girl who was not yet a teenager? Did they really believe that Mary and Charles were in love and ready to settle down in married life? One can only speculate. All that is known is that Fanny agreed to the marriage only after Mary and Charles promised there would be no children until Mary was sixteen.[5] They kept that promise, just barely. Alric, the first of their eight children, was born only three weeks after Mary's sixteenth birthday.

After the marriage, Edwin had an addition built onto the house for Charles and Mary. From that time on, until Wilson Bentley's death nearly fifty years later, the farmhouse was in two parts. The west part was first occupied by Charles and Mary alone, and later with their children; then by Alric alone, and finally by Alric and his wife. The east part, nearest to Bolton Mountain, housed Edwin, Fanny, Melissa, and Wilson. When Edwin died a few years later and Melissa left to get married, Wilson stayed on to take care of his mother. When she died in 1906, Wilson lived on alone in the east part, until his own death in 1931.

With the new addition, the house became one of the largest in the valley. It was white with green shutters, built of wood with a shingled roof. Before the addition, it had a main section with a peaked roof whose end faced the road. There were two stories and each had three windows. Up near the peak of the house, above the middle window on the second floor, was a small triangular-shaped window, probably opening up to an attic. Today, a cut-out of a snow crystal fills this window, large enough to be easily seen from the road. Attached to the east side of the main section, as sort of an ell, was an addition whose roof line extended eastward. A porch and the main door were on this part. Just above the porch roof, a gabled window faced a tiny walk space that was protected by a small railing.[6]

The new addition was an ell similar in design to the one on the main section of the house, though it was slightly larger and on the west side. It too had a gabled window above the porch roof. The central section of the house had two chimneys, one front and back, and each of the ells had a chimney at the end. Attached to the back of the central section and part of the east ell was a sort of sink room or mud room, and attached to that was the unheated woodshed where Wilson worked with his microscope and the snow crystals. A lawn circled the front and both sides of the house. Thirty or forty feet from the front, set back from the road, was a white wooden fence. Several small trees were near the house, but they provided little shelter from winter winds and hot summer suns.

After Mary and Charles had settled down in the new addition, life slowly returned to normal for all in the family except Wilson. Increasingly frustrated in making drawings of snow crystals seen under the microscope, his thoughts turned to photography. He wondered if it would be possible to use what was then a relatively new technology barely out of its infancy, and adapt it to take photomicrographs of snow crystals. It was only a little over forty years before, in 1837, that practical photography was born in the hands of the Frenchman, Louis Daguerre, whose photographic images soon became widely known as daguerreotypes. But it took hours to fix the images in daguerreotypes; thus much effort was invested in new ways to capture the photographic image. In 1851, the wet-collodion process was introduced by an Englishman, Frederick Archer. In his method, a glass plate was coated with potassium iodide and collodion, treated with silver nitrate, and, while still wet, exposed in the camera. Matthew Brady used these wet plates in obtaining his thousands of photographs on the battlefields of the Civil War. The technique was cumbersome, however, requiring development of the picture immediately after exposure. But in the late 1870s, dry plate photography was developed in England, and by the early 1880s was available in America. Dry plates, unlike wet plates, could be exposed, put aside, and developed days or weeks later. This new, easier method of photography arrived just in time for Wilson Bentley.

In the early 1880s, cameras were still a novelty and not used by the average person, much less by farmers' sons in the Mill Brook Valley of Jericho. Indeed, George Eastman, who was later to revolutionize photography by making his Kodak cameras easily available to amateurs, was just then inventing the flexible paper films whose descendants are in widespread use today. So who or what gave Wilson the idea it might be possible to use photomicrography — the taking of photographs through a microscope — to capture on photographic plates all the intricate details of a snow crystal? It's unlikely he heard about it from his parents. Perhaps he read about it in a magazine or book, or maybe an older person, a friend of the family knowledgeable in photography, told him about it and helped him get started. Bentley, in his many articles published years later, never mentioned anyone helping him in his early struggles with photograpy, but there is one person who appears to have been influential.

Henry Seeley, about twenty years older than Bentley, was born in the valley not far from the Bentley farm. He served in the Civil War, and in 1872 opened a photographic studio in Bridgeport, Connecticut. During frequent visits to Jericho, he often talked to Bentley about photography. After Bentley's death, Seeley said:

> He was a genius, known the world over. No question about that.
> . . . I got him his first camera, and showed him the making of
> plates, and whenever there was a new book published on
> photography I used to send it to him, but it was not many years
> before he could send me information.[7]

Seeley does not mention a microscope or photomicrography, so the camera he got for Bentley may have been a small one used for photographing scenes around the valley a year or two before Bentley decided to try photomicrography. Nevertheless, even if Seeley was not directly involved in Bentley's pioneering experiments in the photomicrography of snow crystals, it seems clear that he introduced Bentley to photography. This, and his continued encouragement in the form of books, was all Bentley needed to go where no one had gone before in the photography of the natural world.

Bentley probably read all he could find on photography, especially photomicrography, and concluded he could progress no further in his quest until he had the proper kind of microscope and a camera that could be adapted to it. There was, however, one major problem he had to solve. Where would he get the money to buy such technical equipment? He was still a teenager. Besides, his regular chores on the farm left him little time to work elsewhere to save the money he needed. It was his mother who, with what must have been superb diplomatic skills, convinced a reluctant father that they just had to find the money that young Wilson needed. Years later, Wilson told what happened.

When I was seventeen years old, my mother persuaded my father to buy for me the camera and microscope which I have developed into the apparatus I am still using. It cost, even then, one hundred dollars! You can imagine, or perhaps you cannot, unless you know what the average farmer is like, how my father hated to spend all that money on what seemed to him a boy's ridiculous whim.

Somehow my mother got him to spend the money, but he *never* came to believe it had been worthwhile. He and my elder brother always thought I was fooling away my time, fussing with snowflakes![8]

When the camera and microscope arrived, Wilson must have spent many weeks experimenting, trying different ways to connect them together and to rapidly focus on the ground glass screen at the rear of the camera whatever was on the stage of the microscope. His new compound microscope was the lowest-priced model of about ten made by the Bausch and Lomb Optical Company. It came with a three-quarter inch focal length objective of wide aperture. "Because of its simplicity," the Bausch and Lomb catalog said, "it may be used by inexperienced hands, without detriment or injury to it." The bellows camera, about seven inches square, could be extended nearly three feet. At the back was provision for focusing on a ground or clear glass screen and for the attachment of a photographic plate holder.

But before he could do any experimentation with his new microscope and camera, he had to have something to place them upon. He obtained a wooden table about three feet high, a bit over two feet in length, and slightly more than a foot wide. The four narrow, tapered legs were made sturdy by cross braces on each side. The carpentry skills displayed by the use of screws rather than nails in the table, and by the sanding and rounding of all sharp edges, were in marked contrast to the jury-rigged frame that was built and placed on the table to hold the camera and microscope. The wooden frame, held together only by nails, had the appearance of being slapped together hastily in order to get on with the experiment. One of the nails missed its mark entirely; the end stuck out the side of the board it was nailed into. The nail was not removed but was simply left there! Another nail was pounded in, this time hitting the mark. This suggests that Wilson had obtained the table elsewhere and had himself made the frame which, though crude and by no means elegant, served his purposes admirably for nearly fifty years. In this and in other things, Wilson showed that he believed in that old bit of Yankee philosophy, "If it ain't broke, don't fix it."

The camera took up so much room on the table that, in order to accommodate the microscope, Wilson had to make the frame long enough to stick out about a foot beyond the end of the table. He placed the microscope on the frame extension and bent the upper part backwards ninety degrees around a hinged joint, until the optical axis through the objective and eyepiece was horizontal. By using a variety of shims he made the axis identical with that of the camera. He removed both the eyepiece of the microscope and the lens of the camera, then pushed the microscope toward the camera until the tube or main body had seated itself in a light-tight sleeve attached to the front of the camera.[9] He next used either the fine or coarse focusing knob to get a sharp, magnified image on the camera's ground glass screen of whatever was in front on the microscope stage.

For many people, the focusing would have posed no problem, but for Wilson, slight of build and with short arms, it was nearly insurmountable. Standing at the back of the camera under a large black cloth to keep out stray light, he strained to reach the focusing knob to sharpen the fuzzy image he saw on the ground glass screen. He could not reach it, so he had to take a few steps to the front of the camera to make a slight focusing adjustment. Back behind the camera and under the cloth again, he would see with increasing frustration that the focusing was still not right. He repeated the process again, but soon realized that when he worked with a snow crystal, he would have to move much more rapidly. Somehow, he would have to eliminate these time-consuming, back-and-forth, focusing trips.

He did this in a very clever way. He had noticed that when the microscope was in its bent-back position, the axis of rotation of the fine focus knob was horizontal, parallel to, and below the optical axis of the microscope. On both sides of the frame, opposite the fine focus knob, he attached vertically a short piece of wood that extended upward a few inches to nearly the height of the focusing knob. He screwed in a metal eyelet atop each piece of wood. Near the back of the camera and on both sides of the frame, he attached a wooden disc which had a smaller disc attached concentrically to it. Now, all that remained to do was to take a long piece of string, attach it and wind it once or twice around one of the smaller discs, run it up through the eyelet in front and then a couple times around the focusing knob, on through the other eyelet and back to the other small disc, making sure that the string was taut and wound in the opposite direction on the second disc. With this arrangement Wilson could stand under the black cloth at the back of the camera, look at a fuzzy image on the glass plate and, with his hands on the two larger discs, turn them in one direction or the other until the focusing knob brought the image on the plate into a sharp focus. The beauty of this was that he could do it in just a few seconds.

With the focusing problem solved, Wilson turned his attention to what would have been an impossible task for most people. This was going outside in a snowstorm to select a perfect snow crystal from the few falling among the far more numerous snowflakes, and then quickly putting it on a microscope slide and placing it on the stage of the microscope. Wilson, however, had faced and solved this problem during the long months of earlier winters, when he had tried to draw the crystals he saw under his microscope. He collected the falling snow on a board about a foot square, painted black so even the smallest snow crystals could be seen on it. He attached two wire handles so that his mittened hands would not touch the collecting board. He apparently felt that any heat from his hands escaping through the mittens would be rapidly transferred to the atmosphere by the wire and not to the board. Standing outside the woodshed in the falling snow, he would watch the flakes and crystals falling on the board and occasionally looked at them with a magnifying glass. If he did not see one he wanted to photograph before the board became covered with snow, he would brush the snow off with a turkey feather and start anew. Finally, when he spotted a crystal he deemed worthy of photography, he would rush inside the woodshed to transfer it to a microscope slide.

Here began the most delicate and arduous part of the whole process. Never breathing in the direction of the crystal, he used a small broom splint he had pulled from one of his mother's brooms. Ever so carefully but gently he touched it to the middle of the snow crystal. It stuck to the splint. He picked it up and placed it in the center of a glass microscope slide. To make certain that the crystal was lying flat on the slide, Wilson used the soft edge of a bird's feather to press gently upon it. He needed an unusually steady hand to do this without breaking the crystal. Some of his snow crystals, with their intricate, lace-like patterns, identical on the side branches on all six arms, were only about a sixteenth of an inch across with a thickness no more than one-tenth that of a sheet of paper! Commentating on this in later years, Bentley said, "My hand is perfectly steady. . . . I never have used liquor, tobacco, or any stimulants that affect the nerves."[10]

The delicate part of the process over, Wilson began a race against time. Quickly he placed the slide under an observation microscope — probably the one his mother had given him — to make sure the snow crystal was still unbroken. If it was, he placed the slide on the microscope stage and hastened to the back of the camera. Throwing the black cloth over his head, he rapidly obtained a focus on the ground glass, removed the glass, replaced it with a photographic plate and exposed it to the magnified image of the snow crystal for anywhere from about thirty to three hundred seconds. For light he simply pointed his camera toward a window in the side of the woodshed and allowed the light to pass right through the snow crystal on its way to the photographic plate. Since the legs at the front of the table were nearly two inches higher than those at the rear, the camera was tilted slightly upward. This was probably done to get more light into the camera. Using this technique of transmitted light, Wilson expected his photomicrographs to show not only the surface but the internal structure of the snow crystal. Since he had no use for the camera lens and had removed it, he had no shutter to open and close for the proper exposure time. Bentley made his own shutter in the form of a small black card mounted directly in front of the objective. After the slide in the photographic plate holder was removed to expose the plate, he removed the black card for the required exposure time. Then he replaced it, along with the slide covering the now-exposed plate. The plate was then ready for developing.

Wilson probably completed the camera-microscope assembly late in the fall of 1883 and eagerly looked forward to the first snows of winter. Did he obtain instant success in his photographic quest to capture the image of a snow crystal? He did not. He struggled for weeks on end with the apparatus, but nothing seemed to work.

> Here I was with this expensive apparatus which had been given me so reluctantly. I had been sure that I could do wonderful things with it; but I failed over and over again! . . . If there had only been someone to explain what was wrong! But away off here on a farm there was nobody to help me. Again and again I failed. The winter slipped away, and I was almost heartbroken. But by the next season I had found the secret of my trouble. I began to use a very small 'stop' — a thin plate, with a tiny

opening to shut out most of the light. With this, and a longer exposure, I got a clear image. . . .[11]

The "tiny opening" was probably the smallest of four different-sized holes in a metal disc mounted just beneath the microscope stage. The disc — a revolving diaphragm — could be rotated to bring any of the holes directly beneath the stage and thus control the amount of light passing through the snow crystal and the microscope. The smallest hole had a diameter about one-sixteenth of an inch, the largest was five-eighths of an inch. It appears that during that first winter Wilson used the largest opening in an attempt to get a lot of light rapidly onto his film and thus lower the time required to get the picture. This was fatal. With a large opening, the depth of field was very small, and it was extremely difficult to get a sharp focus. When he finally used the smallest opening on the disc, the resultant increase in the depth of field made it possible to quickly obtain a sharp, crisp focus. A longer exposure was now necessary, but it gave the "clear image" he was seeking.

Bentley later said:

> The day that I developed the first negative made by this method, and found it good, I felt almost like falling on my knees beside that apparatus and worshipping it! I knew then that what I had dreamed of doing was possible. It was the greatest moment of my life![12]

This greatest moment occurred on January 15, 1885. It was a dark, overcast day during which about five inches of snow fell outside the woodshed. With eager anticipation, Bentley probably developed the first of five negatives taken that day, long before he had to turn his attention to the evening chores. Though he did not know it, Wilson Bentley's success that day in the woodshed had produced the world's first photomicrographs of snow crystals. He was still only nineteen years old!

From that moment on, his magnificent obsession with the snow crystals never waned, and he faithfully returned to his studies every winter of the forty-six that remained in his life.

Bentley believed that snow crystals were a metaphor for all things beautiful on earth. In 1904, he wrote:

> The snow crystals . . . come to us not only to reveal the wondrous beauty of the minute in Nature, but to teach us that all earthly beauty is transient and must soon fade away. But though the beauty of the snow is evanescent, like the beauties of the autumn, as of the evening sky, it fades but to come again.[13]

---

[1] Oral communication: Amy B. Hunt to Duncan Blanchard, October 3, 1971.

[2] Mary B. Mullet, "The Snowflake Man," *The American Magazine*, February, 1925, pp. 28–31, 173–175.

[3] Tom Steep, "Scientist devotes thirty-five years to study of snowflakes," *New York Tribune*, September 26, 1920, sec. 7, p. 5.

[4] Marriage certificate on file at the Public Records Division, Montpelier, Vermont.

[5] Letter: Allene Davis to Duncan Blanchard, April 22, 1993.

[6] Description of the house obtained from a photograph given to Duncan Blanchard by Amy B. Hunt.

[7] "Snowflake man found aide here," Article about Colonel Henry Seeley in the Bridgeport, Connecticut, newspaper. Date unknown but probably in the 1930s. Interested readers can obtain a photocopy by writing to Duncan Blanchard.

[8] Mary B. Mullet, *op. cit.*, p. 30.

[9] Details of how Bentley coupled his microscope to the camera and used it to do his snow crystal photomicrography can be found in many articles by and about Bentley. A good description, including photographs, can be found in Bentley's article "Photographing snowflakes," *Popular Mechanics Magazine*, 1922, vol. 37, pp. 309–312.

[10] Mary B. Mullet, *op. cit.*, p. 31.

[11] Mary B. Mullet, *op. cit.*, p. 173.

[12] Mary B. Mullet, *op. cit.*, p. 174. This account, given by Bentley forty years later, has his success at snow crystal photography not coming until the second winter. During the first winter (January to March, 1884) he "failed over and over again." But when I sent the model number of Bentley's microscope to Bausch and Lomb, they said it was not made until 1884. Could it have been made as early as January, 1884, and sent to Bentley immediately? If so, he

could have used it for snow crystal photography in February and March. Alternatively, he may not have received it until late in 1884, but during the earlier winter might have used his mother's old microscope. Forty years later, these details may not have been important to Bentley when he talked to Mary Mullet, the reporter from *The American Magazine*.

[13] Wilson Bentley, "The wonders and beauties of the snow," *The Christian Herald,* March 2, 1904, p. 191.

Chapter 4

The Formative Years

It's fortunate that Bentley's four-year quest to capture the beauty of the snow crystals ended in success in January. Had it not, he might have been so discouraged as to give up any hope of succeeding and probably would have grudgingly agreed that his father was right when he said he was wasting his time "fussing with snowflakes." But success at this particular time was important for another reason. The rest of the family was getting weary of winters in Jericho and were talking of moving either to California or to Florida. Had Wilson not succeeded with the snow crystals, it's possible he would have succumbed to the lures of life in faraway climes. As it was, he did give it some thought.

When and how the decision was made for an exploratory trip south is not known. What is known, however, is that in mid-March of 1885 Charles and Mary arrived in Orange City, Florida, and over the next six months wrote many letters — of which about a dozen have survived — about how wonderful life was in Florida. These letters, ten sent to Wilson and two to Melissa, mention everyone in the family with the singular exception of Edwin.[1] He is very conspicuous by his absence in the letters. Charles had a peculiar style of writing. He used no punctuation whatsoever and capitalized only the personal pronoun *I*. Consequently, his letters were like one long, difficult-to-read sentence that ran from one page to another. Mary's letters were easier to read. Only in portions of her four letters did she neglect her punctuation. It is puzzling as to why Charles wrote in this manner, since he was taught by a mother who had once been a school teacher. Whatever caused Charles's writing problems, it apparently was not catching; it never showed up in later years in Wilson's letters. In the following quotes from the letters, punctuation and capital letters have been added, but the syntax and spelling have been untouched.

With money apparently supplied by his father, Charles wasted no time in acquiring land and a house.[2] This suggests that a decision for certain pieces of property may have been made even before he left Jericho. In a letter to "Dear Brother" on April 4, written only a couple weeks after his arrival in Orange City, Charles said "There is 7 rooms in the house. There is a main part and an ell. . . . Oh, I hope you will all come down. You can come right here and live as long as you wish. The house is large enough."

In addition to the house he bought some property that consisted of:

> . . . four, five-acre lots, or 20 acres. I payed $391 for the whole. They are cheap at that price, not quite twenty dollars an acre. It is good, fine land with a strip of good vegtable land next to the lake. It is as near the landing as this place. Oh, I have got all the land you all will want. I should not have bought them, but I could get them so cheap, and the title is good. . . . I wish you could sit as I do and see orange trees in every direction. There is groves adjoining mine in every direction, and they are the best groves in Orange City.

Charles closed the letter with a sketch of himself eating a "Florida watermelon."

Only three days later, he wrote again:

> If you want to come to the best climate in the world, come to Florida. Oh, I hope you and mother will be down this spring if the rest can't come before June. . . . I guess I will close. How is Grandpa and Grandma?

His concerns for his grandparents must have been prompted by a letter from Wilson, informing him they were in very bad health.

About a week later, Wilson wrote to say that Shelly had died. Charles replied immediately:

> I cannot hardly realize that Grandpa has passed away. Being so far away I cannot make it seem possible, but, as you say, we cannot wish him back to suffer more. It seems sad to think he had to suffer so much before he passed away. I send my sympathy to Grandma in her great bereavement.

Abigail died a few months after Shelly.

In nearly every letter Charles preached the virtues of his newly-found Shangri-la, and told Wilson how much he and the others would enjoy it once they arrived. Wilson, doubtless still excited by his recent success in snow crystal photography, probably did not commit himself initially. But judging from what Charles wrote in his last letter, August 17, it appears that Wilson had made the big decision to move south. Toward the end of the letter Charles said:

> Oh, it seems as though I could not contain myself when I think of your coming so soon. If we don't have some grand sport, I am sadly mistaken. I think you will like Florida. If you like it as well as I do, you will not want to wander.

When Charles wrote on April 4 to tell about the lots he purchased, Fanny worried about it. Wilson immediately wrote to Charles about her fears. On April 10, at the end of a letter to Wilson, he wrote:

> Dear Mother, I will write a line to you. The lots you said you was worrying about are all right. There is four lots or 20 acres. Understand, I pay for the whole $391. That will be all the land you will all want, and more.

One can understand Fanny's worries, especially since there was something else that must have worried her even more. That was the sale of their home and property in Jericho. Apparently it was on the market, and an offer of six thousand dollars had been made for it. When Charles heard about the offer, he wrote to Wilson:

Do not sell the farm for no $6000. There is no use in giving it away. If you cannot sell, hire it out, or hire some one to do the work as you think best, and come down. You can come here and live as long as your a mind to.

Charles then changed the subject, getting back to why living in Orange City was superior to that in Jericho.

Here it isnt as it is up there. You havent got to be shut in the house half of the year . . . but you can move out and air yourself any time of the year without any danger of being froze up. The majority of the nights are plenty cool enough to sleep good.

Perhaps so, but Charles was writing early in April. One wonders if he was as euphoric about the summer nights later in July and August.

The letters show that Wilson was called Willie, a nickname used by the family and his friends in Mill Brook Valley, and that Mary went by the name of May. In the two letters she sent to Wilson, one started with "Dear Willie," and ended with "your affectionate sister, Mary M. Bentley," while the other started "Dear Brother," and ended with "your affectionate sister, May." Though not adopted, as was Melissa, Mary grew up living with the Bentley family and considered Wilson to be her brother more than a brother-in-law.

Continuing his sales pitches for Orange City, Charles worked on two of Wilson's spare time pleasures: his love of fishing and books. Charles wrote that:

I will make your eyes bug out when I take you fishing here. A man told me the other day he caught catfish off from the dock as long as his arm. If you can beat that up in Mill Brook, please inform me.

In another letter he says:

> I want to tell you about the library. By paying, I think, 79 cts,
> you can become a member and have all the reading you want . .
> It would be a cheap way of getting reading matter.

Wilson's love of books and, later in life, his accomplishments and world-wide recognition for his studies of the snow crystals, caused many people in Jericho and beyond to refer to him as Professor Bentley. But it appears that Charles had given him this title many years before. A few months after arriving in Florida, Charles sent Wilson a book titled *Manipulation of the Microscope.* On the inside cover he wrote: "Professor Wilson A. Bentley, Jericho, Vermont, Chittenden County, July 21, 1885. At Orange City, Florida." It's not clear why Charles added the reference to Orange City. Perhaps he thought it might be a further inducement to get Wilson down there. About a month after sending the book, Charles sent a letter to Wilson and playfully started it with "Dear Professor W. A. Bentley."

It's clear that the two brothers had different political views. Charles, who throughout his life loved to talk politics, made clear the difference in his letter of August 17. In responding to a comment made by Wilson, he wrote:

> You seem to be a very patriotic Republican. We will see where your republicanism will go to when you get down here. There was a very respectable Southern Democrat here yesterday. We got to talking on politics. He said there was no difference in principle between the two parties. He said if he was north, he should be Republican, but here in the south he was compelled to be a Democrat. That is just it; you have got to be a nigger or a Democrat. The Republican party here is the nigger party. The south will never be anything but solid south, & I hope it never will be. . . . You know how I felt on the nigger question before I came south.

Although the rest of the family in Jericho may have been slow in making up their mind to move south, there was little doubt that, whatever happened, Charles and Mary had no intention of moving back to Jericho. In his letter of April 16, Charles asked Wilson to speak for him and:

> Tell Mr. B of Jericho Center to go to h___. [Even in a letter to his brother, Charles could not bring himself to write *hell*.] May would not come back for all the tree toads and croaking grasshoppers in the town of Jericho. If he has no other employment than lying, then let him lie. It will not seriously effect us here. We never either of us want to ever come back to Vermont to live. We never enjoyed ourselves so much in this world before as we have here.

At the end of the letter Mary added:

> Dear Brother, I thought I would write a few lines. . . . You tell Mr. B that I have not cried once or teased to come back. I would not come back for all there is in the town of Jericho. Tell him he better find something else to do. Good bye from May.

The mysterious Mr. B was never identified further. It's possible he was someone who objected to the marriage, especially Mary's age at the time, who spread rumors about it and, upon hearing of their move to Florida, ridiculed her by saying she would cry like a baby and want to come back home.

The letters reveal that Wilson was not the only one in the family with musical interests. Charles played the cornet and Mary the violin, but they turned to Wilson whenever musical notes were to be put on paper. In a letter to Melissa, after writing "come as soon as you can," Mary asks her to get "Willie to write the notes to . . . the 'Gov King's March' and 'The Girl I Left Behind Me' and send to me. Tell him that I can play 'Irish Washer Woman' pretty good now."

The curtain closes on this glimpse into the Bentley family life late in August, 1885, with the last of the surviving letters. We do not know what happened later in 1885 to discourage Wilson, his parents, and Melissa from moving south to join Mary and Charles. We do know, however, that the farmhouse and property in Jericho were not sold, ending the only time in Wilson's life when there was a possibility he might leave Vermont. It's hard to imagine he would ever have wanted to move to a land devoid of ice and snow, but perhaps his devotion to his mother, who apparently *did* want to go, overcame any desire to stay behind. The one puzzle left unanswered by the letters is the curious absence of Edwin Bentley. As head of the family and owner of the farmhouse in Jericho, why was he not even mentioned when Charles wrote Wilson and told him not to sell the property for six thousand dollars? Surely that was Edwin's decision to make. His absence in the letters might suggest he had died, but that was not the case. He had two more years to live. In February, 1886, he made his will, and this revealed that not only was he very much alive but he was the one who had paid for all the property in Orange City.[3] He left to Fanny, Charles, Wilson, and:

> . . . to my daughter Melissa Bentley twenty acres near Orange City . . . to be divided equally between them." In addition, he left to all but Melissa "a five-acre grove and house in Orange City . . . and all the remainder of my estate real and personal in the town of Jericho.

What began as an idyllic, adventurous trip to Florida ended in disaster and disillusionment for Mary and Charles. In December, 1886, or perhaps the following winter, a severe freeze hit northern Florida, and overnight they lost all their oranges and several thousand dollars. Discouraged, they sold the grove for what they could get.[4] Though they had vowed never to return home for all the "croaking grasshoppers in the town of Jericho," they did just that. They moved into the west part of the big house and proceeded to raise a family of four boys and four girls. In May, 1887, little more than a year after making his will, Edwin Bentley died at age fifty-eight of a liver illness. He left behind a ten-cow dairy farm that was to provide a living for Charles and Wilson and the rest of the Bentleys.

❈

Starting in 1885 with his first successful photomicrographs of snow crystals, Wilson Bentley began keeping records in two separate sets of notebooks, and continued this for the rest of his life. In the first notebook he kept records of his photography. By far most of the entries were for snow crystal photography, but some were for the photography of frost on windowpanes and on leaves and blades of grass, of pond ice, dew, clouds, people, and anything else that interested him. He wasted no words in the entries on snow crystal photography, probably a reflection of the speed with which he had to work. He recorded the date, a brief description of the weather, the number of photographs taken, and for each photograph the exposure time and the extension of the camera bellows. The smaller the crystal, the larger was the magnification needed to give the desired size of the crystal on the photographic plate, and the farther out the bellows had to be extended. With the one-half inch focal length microscope objective he acquired in 1894, and with the camera bellows fully extended, he was able to obtain the maximum magnification of sixty.

Over the years Bentley filled five photographic notebooks that together cover some four hundred pages.[5] Sprinkled at random throughout the pages, and often at the end of each notebook, he would record things that had nothing to do with photography. He would list the names of people to whom he wanted to send reprints of his articles, and the birthdays of his brother's and neighborhood children. Often he would itemize very practical things such as the names of farmers in the valley, along with the number of tons of hay they had bought from him and the money they still owed him. Incidentally, in 1890 he was selling his hay for six or eight dollars a ton, the difference in price presumably reflecting a difference in quality of the hay. Sometimes he would get very practical indeed, and personal. After the entries about the hay, he wrote, "Size of winter pants for W.A.B., 32 waist, 30 leg."

His second notebook was a weather notebook. Though he recorded the weather in his photographic notebooks, he did so only on the days when he photographed something. Sometimes weeks or months would pass between entries. But in his weather notebook Bentley recorded the weather every day. If he was to be away for several days, he would get someone else to record it for him. He developed a concise, compact method of recording the weather, and he never deviated from it. Each month took only one page and each day only one line. About in the center of the line he drew a square surrounded on both sides by larger rectangles. The first rectangle was for the forenoon weather, the square for afternoon, and the second rectangle for the evening weather. Festooned along the sides and tops of the squares and rectangles were symbols representing rain, snow, thundershowers, cloud types, and optical phenomena such as the aurora. Two pairs of numbers, representing the maximum and minimum temperatures for the morning and afternoon, also appear. In the evening rectangle Bentley often drew a large circle with a number of lines going outward radially from the top half of the circle. Looking like a giant eye staring out of the page, this represented an aurora he observed that evening. At the end and beginning of the line, in his small, crabbed handwriting, he would squeeze in more data. If it was snowing, he would note the crystal types by a letter code. And every spring, usually late in March or early in April, he would write for several days entries such as "sap runs well." Anyone looking at the maze of numbers, symbols, letter codes, and geometrical figures in Bentley's weather notebooks would, without knowing their meaning, be as confused as if he were looking at the hieroglyphics on a long-lost Rosetta Stone. But these data, taken and recorded by Bentley for forty-seven years, give mute testimony to his patience, perseverance, and superb observational skills.

After his initial success in snow crystal photography in January 15, 1885, there was no letting up. Bentley eagerly awaited the next snowstorm. In little over a week it snowed again, and he captured three more photographs. He photographed snow crystals in each of the remaining eight snowfalls of that winter. By the last one on March 12 he had a total of twenty. It wasn't much, compared to what he did in later years when he had learned how to work faster and more efficiently, but it was a good start on the many thousands he would take before his death.

Each winter Bentley had his camera set up long before the first storm blew in over Jericho. And each winter he photographed more jewels from the winter storms. On Sunday evening, March 11, 1888, his camera ready in the back shed, he went to bed not knowing that what would be the most disastrous snowstorm in American history was fast gaining strength and bearing down upon him. Within hours the fury of this churning maelstrom turned into a blizzard with gale force winds, low temperatures, and a heavy blanket of snow that began to settle over the northeastern United States. Though by now a superb observer of the weather, why should Bentley have had any suspicion of what was to come the next day? The United States Signal Service, the forerunner of today's National Weather Service, certainly did not. Their forecast issued on Sunday was, "Fresh to brisk easterly winds, with rain, will prevail tonight followed on Monday by colder, brisk westerly winds and fair weather throughout the Atlantic States."[6] But on Monday morning residents of New York City were greeted with a blizzard and ten inches of snow already on the ground, while up in Jericho Bentley realized that an extraordinary snowstorm had descended upon him. He probably did only the absolutely necessary chores around the house and barn that morning, then turned his attention to snow crystal photography. He photographed twelve snow crystals, the most he had ever taken in a single day. In his notebook he wrote, "All splendid crystals. . . . taken in great blizzard. Cloudy. Snowing hard. Taken between 9 & 3 oclock in back room. . . . Therm. 18 going down to 2 above at dusk." The blizzard raged on for another two days, but Bentley obtained no more photographs. In fact, they were the last ones he took that winter.

By 1890 his collection of photomicrographs numbered one-hundred-fifteen. His interests in photographing and studying the forms of water in the atmosphere were expanding beyond the snow crystals to include frost, dew, raindrops, and clouds. He had obtained other cameras to do this, including one with a double combination stereo lens. When not pointing his camera at some of the water wonders of the atmosphere, Bentley was pointing it at the people and views around the valley. He got pictures of Bolton Mountain, Mount Mansfield, neighbors houses, and mayflowers in the woods. Closer to home, he took pictures of his mother, Melissa, and Mary and Charles's two youngsters. And to prove that he was utilizing his musical talents, he took pictures of the Bolton Band and "Charlie and me in uniform."[7]

About this time, and unknown to Wilson Bentley, scientists on the other side of the Atlantic were starting work on the photomicrography of snow crystals. In 1893, a Swedish scientist, Dr. G. Nordenskiold, published an article on some photographs he had taken of snow crystals. In the same year, Professor Dr. Gustav Hellmann, an eminent German meteorologist working in Berlin, published his photomicrographs of snow crystals in a small book.[8] He discussed the different forms of snow crystals and gave a brief historical account that went back through the centuries to those who had been captivated with the beauty and symmetry of snow crystals and, like Bentley, had tried to make drawings of them. Since Bentley had yet to publish any of his snow crystal photographs, Hellmann did not know about his work and, consequently, made no mention of it in his book. Years later, however, their paths would cross in the scientific literature. Sparks would fly from a clashing of verbal swords, and Bentley would emerge the winner.

Sometime in the early 1890s, Bentley developed his "blocking-out" method to enhance the beauty of the snow crystals.[9] Most people would have been overjoyed to obtain a sharp, clear image of a snow crystal on their three-by-four-inch glass photographic plate, and would have considered it a job well done. But not Bentley. There was much more work to do before he was satisfied. He was so impressed and moved by the beauty of the snow crystals that he felt nothing should detract from them. They should be seen against a black background. But this was impossible, since the photomicrographs were taken with transmitted light, and thus the prints showed the white crystals against the white of the snow-filled sky. Or was it impossible? Not quite. After experimenting unsuccessfully with several techniques, he developed one that worked. Using a small, sharp penknife, he slowly and very carefully scraped away the emulsion on the glass plate negative that surrounded the snow crystal, leaving only clear glass. Now when the positive print was made, the snow crystal stood sharp and clear against a jet black background like a bright star in a midnight sky.

Bentley was well aware that some scientists or photographers might criticize this blocking-out method and accuse him of sharpening up the edges of the snow crystals, or, worse, mutilating them. To avoid such criticism, he never touched his original negatives. From the original negative plate he made a contact-positive plate and from that a duplicate negative. All of this was done with the light from a lantern whose chimney was kept very clean. It was this duplicate that he operated on with his penknife. He held the negative firmly in a small frame at an angle of about forty five degrees to the horizontal and, depending upon the complexity of the snow crystal, spent the next thirty minutes to four hours carefully scraping away the emulsion from around the crystal. All of his snow crystal photographs that appeared later in numerous newspapers, magazines, and books were made from negatives laboriously prepared in this manner. But he always kept the original, untouched negatives to show anyone who felt he had grossly distorted the crystal by the blocking-out method. Testimony to this labor of love can be found today in the thousands of negatives at the Buffalo Museum of Science.

Most of the 1890s were uneventful years for Wilson Bentley. He continued taking photographs of snow crystals, but he did not write about them or publish any of the photographs. In 1893, Melissa left to marry Edwin McGee and they settled down to raise a family in Bolton. Wilson and his mother were left to live a quiet life in the eastern part of the house. But the quiet in their side of the house was balanced by the increased noise and commotion provided by the four children of Charles and Mary in the other side. The income for both families continued to come from the sale of milk and hay from their farm. Wilson's share of the profits, however, was not quite enough to live on, considering that he had an extra expense in all the photographic plates, developing solutions, and other materials he used with ever-increasing frequency.

> During these years . . . no appreciation came, no photographs were sold, it was all 'out' and nothing coming in. . . . I was hampered by lack of means, yet carried on nevertheless. . . . I had to teach music to keep alive and to get funds.[10]

All this changed during the winter of 1898. Two things happened that propelled Bentley out of obscurity and made his name known far beyond the borders of Jericho. To begin with, he made what apparently was his first sale of snow crystal photographs. Second, and perhaps just as important, he published his very first article on snow crystals. He may have known at the start of the winter that both things were going to happen, for he eagerly turned to his photographic quest and obtained over twice as many photographs, ninety-four, as he had in any previous winter. By the end of February, 1898, he had a grand total of just over four hundred. All of these were bought by the Harvard Mineralogical Museum. An article about the purchase in the distinguished *Proceedings of the American Academy* said that the Bentley collection was "for study and public exhibition."[11] It went on to praise Bentley for the copious notes he made on the meteorological conditions at the time of each photograph and for his "superb technique" in photography. It ended by saying that "this large and perfect collection . . . may justly be called a monument to the patience, skill, and enthusiasm of the maker." There is no record of Bentley's reaction to any of this; but who could not have been anything but pleased and excited upon hearing that his work of fourteen winters went on public display at one of the world's great universities!

With his work receiving such high praise, why hadn't Bentley made an effort to publish it? Apparently he had. "I took some prints and wrote an article and sent it to a New York paper," he told a reporter years later. "It was very crudely written. I can't write well, you know. . . . They sent it back to me. . . . I didn't try again for years, but I kept on with my work."[12] The urge to make another attempt to write about his work may have been rekindled when his photographs were accepted for display at the Harvard Mineralogical Museum. "I wanted to share my treasures with somebody, and I couldn't," Bentley said. "Finally I took them to the University of Vermont [in Burlington] and showed them to a professor there."

By 1898, Professor George Henry Perkins, a Ph.D. from Yale, had been teaching at the University of Vermont for nearly twenty years.[13] Highly respected as both teacher and administrator, he was the Howard Professor of Natural History and Dean of the Department of Natural Sciences. A kindly man with a gentle disposition and understanding, he had the confidence and affection of both faculty and students. A Fellow of several scientific societies, his interests in the natural sciences seemingly knew no bounds. He had published numerous articles on botany, zoology, archeology, entomology, and geology. As if his academic duties were not enough to keep him busy, he was appointed state geologist in 1898; over the years he wrote about fifty articles for the Vermont Geological Survey. Whether by chance or by choice, Wilson Bentley could not have picked a better person with whom to share his "treasures."

When Professor Perkins saw the photographs that Bentley spread before him, he was amazed at their quality. He told Bentley that he absolutely must write about them. Bentley went home and made an attempt to write but could not do it. "I tried," Bentley said, "and I went back to him with the data, and he said he would write the thing for me, and he did. And a magazine took it." In May, 1898, the article "A study of snow crystals," by W. A. Bentley and G. H. Perkins appeared in *Appleton's Popular Science Monthly*. In a footnote, Professor Perkins wrote that though he put the pages together from Bentley's notes and photographs, the "facts, theories, and illustrations are entirely due to [Bentley's] untiring and enthusiastic study of snow crystals."

In this first article, Bentley revealed two sides to his personality; both were to appear again and again in future writings. There was the scientific side in which he wondered about the shapes and structure of the crystals, how they originated, and what portions of the storm they came from. Then there was the other side that revealed the artist, the poet, and the dreamer within him. The scientist in Bentley wrote about the details of taking the photomicrographs and the complicated internal structure of the snow crystals. He was aware that the structure of the crystal changed with temperature as it fell down through the atmosphere. The poet in him wrote:

> A careful study of this internal structure not only reveals new and far greater elegance of form than the simple outlines exhibit, but by means of these wonderfully delicate and exquisite figures, much may be learned of the history of each crystal and the changes through which it has passed in its journey through cloudland. Was ever life history written in more dainty hieroglyphics!

Because of Bentley, every schoolchild today is taught that no two snowflakes are alike. Bentley made this bit of wisdom popular by stating it in many of his lectures and articles, but here in his first article he was wordy and cautious. The closest he came to a concise statement of this fact was that while "it is not difficult to find two or more crystals which are nearly if not quite the same in outline, it is almost impossible to find two which correspond exactly in their interior figures."

The article ended with an eloquent statement of the beauty and mystery that Bentley saw in the snow crystals.

> There is no surer road to fairyland than that which leads to the observation of snow forms. To such a student the winter storm is no longer a gloomy phenomenon to be dreaded. Even a blizzard becomes a source of keenest enjoyment and satisfaction, as it brings to him, from the dark, surging ocean of clouds, forms that thrill his eager soul with pleasure.

And this from a man who said he could not write!

Although Bentley took the first photographs of snow crystals, there were many before him who had observed their delicate beauty, six-fold symmetry, and near inexhaustible variety of shapes. To meet these people we must journey back through the centuries to the dawn of recorded history.

[1] Copies of the letters were given to Duncan Blanchard by Amy B. Hunt, July, 1973.

[2] Edwin Bentley's last will and testament, Jericho, Vermont, town hall.

[3] *Ibid.*

[4] Oral communication: Amy B. Hunt to Duncan Blanchard, October 3, 1971.

[5] His notebooks are at the Buffalo Museum of Science, Buffalo, New York.

[6] Paul J. Kocin, "An analysis of the blizzard of '88," *Bulletin of the American Meteorological Society*, 1983, vol. 64, pp. 1258–1272.

[7] Bentley's first notebook.

[8] *Schneekrystalle,* published by Rudolf Muckenberger, Berlin, 1893.

[9] Wilson A. Bentley, "Photomicrographs of snow crystals and methods of reproduction," *Monthly Weather Review,* 1918, vol 46, pp. 359–360.

[10] James Powers, "Fame comes to Snowflake Bentley after 35 patient years, *The Boston Sunday Globe*, January 2, 1921, p. 2.

[11] J. E. Wolff, "Exhibition and preliminary account of a collection of microphotographs of snow crystals, made by W. A. Bentley," *Proceedings of the American Academy,* 1898, vol. 33, pp. 431–432.

[12] James Powers, *op. cit.*

[13] *Dictionary of American Biography*, Charles Scribners Sons, 1934, vol. 7.

Chapter 5

The Pioneers

Who was the first to notice snow crystals? We will never know, but surely it must have been many tens of thousands of years ago when some curious, inquisitive creature, a member of our species *Homo sapiens*, first noticed the infinite variety of snow crystals and their six-fold symmetry. Perhaps it was a hunter, returning to his cave after a long hunt, who stopped momentarily to rest when a light snow began to fall. Peering through matted hair, he may have pondered those curious, six-sided pieces of ice that fell intact on the fur of the animal pelts wrapped around him for warmth. Or perhaps the special shape of snow crystals was first seen by a woman who, when leaving the warmth of the cave to get wood for her fire, noticed the crystals on sticks she picked up. We can imagine that she might have told her children back in the cave of these magical, six-sided flowers of ice that fell from the sky. *Imagine* is all we can do, for until written languages were developed, no permanent record of the nature of snow crystals could be made.

One might suspect that the first written record of the hexagonal symmetry of snow crystals would be found in the writings of the early Romans, Arabs, or Greeks. But none has been found. Even Aristotle, whose writings covered a vast variety of subjects, had nothing to say about the shape of snow crystals.[1] Could this be because Aristotle and the other observers of the natural world lived in the Mediterranean region and were little exposed to falling snow? Whatever the reason, scientists and philosophers in the West were silent on the shape of snow crystals until well over a thousand years after the subject appeared in the literature of the East.

The oldest observation on record is very old indeed. It appeared in the Chinese literature about 135 B.C. in a book of the former Han dynasty written by Han Ying. In it is the statement "Flowers of plants and trees are generally five-pointed, but those of snow are always six-pointed." This difference between the shape of plant flowers and snow crystals became well known in the centuries after Han Ying's book. In a poem by Hsiao Thung (A.D. 501 to 531) are the lines "The ruddy clouds float in the four quarters of the cerulean sky. And the white snowflakes show forth their six-petalled flowers." The Chinese, however, having discovered the hexagonal symmetry of snow crystals, did nothing to advance their understanding of crystal structure. They appeared to accept the symmetry as a fact of nature that required no further study. Indeed, in A.D. 1189, over thirteen hundred years after Han Ying, the physician Chang Kao in his book *I Shuo* (*Medical Discourses*) writes "Plants and trees all have the five-fold pattern; only the yellow berry (*chih tzu*) and snowflake crystals are hexagonal." Little progress here.

We cannot fault the Chinese for their lack of progress in the understanding of snow crystal structure. In Europe, where we now must turn, progress had been halted on many fronts during that long intellectual hibernation known as the Dark Ages. Well over thirteen hundred years had to pass before significant advances were made over the teachings of Aristotle and the great Greek physician Galen.

The first mention of snow crystal structure in the European literature was about A.D. 1260 in the meteorological writings of Albertus Magnus. He thought that the crystals were star-shaped, but believed that they fell only in February and March. Nearly three hundred years passed before the subject was taken up again. In 1555, the Scandinavian bishop Olaus Magnus published a book in which a brief chapter was devoted to snow crystals. A woodcut, widely reproduced by others in later writings, supposedly shows the wide variety in shapes of snow crystals. Twenty-three strangely-shaped objects can be seen falling from the bottom of a cloud. Only one of these, however, a six-pointed star, resembles a snow crystal. The rest show curious shapes like arrows, bells, and a king's crown. One even looks like a human hand! It can't be said that the good bishop did not recognize the endless variety of shapes of snow crystals, but he did miss the most important thing of all — their hexagonal symmetry. The first in the West to recognize that was one of the greatest scientists of the Middle Ages.

In 1610, Johannes Kepler was famous for having discovered in the previous year that the planets did not move in a circular path, as had been taught for centuries since the time of Aristotle and the Greeks, but in an elliptical one. For this great discovery he had been appointed imperial mathematician to the court in Prague. One day, probably in December, he was walking outdoors wondering what he could give as a New Year's gift to his benefactor in the court. While crossing a bridge serendipity struck, and he later wrote:

> Just then by a happy chance water vapor was condensed by the cold into snow, and specks of down fell here and there on my coat, all with six corners and feathered radii. . . . Here was the ideal New Year's gift. . . the very thing for a mathematician to give.

Further observation and much thought resulted in the gift of the essay *On the Six-Cornered Snowflake*.[2]

Kepler not only recognized the hexagonal symmetry of snow crystals, but he was the first to use a rational scientific approach in an attempt to understand it. He stated the problem with amazing clarity:

> There must be some definite cause why, whenever snow begins to fall, its initial formations invariably display the shape of a six-cornered starlet. For if it happens by chance, why do they not fall just as well with five corners or with seven? Why always with six, so long as they are not tumbled and tangled in

masses by irregular drifting, but still remain widespread and scattered?

He also wondered why the crystals were flat and grew only in two dimensions. These were excellent questions. Kepler considered the packing of spheres and hexagons but got nowhere in his quest. Noting that substances other than water, such as salt, crystallized in different shapes, he ended his essay by posing an interesting problem to chemists that is still relevant today: "So let the chemists tell us whether there is any salt in a snowflake and what kind of salt, and what shape it assumes otherwise."

About a quarter century later, in 1635, another intellectual giant, the mathematician and philosopher Rene Descartes, having read Kepler's essay, published drawings he made from his own observations of snow crystals.[3] Unlike the drawings of Olaus Magnus, of which only one made any sense, most of Descartes', though crude, showed hexagonal symmetry. Because of this, they must be regarded as the first scientific records of snow crystals. Amazingly, among his drawings is a relatively rare form of snow crystal consisting of a hexagonal column capped on both ends by six-pointed crystals. Descartes, like Kepler, believed there was some unknown relationship between the way particles were packed in two dimensions and the hexagonal patterns of the snow crystals.

Another quarter century passed. In Copenhagen, in 1660, Erasmus Bartholinus published snow crystal drawings that showed, though not quite in their proper orientation, the fine branches that often protrude from each of the arms of the hexagonal stars. In the remaining years of the 1600s, three other men in rapid succession contributed to the increasing store of accumulated knowledge on snow crystals.

The first was Robert Hooke, an eminent scientist in his own right, but who unfortunately had to do his work in the shadow of the great Isaac Newton. Hooke was one of the first to use the newly-invented microscope to explore the world of commonplace objects whose detailed structure was beyond the limits of the human eye. In 1665, he published his now-classic book

Micrographia.[4] It contained numerous drawings of things seen through the microscope, such as an ant's head, pores in wood, a razor's edge, a human hair, and of course, snow crystals. He collected the crystals by:

> . . . exposing a piece of black cloth, or a black hatt, to the falling snow. I have often with great pleasure, observ'd such an infinite variety of curiously figur'd snow, that it would be as impossible to draw the figure and shape of every one of them, as to imitate exactly the curious and geometrical mechanism of nature in any one.

Hooke was well aware of the six-fold symmetry of the snow crystals. He wrote that "whatever figure one of the branches were, the other five were sure to be of the same." But when he looked at them very closely through the microscope, he:

> . . . found them not to appear so curious and exactly figur'd as one would have imagin'd, but like artificial figures, the bigger they were magnify'd, the more irregularities appear'd in them; but this irregularity seem'd ascribable to the thawing and breaking of the flake by the fall, and not at all to the defect of the plastic virtue of nature. . . . I am very apt to think, that could we have a sight of one of them through a microscope as they are generated in the clouds before their figures are vitiated by external accidents, they would exhibit abundance of curiosity and neatness.

Hooke realized, as did Bentley over two hundred years later, that quickness and manual dexterity are the keys to success in looking at snow crystals through the microscope.

Ten years after Hooke's work, Friedrich Martens, in 1675, published drawings of snow crystals he had seen in the Arctic, where he had gone as a barber on a whaling ship. An accomplished amateur naturalist, Martens was the first to note the meteorological conditions when he made his drawings. Some barber! In 1681, the Italian, Donato Rossetti, contributed another first when he drew in detail not the star-shaped snow crystals earlier observers had seen but hexagonal plates.

During the 1700s, a number of people made drawings of snow crystals, some of them clearly in error, and in general little advance was made. Indicative of the lack of progress in the eighteenth century, the most significant piece of new information was not an observation but only a suggestion by Guettard in Warsaw in 1762 that the shape of the snow crystals should be related to the temperature at which they form. In this, Guettard was correct, but confirmation of his idea did not come until the next century.

As if to make up for the lack of progress in the 1700s, the 1800s presented us with the amazing William Scoresby who did as much for snow crystal science as all previous workers combined.[5] Scoresby went to sea at age ten aboard his father's whaling ship and by sixteen was Chief Officer on a trip to the Arctic. The next two years found him at Edinburgh University studying physics and chemistry, but on his twenty-first birthday his father gave him command of a whaler. During the next ten years he made a number of trips to the Arctic. In addition to the business of catching whales, Scoresby made hydrographical surveys, observations and measurements on the biology and chemistry of seawater, and significantly advanced what was known of the meteorology of the Arctic. His findings were published in 1820 in a monumental two-volume treatise *An Account of the Arctic Regions*.

In the section on meteorology, Scoresby wrote in some detail about the many forms of snow crystals he observed. Though he does not mention looking at them through a microscope, he had one on board ship and it is quite likely he used it to examine some of the crystals. He made drawings of ninety-six crystals that included the majority of forms that are known today, including the relatively rare capped hexagonal columns — similar to those that appeared in Descartes' drawings — and the very rare twelve-sided crystals that occur when two regular, six-sided snow crystals grow independently but on opposite sides of a cloud droplet that has frozen. Though each of his crystals was unique, Scoresby found that he could classify them under five general categories, with two or more subsections for some categories. But best of all, he was able to show for the first time that crystal type was determined by the temperature of the air. Within a given type, however, he found the variations in crystal design to be endless. He was puzzled by this and said that the explanation:

> . . . can only be referred to the will and pleasure of the Great First Cause, whose works, even the most minute and evanescent, and in regions the most removed from human observation, are altogether admirable.

Halfway around the world from Scoresby, Toshitsura Doi, a feudal lord in Japan, spent many years carefully observing the shapes and structure of snow crystals. In 1833, Doi published *Sekka-Zusetsu (Illustrations of Snow Crystals)*, a small book that contained eighty-six illustrations.[6] They were painstakingly drawn and many were the equal of those sketched by Scoresby. What is remarkable about the book is that it appeared at the very beginning of the dawn of science in Japan. In 1840, Doi published a supplementary volume of the *Sekka-Zusetsu* that contained an additional ninety-seven drawings of snow crystals. After Doi, studies of snow crystals in Japan lapsed for nearly a century. But in 1932, the year after Wilson Bentley's death, Ukichiro Nakaya at Hokkaido University began his classic studies of snow and snow crystals. Nakaya's lifetime quest to understand the mysteries of the snow crystals was carried out with such enthusiasm and dedication that he attracted many young scientists to his laboratory. Today, these scientists and their students are among the world leaders in studies of snow crystals and all forms of ice that occur in the atmosphere.

The snow crystal sketches of Doi and Scoresby, though better than any done before them, could not match the intricate detail in those done in England by James Glaisher.[7] Though trained as an astronomer, Glaisher early in life turned to meteorology. His research and administrative abilities were soon recognized, and he was placed in charge of the British Meteorological Department. With a strong interest in instrumentation, he organized a series of studies that resulted in more accurate thermometers being placed in the hands of observers that were carefully selected and trained. Not content to sit in an office, Glaisher took part in many experiments. In one of a number of high altitude balloon ascents in the 1860s, Glaisher and a colleague nearly lost their lives when the balloon reached an altitude of about 29,000 feet. Glaisher had become unconscious and his colleague, whose hands were nearly frozen, had to use his teeth to pull a cord to release gas to allow the balloon to descend.

Glaisher was a co-founder of the British (now Royal) Meteorological Society and soon became its President. But he was also active in many other organizations. He became the first President of the Royal Microscopical Society and was for many years President of the Photographic Society. At age forty he was elected a Fellow of the Royal Society of London. With such wide-ranging interests it is not at all surprising that Glaisher turned his attention to the snow crystals. In 1855, he published about one hundred fifty amazingly detailed drawings of crystals he had observed under a magnifying glass. "Their forms were so varied," he wrote, "that it seemed scarcely possible for continuous observations to exhaust them all." As with others before him and since, he not only was aware of the six-fold symmetry of the snow crystals but was awed by their elegance and beauty. He wrote that at the center of every crystal was:

> . . . a hexagon of six rays. These rays, in passing through successive stages of crystallization, become encrusted with an endless variety of crystalline formations, some consisting of thin laminae alone, others of solid but translucent prisms, heaped one upon another, and others gorgeously combining laminae and prisms in the richest profusion.

Glaisher was aware that the form of the snow crystals changed with temperature, but had little more to say about it. With the typical caution of the scientist, he said he wanted to continue his investigations and "to defer all conclusions for the present."

It is hard to imagine anyone having the perseverance and the ability to produce better drawings of snow crystals than Glaisher's. Perhaps the young Wilson Bentley did, but we'll never know since his drawings have not survived. Glaisher's work came at the dawn of the age of photography, an age that was soon to bring us the photographic successes of Bentley and those who followed him. This brought to an end the centuries-long quest to capture in drawings the intricate and beautiful structure of the snow crystals.

This brief excursion into history cannot end without mention of the only known American before Bentley who tried to capture the shape of snow crystals. In 1864, the year before Bentley was born, a charming little book titled *Cloud Crystals, A Snow Flake Album* appeared.[8] Its author was identified only as "a lady" from Portland, Maine. She made not drawings but paper cutouts of snow crystals that fell upon her window sill. "The crystals are caught upon dark fur or cloth," she wrote, "a strong magnifier placed over them to assist the eye, and the figure immediately cut from memory." Her book contained nearly sixty short articles, most of them poems by others extolling the beauty of winter and snow, but sprinkled liberally among them were nearly a hundred of her snow crystal cutouts.

Apparently she had sent some of her crystal cutouts to Louis Agassiz, the great biologist and popularizer of science who was then a professor at Harvard. He wrote back with the good advice that should she publish the cutouts, she should also mention the weather conditions at the time the crystals fell. In addition she should:

> . . . furnish the internal evidence that they are all copies from nature, and not fanciful imitations of the general aspects of snowflakes, embellished by an active imagination; otherwise the whole would be useless to students of nature, and only to be

looked at as an elegant toy, fit to excite the curiosity, but not to impart information.

Replying to Agassiz's admonition in the introduction to her book, our lady said "all is fact and not fanciful embellishment. As far as the eye and the hand could be trusted, every delineation is strictly truthful." But a few lines later she admitted that:

> It will not be supposed that the *whole* impression can thus be given. One might as well attempt to copy the frostwork upon the windows on a winter's morning. Many of the embellishments are inimitable.

Our lady did *not* take Agassiz's advice to mention the weather conditions associated with each of the cutouts in her book, though it appears she knew them. She said that "a slight change of temperature, or any other atmospheric variation, soon changes the entire form of the falling crystals." And despite her promise to stay away from "fanciful embellishment," some of her cutouts, in defying the laws of snow crystal architecture, were exactly that. The best of her cutouts, though apparently accurate, do not contain the intricate detail found in Glaisher's drawings. Her difficulties, however, in capturing the exact shape and beauty of the snow crystals should not detract from her valiant attempt to do so. It is likely that about fifteen years later, Bentley, sitting in that cold shed peering through his mother's old microscope and trying to draw a rapidly subliming snow crystal, was forced to do a bit of embellishment himself. But perhaps he realized this. It may have been a factor in causing him to turn to the new science of photomicrography where he became the first to capture without embellishment the fragile and fleeting beauty of the snow crystals and to introduce it to millions of people around the world.

---

[1] Much of the history of the early work with snow crystals discussed in this chapter can be found in Joseph Needham and Lu Gwei-Djen, "The earliest snow crystal observations," *Weather*, 1961, vol. 16, pp. 319–327.

[2] L. L. Whyte, ed., *The Six-Cornered Snowflake,* Oxford University Press, 1966.

[3] B. J. Mason, *Ibid.* pp. 47–56.

[4] Robert Hooke, *Micrographia*, first published by the Royal Society of London, 1665; reprinted 1961 by Dover Publications, Inc.

[5] William Scoresby, *An Account of the Arctic Regions with a History and Description of the Northern Whale-Fishery*, vol. 1, *The Arctic*, first published in 1820 but reprinted by Augustus M. Kelly, Publishers, New York, 1969.

[6] Ukichiro Nakaya, *Snow Crystals*, Harvard University Press, 1954, p. 2.

[7] James Glaisher, "Snow crystals," *The Illustrated London News,* February 24, 1855, p. 192.

[8] A Lady, *Cloud Crystals, A Snow Flake Album*, D. Appleton & Co., 1864.

Chapter 6

The Treasures of the Snow

The public exhibition of Bentley's photomicrographs of snow crystals at the Harvard Mineralogical Museum in 1898, and the publication in the *Popular Science Monthly* of his first article, must have made Bentley's work known to thousands. Letters probably poured into the Bentley farmhouse on Nashville Road, urging him to continue with his work. It's doubtful that he needed this urging. Winter after winter since 1885 had found him pursuing his labor of love, in spite of his father's and brother's feeling that he was wasting his time. Within the family, only his mother encouraged him. By the end of 1898, Bentley was secure in the knowledge that his work was being appreciated by others far beyond the borders of Jericho. He did not hesitate, as he might have a year or two earlier, to write to people of prominence in the sciences. On May 17, 1899, he penned a letter to Abbott L. Rotch, founder and director of the famed Blue Hill Meteorological Observatory.

Abbott Rotch was born with the proverbial silver spoon in his mouth.[1] The descendent of a long line of Rotchs, all successful businessmen, A. L. Rotch was born in 1861 in Milton, Massachusetts, a town south of Boston and just north of the Blue Hills. His parents were well-known in Boston, being active in the arts, politics, and social life of the city. The youngest of seven children, Rotch, along with his parents and siblings, traveled abroad on trips that sometimes lasted many months. While abroad, he often attended schools in Paris, Berlin, and Florence. By an early age he was proficient in foreign languages. At age sixteen he became interested in science and mathematics, and the following year began a series of detailed meteorological observations that were carefully recorded in a weather diary. He graduated from the Massachusetts Institute of Technology in 1884 with a degree in mechanical engineering, but with no burning desire to pursue that profession. He did not have to pursue *any* profession. His father had died two years before, leaving him with an income sufficient to live on. He was active and popular in Boston circles. He liked people and had traveled widely, but he had little idea what to do for the rest of his life.

One day, not long after graduation from MIT, he climbed the Great Blue Hill — 636 feet (194 meters) above sea level — the tallest of the Blue Hills. The visibility was excellent; he could see for miles in all directions. A few weeks later the thought occurred to him that Blue Hill would make a splendid site for a meteorological observatory. He had found his life's work. In less than half a year he purchased land and built the observatory. At midnight on January 31, 1885, just sixteen days after Wilson Bentley had obtained his first successful photomicrograph of a snow crystal, Abbott Rotch, amidst bonfires and the firing of rockets, celebrated the opening of the Blue Hill Meteorological Observatory. Over the next dozen years, Rotch engaged in a whirlwind of activity. He added people to the staff of the observatory. He made numerous trips to Europe where he met and consulted with all the eminent meteorologists of the day, always returning with the latest in meteorological instrumentation to supplement that being built and used in the observatory. When Bentley wrote his letter to Rotch, the Blue Hill Meteorological Observatory was one of the best in the world. Much of its eminence was due to Rotch, who not only gave numerous lectures on meteorology but also was a prolific writer on the subject. By 1899, he had written eighty-five scientific articles, most in English but some in French or German for publication on the continent.

Bentley's letter to Rotch, written on lined paper, read as follows:[2]

Dear Sir,

I have been advised by one of the Professors in Wellesly [*sic*] College, to write to you, & to send you samples of microphotographs of snow crystals secured by me here in Vt during the last 15 Winters. I take pleasure in enclosing a few of them. The authority referred to, thought you might wish to secure a collection of such, for yourself, or for exhibition in the observatory. Should you wish to do so, price is 5 cts each photo, unmounted.

Very Truly Yours,

W. A. Bentley

In the left hand margin he added "Lantern Slides furnished, if desired."

Rotch wrote back on June 3. His letter has been lost, but he apparently asked for details. Bentley replied on June 7:

Dear Sir,

Yours of the 3rd inst. at hand. In reply to your inquiry, will say that I have a record of temperature, number of cloud strata, and approx. height of each (in many instances), also direction of drift of clouds & lower air, etc. taken when the snow crystals were photographed. I have also noted down in most instances portion of storm from which the crystals photographed fell from, i.e., whether southern, central, northern, etc. I have secured sets of from 4 to 20 specimens from almost all the great snow storms & blizzards from March 12, 1888 to March of this year. Should you wish for one or two hundred photos, I shall be glad to furnish this data, if desired, without extra charge. If you are greatly interested in the causes and conditions that determine the selection & modification of the different snow forms, I shall be very glad to write you a long letter telling you something of what I have observed and learned during my over 15 years study of them. It will give me great pleasure to receive an order from you, for a collection of these gems, wrought by the blizzards.

Very Truly Yours

W. A. Bentley

Rotch, now satisfied by what Bentley said in his letter, wrote back on June 22 with an order for snow crystal photographs.

Dear Sir,

Referring to your letter of the 7th inst., I should like to purchase 100 prints of various photos of cloud crystals, unmounted, & I enclose money order for five dollars, in payment. I should like to have any notes which you made of the weather conditions at the time of photographing the crystals, as well as any deductions which you have drawn from your observations during fifteen years.

Glaisher, the English meteorologist, many years ago published drawings of snow crystals & about 30 years ago a lady in Portland, Maine, did the same. The only photos I know of besides yours are by Dr. Neuhauss of Berlin.

Yours truly,

A. L. Rotch, Director

During the following week Bentley probably angered his brother Charles by spending less time on chores around the farm and more time on the selection of snow crystal prints for Rotch and the preparation of a long letter. On June 29, exactly a week after Rotch had written, Bentley pulled his thoughts together and wrote back. His letter began: "I send you by to days [sic] reg. mail 150 micro photos of snow crystals. I send the extra ones, so that you can make your own selection returning the excess over 100." It's clear that Bentley had been selling photos to others, since he mentions a technique of mounting the prints that has been used by the "Am. muzeum [sic] of Natural History, at Central Park, N.Y. & elsewhere" The major part of his letter, however, was what he called "Major deductions and other facts of interest." He said that his photos do not represent the average: "the average forms are much less perfect & beautiful." He wrote about what portion of the storm the most beautiful crystals emerged from, and how the temperature and other conditions determined their structure. He stated you do not need visible clouds for the formation of snow crystals.

> A striking proof of this interesting fact was afforded the past winter on February 4, 1899. Most of the exquisitely beautiful snow forms falling in that day, fell from out a bright blue unclouded sky.

He penned a few lines about the nuclei of the crystals and his suspicion that the electromagnetic nature of the cloud helps determine the crystal structure. Much of what Bentley said would appear two years later in the first of his technical articles.

On July 7 Rotch, in a brief reply to Bentley, said:

> The 150 microphotos received & I am much pleased with them. Instead of returning the 50 not ordered, which you sent for inspection, I will keep them and send $2.50 in payment. It is possible that I shall send some to Germany. I should like to know the magnifying power used and whether it was the same in all cases.

This ends the known correspondence between Bentley and Rotch. A number of interesting things can be gleaned from it. First, both Bentley and Rotch, in referring to the photographs of the snow crystals, persisted in using the incorrect term *microphotograph*, which means a small photograph, and not the correct term *photomicrograph*, a photograph of something very small. Back at the turn of the century, photomicrography was in its infancy, and confusion in the terminology must have occurred frequently. Though Bentley and Perkins used the correct term in their 1898 article, Bentley, in his next two articles lapsed back into incorrect usage. But by 1902, he finally got it right and never again confused the two words.

Bentley's charge of five cents for each of the 3-inch-square (7.6-cm-square) snow crystal photographs is ludicrously low by today's standards but perhaps not by those of his day. He never increased the price. Until the day he died over thirty years later, the charge for a snow crystal photograph was still only five cents!

These photographs and the 3-by-4-inch lantern slides were in great demand over the years. A quarter century later he said, "There is hardly a university in the United States or Canada that does not have some of my slides for use in class work."[3]

Did Bentley then make money from the sale of his slides and photographs? Hardly. He went on to say:

> The recognition has been very gratifying, but not very remunerative. . . . I am a poor man, except in the satisfaction I get out of my work. In that respect I am one of the richest men in the world. I wouldn't change places with Henry Ford or John D. Rockefeller for all their millions! And I wouldn't change places with a king; not for all his power and glory. I have my snowflakes!

Putting it in more realistic terms, he said:

> From a practical standpoint I suppose I would be considered a failure. It has cost me $15,000 in time and materials to do the work and I have received less than $4,000 from it.[4]

Bentley's comment about snow crystals falling from "a bright blue unclouded sky" may have caused Rotch momentarily to wonder about his observational skills and general intelligence. After all, isn't the belief that snow can fall from a clear sky in the same category as believing that rain can fall from a clear sky? Many people have said they saw rain fall from a clear sky and believed that it actually formed there. What undoubtedly happened, however, was that the rain formed in the usual manner in a cloud, and during the ten to fifteen minutes it took the raindrops to fall to the ground, the cloud either evaporated or was carried far away by winds that generally move faster up where the clouds are than winds near the ground. Consequently, when people feel raindrops hit them and look up to see a clear sky, they jump to the conclusion that the rain somehow formed there. Could not a similar thing have happened with Bentley's snow crystals? Perhaps, but Bentley was far too good an observer to be fooled in that manner. Besides, Bentley was not the first competent observer to report seeing snow crystals fall from a clear sky. No less an observer than William Scoresby saw the same thing two centuries before Bentley.

The explanation of this curious phenomenon has to do with the fact that the vapor pressure of ice is slightly less than that of water at all temperatures below thirty-two degrees Fahrenheit (zero degrees Celsius). Vapor pressure is the pressure exerted by water vapor evaporating from ice or water. Consider first the formation of a cloud. When the relative humidity of ascending air reaches and slightly exceeds one hundred percent, water vapor condenses on tiny, submicroscopic particles in the air to produce cloud droplets. Even when the droplets form in air at a temperature below thirty-two degrees Fahrenheit, they remain liquid and seldom show any tendency to freeze until the temperature cools another ten degrees or more. The droplets are said to be supercooled. Now, if the nucleus of a snow crystal forms in the midst of the cloud of supercooled water droplets (for example, by the freezing of a single cloud droplet), the tiny crystal finds itself in an environment where the vapor pressure is controlled by that of all the nearby water droplets. The vapor pressure at saturation produces a relative humidity of 100 percent with respect to the liquid water. But since this is higher than the vapor pressure at the surface of the snow crystal, water vapor will flow quickly toward the snow crystal, causing it to grow rapidly. The growth continues while the surrounding cloud droplets decrease in size as they supply water vapor to the snow crystal. From the point of view of the growing snow crystal, the surrounding air is supersaturated with water vapor.

Imagine next a situation in the atmosphere where the relative humidity is less than one hundred percent but still high, say ninety-eight percent. No cloud will form. In Bentley's words, the sky may be "bright blue." But the vapor pressure, while not high enough to produce saturation for liquid water, is quite high enough to produce a supersaturated vapor pressure for ice. If at this time some special submicroscopic particles that go by the name of ice nuclei wander into the region, water vapor from the surrounding air will flow rapidly to the nuclei, causing them to grow into visible snow crystals. The growth will continue until the vapor pressure (and relative humidity) of the environment decreases to that exerted by the snow crystal. Such snow crystals, formed in a clear, cloudless sky, seldom grow very big. Indeed, Bentley observed just that on February 4, 1899, when he wrote in his notebook that "the crystals gradually became smaller, until 1 o'clock when they became too small to photograph."

Neither Bentley nor any other meteorologist at the turn of the century had any idea of the importance of the role of vapor pressure differences between ice and water in the growth of snow crystals. When this was realized in the mid-1930s, a few years after Bentley's death, it was used to explain the rapid growth of snow crystals in supercooled clouds. But no one thought to use it to explain the curious production of snow crystals in clear air where the water vapor was supersaturated with respect to ice but not to water. If they did, it would have had to remain an interesting conjecture, for there was no way to test the idea by experiment in the atmosphere. At that time, no one knew of any way to inject into the air prodigious numbers of submicroscopic ice crystals to test whether they would grow to snow crystals large enough to be seen falling to the ground. But all this changed right after World War II when two famous discoveries were made that led to modern-day cloud seeding. In 1946, Vincent Schaefer, a scientist at the Research Laboratory of the General Electric Company in Schenectady, New York, discovered that dry ice, when dropped through a supercooled cloud of water droplets, left behind a trail containing immense numbers of tiny ice crystals.[5] A few months later his colleague, Bernard Vonnegut, discovered that submicroscopic crystals of silver iodide could also initiate snow crystal formation in a supercooled cloud.[6] Among the many experiments these scientists performed was clear air seeding. With their seeding agents they were able to produce in clear air, where the relative humidity was high, a visible cloud of snow crystals that settled slowly earthward. A half century after Bentley saw snow crystals falling from a clear sky, scientists finally were able to reproduce the experiment that nature had done so easily for him.

❄

On January 3, 1900, Bailey Willis, a geologist in the US Geological Survey, wrote a letter to Willis Moore, Chief of the US Weather Bureau. It read in part:

> I have recently come into correspondence with Mr. W. A. Bentley of Nashville, Vt. . . . He has accumulated a collection of over 500 forms of crystals, showing great variety of development. . . . Mr. Bentley furnishes photographic prints from his negatives at the moderate charge of 5 cents a print. It has occurred to me that you might be interested to secure a set for your Bureau, that the data might be worked up into a contribution of some value for meteorologists. I have a collection of 100 prints from Mr. Bentley's negatives, and should be glad to show them to you.

Moore replied two days later:

> While the Weather Bureau is not at present engaged in any investigations relative to the formation of snow crystals, we should like to see the prints now in your possession. If it would be convenient for you to bring them to the Cosmos Club or the Weather Bureau some day next week we shall [consider them].

Chief Moore must have passed Willis's letter on to Professor Cleveland Abbe to get his advice on the matter. Abbe, knowledgeable in many aspects of meteorology, was editor of the *Monthly Weather Review*, an official publication of the Weather Bureau and the only technical journal in the United States that published original articles on meteorological research. His advice to Moore left no doubt about his appreciation of the importance of Bentley's work:

> The study of a great collection like the five hundred secured by Mr. Bentley promises to give us definite and most important information. I think that the whole set should be secured for our

library. . . . Furthermore, Mr. Bentley should be encouraged to continue his work until the subject is thoroughly understood.[7]

Like Professor George Perkins two years earlier, Professor Abbe recognized that behind these amazingly clear and detailed photographs was an intellect that passionately wanted to understand the origin of snow crystals, why they were all different, and how they were modified during their long journey from the clouds to the ground. Once again, quite by chance, Bentley had found an influential person who would champion his efforts.

Abbe was interested in everything.[8] In 1868, at age thirty, he became director of the Cincinnati Observatory, Cincinnati, Ohio, and immediately wanted to extend the scientific work of the observatory to astronomy, meteorology, and magnetism, and to apply these sciences to "geography and geodesy, to storm prediction, and to the wants of the citizen and the land surveyor."

Needless to say, all this could not be done at once, so Abbe's interests slowly centered on meteorology. He began to draw weather maps based on telegraphic reports of the weather. When the Weather Service of the United States was inaugurated in 1870, Abbe became the first official forecaster of the weather, issuing his forecasts in terms of the "probable" weather to be expected. First published only for the Cincinnati region, they were later published throughout the country as official weather bulletins named *Probabilities*. Abbe soon was known by the nickname of *Old Probabilities*.

When Abbe gave up forecasting, he turned his attention to the running of the *Monthly Weather Review*, the writing of nearly three hundred articles on weather phenomena, and sending many thousands of letters encouraging others to become as excited as he was about the atmosphere and its many mysteries. Abbe's weather forecasts in the 1870s were so well-known that Mark Twain spoofed them in an after-dinner talk on the difficulty of forecasting New England weather.

Old Probabilities has a mighty reputation for accurate prophecy, and thoroughly well deserves it. You take up the paper and observe how crisply and confidently he checks off what to-day's weather is going to be on the Pacific, down south, in the Middle States, in the Wisconsin region. See him sail along in the joy and pride of his power till he gets to New England, and then see his tail drop. *He* doesn't know what the weather is going to be in New England.[9]

In March, 1900, Bentley published a short article on snow crystals in *Popular Science News*. In the following issues, two more of his articles appeared, one on frost, the other on raindrops. Though brief, they showed his wide ranging interests in atmospheric phenomena. By the end of the year over twenty universities and museums, including the British Museum, had bought prints of his snow crystal photographs.

The year 1901 was remarkable for Wilson Bentley and his snow crystals. It was not because he had obtained 127 new snow crystal photographs, the most he had ever photographed in a single winter, nor was it because on January 28 he captured on film thirty-two snow crystals, the most ever in a single day. These records did not concern him, for he made no mention of them in his notebook. On January 28, some of his notebook entries were:

Great blizzard extends from Florida to north of Quebec. . . . Snowfall 6 or 8 inches during day. . . . Very beautiful perfect forms all afternoon. . . some large [ones] at dusk. . . . Saw a very odd crystal shaped like a sawhorse.

The year was remarkable for the variety of ways in which Bentley's work was brought before both scientists and non-scientists, in this country and abroad.

It all began in March when Cleveland Abbe devoted a full page in the *Monthly Weather Review* to Bentley's work. He reminded readers that during the previous year he had mentioned Bentley's extensive collection of snow crystal photographs. And then, as a sort of advertisement of what was coming soon in the *Review*, he said:

> Mr. Bentley has kindly promised that the readers of the *Monthly Weather Review* shall be favored with a very complete series of photographs and notes, and the Editor hopes by this publication to contribute to the foundations of our knowledge of the formation of clouds and rain.

As if this were not enough of a preview of things to come, Abbe reprinted several paragraphs from Bentley's article in the *Popular Science Monthly*.

Bentley's article appeared in the May issue of the *Review*. It was the first one he had ever written just for meteorologists. It was brief and somewhat tentative. One had the feeling that Bentley was as unsure of his writing skills as he had been earlier when Professor Perkins urged him to write about his work. Nevertheless, his 1.5-page "Twenty years study of snow crystals," accompanied by twenty-six exquisite photographs of snow crystals, had a number of interesting and provocative ideas. At the start he made it clear that all snow crystals are different. Throwing caution and wordiness to the winds, as he had not in his earlier article with Perkins, he simply stated that he had taken several hundred photographs of snow crystals over the years, "no two alike." He reiterated what he had said earlier, that the most perfect crystal forms fell from the western and northwestern portions of the storms. He added that the temperature and relative humidity at the ground was not as important as "generally supposed in determining the form and size of the crystals." What is important, he said, are the conditions aloft. Tiny crystals come into being and are carried upward by air currents. When they become large enough to fall down through the currents, "the crystals will in all probability be greatly modified by passing through atmospheric strata varying so greatly in density, temperature, humidity, etc." As proof of this conjecture he asked his readers to look at the nucleus (center) of many of his photographs, one of which came from the Great Blizzard of 1888. This showed the shape of the crystal when it was first formed. Then, Bentley said, move outward from the center and observe how the crystal shape often goes through a variety of shapes, some ending up more or less as hexagonal plates, others the feathery, stellar shapes most people identify with a typical snow crystal. This, Bentley contended, results from and reflects the varying atmospheric conditions the crystals encountered on their journey through the clouds to the earth.

Bentley wondered whether the electrified state of the atmosphere played a role in determining crystal shape, or whether also "greater or less amounts of various gases and vapors in the atmosphere may be controlling factors."

Pulling all his ideas together, he made a suggestion for future work involving other observers that is as pertinent today as it was then.

> Simultaneous observations of the forms and changes the crystals undergo from hour to hour during our great blizzards should be made by many skilled observers, stationed along a general line extending north and south. . . . This study should include observations of the kind and approximate height and direction of drift of the various clouds, direction and force of the surface wind, temperature of the air, and amount of moisture at the earth's surface; also its electric condition, whether negative or positive, and the portion of the storm from which the crystals emanate.

While meteorologists were being exposed to his technical accomplishments, another aspect of Bentley's creativity was revealed in May. The opening of the Pan-American Exposition in Buffalo, New York, allowed thousands of visitors to see a sensitive artistic side to his talents. The Exposition, the most important ever to be held in the United States up to that time, had a midway, numerous illuminated fountains, and hundreds of exhibits, both from the United States and other countries, that touched on religious, philosophical, musical, artistic, and scientific themes.[10] It is not known with any certainty how Bentley happened to exhibit there or how much of his work was used. But it is likely he was asked to do so by the Weather Bureau. A year before, when the Bureau was making plans for their own displays in the Exposition, a memo from one Bureau administrator to another said that Bentley's photographs of snow crystals "if enlarged could possibly be suitable for exposition purposes."[11] Undoubtedly the enlarged photographs were on exhibit. Their beauty must have been appreciated by all whose eyes fell upon them, but most of the admiration had to be reserved for a single work of art.

Bentley had made a large montage of a snow crystal from 125 of his snow crystal photographs. The individual crystals, both large and small, were placed upon a jet black background in such a way as to make a montage nearly three feet in diameter. It had a certain abstract quality to it. Most people looking at it probably saw first a simple six-pointed star, each of whose arms was made from five of the largest snow crystals in the montage. To keep the six-fold symmetry, Bentley placed a single crystal at the very center to be shared with each of the six arms. Superimposed on all of this and composed of slightly smaller crystals was a Star of David, two equilateral triangles interlaced one with the other. The six points of the Star were placed not upon but between the points of the simple star, whose six arms moved radially outward from the center. By using smaller crystals for the Star of David, Bentley achieved a three-dimensional aspect to his creation; it appeared to be set back from the simple star.

But that was not all. Toward the center of the montage, he placed thirty-six very small crystals in the form of a smaller Star of David that showed only the six points. Within this, but now using much smaller crystals that showed up mainly as tiny dots, were two more modified Stars of David, interlaced but still surrounding the crystal at the very center. The decreasing size of the crystals that made up the interior Stars gave a further three-dimensional aspect to the montage, making it appear as though the central crystal sat in some special position at the end of a long tunnel that receded far into the background. Looking at the montage as a whole, the eye moved back and forth unconsciously between the two types of stars, first seeing one, then the other, then both together. The six-pointed star in the foreground gave the viewer the feeling that the montage primarily depicted those stellar snow crystals so often associated with the snowflakes, but if one focused on the bold hexagonal outlines that both stars together make, the montage appeared to be that of a hexagonal plate, the most popular of the snow crystals in the public eye after the stellar. As beauty is in the eye of the beholder, so is the type of snow crystal that could be seen in this splendid work of art. But perhaps Bentley had that in mind when he created it.

Curiously, after the Exposition, Bentley never again used the montage. Since he was so enchanted with the beauty of the snow crystals, one would have expected him to use it in some of the many articles he would later publish, but he never did. He did, however, make a lantern slide of it, and a large photograph of the montage was found in his farmhouse after his death. Surprisingly, Bentley had made a similar montage many years before the Exposition, possibly as a teenager. One of his nieces years later said it was made "just from sketches he'd made of snowflakes that he examined under the microscope. That's when he was around fifteen, sixteen years old."[12] She went on to say that her uncle had it framed and hung on the wall, but one day it fell and the glass broke. She said "uncle didn't take care of things. . . . It was long before he died that [the montage] had been thrown out."

A month after the Exposition opened, Bentley's work reached yet another audience, this time in England. The *Quarterly Journal of the Royal Meteorological Society*, published in London, devoted a page to summarizing his article of two months before in the *Monthly Weather Review*. Bentley had to be pleased at all the attention his work was getting. No doubt his mother was, and it's likely that the older nieces and nephews on the west side of the farmhouse were boasting to other children in the neighborhood about how famous their uncle was becoming far beyond Jericho and Vermont.

※

By 1901, Mary and Charles's family was nearly complete. After the birth of Alric in 1885, children arrived at regular intervals and all had names starting with the letter *A*! There was Agnes, Arthur, Alice, Archel, Amy, and, in 1901, Anna. The last of the children, Alwyn, would be born in 1905.

Wilson Bentley loved his nieces and nephews as if they were his own, and by all accounts the love was reciprocated. Mary and Charles called him Willie or simply W. A., the initials of his first and middle names. The children picked up on this and referred to him as Uncle W. A. or Uncle Willie. Bentley never minded the frequent visits the children made to his side of the house. In fact, it appears that he encouraged them. Charles, however, sometimes discouraged them. Years later, Amy said that her father thought that Uncle W. A.:

> . . . was spending too much time with his head in the clouds. I know that they used to now and then have a problem, and he'd prevent us children from going over there. But we were always over there. There wasn't a night that went by but we were over there sitting on the wood box listening to his stories and things that he would tell us.[13]

Alice, too, had fond recollections of her uncle.

> Uncle W. A. always had some project going. He had his croquet games Sunday afternoon, and there was always lots of lemonade, cookies, ice cream some days, and he had a special fudge he made from white sugar, and what they used to call vanilla drips. It was delicious. . . . And he had evening parties when we'd hang out Japanese lanterns. One Halloween he scared everybody to death. He fixed up a large bough from a balsam tree. . . . It was wrapped in sheets and he had a face with a florescent design, built like a skeleton. It came out of the third floor window.[14]

The summer of 1901 probably was a happy one for Bentley, but storm clouds were gathering. On the happy side, he was in good health. Though no more than five feet, three inches in height and one-hundred-twenty pounds in weight, he was wiry, agile, and extremely well coordinated. His many chores in the barn and in the fields left him with muscles that gave above average strength for his slim frame. He had delicate, rounded facial features, a small nose, and a forehead that appeared high because of the dark hair that slowly began to recede when he was in his twenties. Sometime in his twenties he grew a mustache that hugged his upper lip and extended out about half an inch to either side of it. It stayed with him for the rest of his life.

His mother, however, had anything but good health. When Edwin died in 1887, Fanny had only Wilson to cook for in the east side of the house. She continued to do this until sometime in the mid to late 1890s when her health began to fail. Soon Wilson was doing the cooking for both of them. Amy said that her grandmother:

> . . . got crippled up with rheumatism. Now they call it arthritis.
> So for years she was bedridden. She couldn't go downstairs....
> [My uncle] took care of her but my mother always went over
> and helped him change things, but he took most of the care of
> her.[15]

Though the warm summer days of 1901 often found him entertaining his nieces and nephews along with some of the neighborhood children, every day found him going up the stairs to the second floor bedroom to attend to the needs of his mother.

During the previous summer Fanny and her two sons must have realized she would never get better. A legal document was drawn up in which she turned over her one-third share of the house and all other property to be divided equally between Wilson and Charles.[16] In return for this, Charles had to give her fifty dollars a year for the rest of her life. Presumably most of this was turned over to Wilson for her support. His part of the agreement was to furnish "her at all times with sufficient and proper food, clothing, medicines, and medical care in sickness and health." In addition, since Wilson would be spending a great deal of time taking care of his mother, Charles had to agree that as long as she lived he would "carry the milk of the said Wilson A. to the creamery each and every day that there may be milk to carry." And finally, since Fanny apparently foresaw some squabbling among her sons, the document spelled out precisely which rooms of the house would be occupied by Charles and his family and which by Wilson and his mother. Most importantly, Charles had to agree that "this arrangement is to continue after the decease of said Fanny E. Bentley." With this document Fanny had very cleverly eliminated problems that almost certainly would have come between her two very different sons after her death. One was a practical, hardworking farmer, the other was a sensitive dreamer who did as little farming as possible, whose main mission in life was to understand and photograph the water wonders of the atmosphere.

Sometime during the autumn, probably in October, Cleveland Abbe wrote to Bentley and asked if he would prepare a much more extensive article for the *Monthly Weather Review* than the one he had done earlier in the year. Bentley eagerly agreed to do so, and on November 26 wrote to Abbe with the news that he had started work on the project by taking the first snow crystal photographs of the winter. He went on to say that:

> . . . it occurs to me that if I had a copy of the weather map. . .
> the one that tells approximately of the geographical position of
> storms from day to day, it would greatly help me to know and to
> state more exactly the portion of such storms that the crystals at
> any given time emanate from. As I am, in one sense a
> government observer, can you not arrange to have these sent to
> me?[17]

Abbe wasted no time in making the arrangements. Starting the first week in December, a daily weather map was sent to Bentley from the Boston office of the Weather Bureau.

The year in which Bentley's name and work was thrust before the public ended in December with his publication in *Harper's Magazine* of "The story of the snow crystals." With its fifteen photographs of snow crystals, the article came alive with

82

his enthusiasm. Gone were the fears of not being able to write well that he had expressed to Professor Perkins. Here was a Bentley sure of himself, who, through a masterful control of simile and metaphor, conveyed to his readers some of the beauty and magic he saw in the snowy winter skies. Listen to how he described the falling and arrival of snow crystals upon his blackboard.

> Quick, the first flakes are falling, the couriers of the coming snowstorm; open the skylight, and directly under it place the carefully prepared blackboard, on whose ebony surface the most minute form of frozen beauty may be welcomed from cloudland. . . . Here they come. . . . Glancing eagerly over the surface of the board, the eye discerns some snow crystals of perfect symmetry and unusual shape. It is a delicate puzzle of geometrical beauty, this tabletop from fairyland, like a spider's web frosted as it floated through the air. Lifted on the point of a broom splint, flattened on the plate by a feather, this prize specimen is soon photographed.

Bentley wrote about how he got started, his early attempts at making drawings of the crystals, and his success with photography in 1885. And he mentioned at least twice that "No two are alike." But he went on to say that:

> Of the tens of thousands now filling the air, an infinitesimal proportion fall on this board; nor is there any good reason to doubt that when they started from equal heights on their journey earthward, many of the snow crystals were exactly alike in shape and size, and probably in density.

Atmospheric scientists today agree with Bentley that if any two crystals are to be alike, it will be soon after they are formed nearly side by side in the cloud and initially exposed to identical conditions. In confirmation of this, in 1988, Nancy Knight, a scientist at the National Center for Atmospheric Research in Boulder, Colorado, collected snow crystals from a high-flying aircraft and *found two that were alike*.[18] Bentley would have been pleased.

By the end of 1901, Wilson Bentley, more than any other person on earth, could answer with a joyous and resounding "Yes!" the question God had asked of Job: "Hast thou entered into the treasures of the snow?"

[1] John H. Conover, *The Blue Hill Meteorological Observatory*, American Meteorological Society, 1990, p. 1.

[2] Letters between Bentley and Rotch are by permission of the Houghton Library, Harvard University, shelf mark bMS Am 1271.5 (8) [1–3].

[3] Mary B. Mullet, "The Snowflake Man," *The American Magazine*, February, 1925, pp. 28–31, 173–175.

[4] "Snowflake hides beauty secret from her most persistent suitor, *Philadelphia Public Ledger and North American*, April 4, 1926.

[5] Vincent J. Schaefer, "The production of ice crystals in a cloud of supercooled water droplets," *Science*, 1946, vol. 104, pp. 457–459.

[6] Bernard Vonnegut, "The nucleation of ice formation by silver iodide," *Journal of Applied Physics*, 1947, vol. 18, p. 593–595.

[7] The correspondence between B. Willis, W. Moore, and C. Abbe is in the records of the Weather Bureau, Record Group 27, general correspondence file 1894–1942, File No. 135, National Archives, College Park, Maryland.

[8] "Cleveland Abbe, 1838–1916," *Monthly Weather Review*, 1916, vol. 44, pp. 517–518; *Dictionary of American Biography*, Charles Scribner's Sons, 1964, vol. 1, p. 1.

[9] Mark Twain's *Speech on the Weather* at the New England Society's Seventy-First Annual Dinner, New York City, date unknown.

[10] "Pan-American Exposition," *The New York Times*, 1901, May 2, p. 5.

[11] This memo is in the records of the Weather Bureau, Record Group 27, general correspondence file 1894–1942, File No. 135, National Archives, College Park, Maryland.

[12] Oral communication: Alice B. Hamalainen to Duncan Blanchard, October 3, 1971.

[13] Oral communication: Amy B. Hunt to Duncan Blanchard, July 26, 1969.

[14] Oral communication: Alice B. Hamalainen to Duncan Blanchard, June 26, 1971.

[15] Oral communication: Amy B. Hunt to Duncan Blanchard, July 26, 1969.

[16] Town Records, Jericho, Vermont, 1900, vol. 19, pp. 580–582.

[17] Bentley's letter is in the records of the Weather Bureau, Record Group 27, general correspondence file 1894–1942, File No. 8807, National Archives, College Park, Maryland.

[18] Nancy C. Knight, "No two alike?," *Bulletin of the American Meteorological Society*, 1988, vol. 69, p. 496.

Chapter 7

Even on Christmas Day

On June 10, 1902, Wilson Bentley walked into the Jericho post office with a bulky package addressed to Cleveland Abbe. It contained the manuscript of the longer article for the *Monthly Weather Review* that Abbe had requested and Bentley had agreed to write. Published at the end of the year, it ran to nearly ten pages of text, but the crowning glory of the article was 255 photographs of many forms of snow crystals, most of which had been obtained the previous winter.[1] Never again would Bentley write such an extensive article on snow crystals, and with the exception of his book published the last year of his life, none of his future writings would contain such a massive collection of photographs.

Bentley must have spent the winter in a frenzy of activity, hurrying or neglecting some of his farm chores and sometimes, under the pressure of work, discouraging the visits of his nieces and nephews from the other side of the farmhouse. On each of the twenty-four days it snowed, he worked in the back shed, even on Christmas Day when he took photographs from 8:30 in the morning until 2:30 in the afternoon![2] His efforts produced 239 snow crystal photographs, the most he had even taken in one winter. At times he needed help in changing and numbering the exposed plates. This he got from E. H. Nash, a neighbor and one of the many Nash's after whom Nashville Road was named. Bentley was not exaggerating when he wrote in his article: "No time, pains, or expense have been spared to make this sketch of the past winter's work as complete as possible."

Although he tried to get characteristic photographs from each storm:

> This proved the most difficult task of all, because the old habit of seeking for the beautiful and interesting, rather than the characteristic types, was very difficult to overcome. For this reason, I fear the winter's photographic record portrays far more fully the general character of the beautiful and interesting than it does the broken or unsymmetrical types. And yet there are few, perhaps, who after viewing the feast of beauty filling these pages will regret our shortcomings in this regard.

With the help of the daily weather maps Abbe had arranged to send, Bentley confirmed the conclusions he reached the year before — the more perfect snow crystals came from the western segments of the storms. He argued that there was less turbulence to cause crystal breakup. He reiterated his agreement with others that the shape of the central part of the crystals reflected the temperature and altitude at which the crystals formed. In a discussion of the various names given to different types of snow crystals, he wrote that:

> Crystals of more or less open structure possessing solid tabular nuclei [hexagonal centers], for want of a better name, will be referred to as *stellar*. Those possessing centrally open structure and devoid of solid tabular nuclei, resembling ferns, are the *fern-stellar*.

The name *stellar*, originating with Bentley, is still used by scientists today to describe that beautiful, six-sided feathery snow crystal most associated in the public eye with snowflakes.

Bentley presented his data in several tables, one of which showed the frequency of occurrence of the various types of snow crystals from a variety of cloud systems, including cirrus, stratus, and cumulus. The data showed that snow crystals "are most frequently precipitated when two or more cloud strata exist." Most curiously, Bentley, after close examination of his photographs, found evidence of tiny tubes of air embedded within the solid ice structure of the interior portions of some of the crystals. With this finding he confirmed the discovery of air tubes made some years before by the Swedish scientist G. Nordenskiold. Today, scientists accept the existence of air tubes and cavities of other shapes embedded within snow crystals, though the exact mechanism of their formation is still unclear.

It is clear that Bentley was not in scientific isolation in Jericho but was aware of the research on snow crystals being carried out by other scientists. Throughout his article he mentioned not only the work of Nordenskiold in Sweden, but experiments done by Hellmann and Neuhaus in Germany, Sigson in Russia, Squinabol in Italy, and several scientists in the United States. Though no correspondence has survived to confirm the fact, it is quite likely that he had an exchange of letters and ideas with some of these scientists.

Little seems to have escaped Bentley in his meticulous examination of snow crystals. He wrote about crystals covered with granular coatings caused by the freezing upon impact of supercooled cloud droplets. He postulated that these crystals can clump together, fall, and subsequently melt to form raindrops. He speculated on how wind and turbulence could cause crystals to break. Looking closely at some crystals through his microscope he saw "a phenomenon that has been quite frequently observed by me, but rarely if ever mentioned by other observers . . . the occurrence of colors of red or green, or a combination of both, within the well-defined nuclear [central] portions of certain tabular [hexagonal] forms." He said that the colors were seen "only by reflected light when the crystals are viewed obliquely from a certain angle." Though Bentley did not say, it appears that he was seeing what are called interference colors similar to those produced from soap bubbles and thin films of oil on a wet pavement. Interference colors, however, are produced by the interference of light when reflected both from the front and back of a thin film of water or ice very much thinner than the crystals he was observing. Consequently, it remains a mystery as to what caused the colors in Bentley's snow crystals. No scientists today have ever seen them.

In the final four pages of his article, Bentley discussed the relationship between cloud structure and crystal type. In the midst of several paragraphs of a technical and unemotional discourse, his love and enthusiasm for the snow crystals would bubble to the surface, overwhelm him, bringing about a sudden change in his writing style. Consider this: "As the last belated cloud legions . . . were passing overhead . . . they contributed a few more choice examples of snow crystal architecture as souvenirs of the skill of the Divine Artist." He ended the article on a similar theme:

> It is extremely improbable that anyone has as yet found, or, indeed, ever will find, the one preeminently beautiful and symmetrical snow crystal that nature has probably fashioned when in her most artistic mood.

Bentley would return to this idea of "the one preeminently beautiful" snow crystal again and again in his future writings. It haunted him long after his search for scientific understanding had diminished. It was this quest, like Sir Galahad's for the Holy Grail, that sustained and nourished Bentley with undiminished enthusiasm until his dying day.

Bentley's article must have been read by many readers of the *Monthly Weather Review*, and those who did not still had to be impressed with the "feast of beauty" on the many pages of photographs of the snow crystals. Across the Atlantic in London, the editors of *Nature*, the prestigious international journal covering all aspects of science, requested and received permission to reprint large sections of the article. The June 11, 1903, issue of *Nature* contained three pages of material that had been extracted from the article and sixty of the photomicrographs.

At the headquarters of the Weather Bureau in Washington, DC, Cleveland Abbe, in a determined effort to get money for Bentley to continue his work, wrote the first of what eventually would be a dozen memos that in the next two weeks quickly bounced back and forth like a game of musical memos between

Abbe, the Chief of the Bureau, and two high officials in the Bureau.[3] The first, on June 13, 1903, from Abbe to the Chief, read:

> Mr. W. A. Bentley of Jericho, Vermont, who made the beautiful photomicrographs of snow crystals lately published in the *Monthly Weather Review*, would like to enlarge his facilities and do better work during the coming winter. He does all this as a voluntary observer, without expense to the Bureau, and we can but believe that a prosecution of his work will eventually tell us very much as to how snow and rain are formed in the clouds. He has sent me the following items of expenses that he would like to incur in studying the internal structures of the snow crystals by oblique illumination, and I recommend that you allow the expenditure of $118 by him under my supervision.

The $118 was to cover photographic supplies, a new microscope objective, and the services of an assistant, possibly E. H. Nash.

It appears from this memo that Bentley requested the money in a letter to Abbe, but one wonders. A memo a few days later from Abbe to a Dr. Phillips begins: "In order to encourage further studies on snow crystals, I have asked Mr. W. A. Bentley to give me an estimate of the expense of the proposed work." Here it appears that it is Abbe, not Bentley, who would like to see enlarged facilities and more work done. It is possible that Abbe had written to Bentley, encouraging him to do more, and asking him to submit an estimate of the expense involved. Bentley would have responded, and why not? He certainly intended to continue his work with the snow crystals, and he could use the money. But why then, if this scenario is true, did Abbe in his memo to the Chief make it appear that the request for the money came from Bentley? Probably because Abbe knew that the Chief would be more likely to approve the request if it had been initiated by Bentley. Any scientist, anyone doing creative work of any kind, is much more excited, motivated, and will do a far better piece of work if he initiates an idea himself rather than being told to do something by someone else. Another reason for thinking that Bentley did not initiate the request for the money is that it's hard to imagine he could do any more than he had done in his Herculean efforts in the previous few winters. He might have liked "enlarged facilities" but where would he get the time to use them? After all, he was still running the farm and sharing the work with his brother Charles. It would be a decade or more, and long after his mother's death, before he brought in another person to do most of the farm work and to run the farm on shares.

The Chief apparently approved Abbe's request for money and sent the memo to the Bureau's accountant for action. The accountant, in a memo to Abbe, said there would be complications if they gave the money directly to Bentley, since the microscope objective was unexpendable property. He suggested they pay Bentley a certain rate for lantern slides. Further memos flew between the accountant, Dr. Phillips, and Abbe. A counter suggestion was made that the Bureau hire Bentley as a special agent for four months at twenty-five dollars a month. No consensus was reached as to what to do, and finally the Chief withdrew his approval for any sort of compensation to Bentley. In a final memo to the accountant, Abbe said "Mr. Bentley knows nothing about the proposition that he be employed by the Weather Bureau, hence I see no need of writing him and recommend that these memos be filed and the matter closed." But the matter could not be completely closed until Abbe wrote Bentley to explain why the request for $118 was turned down. One can only guess what he said in his letter; it has never been found.

Toward the end of 1903, Bentley published in the *American Annual of Photography* the first article in what would become a yearly event, not ending until the tenth article in 1912. These writings painted a wide and varied picture of how to capture nature with the camera lens, from the photography of snow crystals to that of frost, dew, and the clouds. In this first article, *How to Photograph Snow Crystals*, Bentley gave the most complete description up to that time on how to select the proper microscope objective, collect the crystals, place them on the microscope slide, and obtain the proper exposure.

But what he did not give, nor would he ever give in any of his writings, was how, in a farmhouse devoid of electric lights and running water, he was able to make contact copies of his glass plate negatives and prints and then to thoroughly wash them. His notebooks reveal part of the story and his nieces have completed it. Under the stairs that led upward from his kitchen was a small, cramped area that he used for a darkroom. Here he developed his plates. His niece Amy said:

> In the winter, those glass plates after developing had to be washed a long time. . . . He made these little corrugated things out of galvanized tin. He'd put the plates in and stand them up in the brook so the water could wash through them. He'd go up there with his lantern on a cold winter night. It wasn't Mill Brook. It was a small brook that came from springs up on the hill, but it ran into Mill Brook. . . . In later years he took them down to the barnyard where the water was running in and out all the time, and he'd wash them there.[4]

Since he never touched or modified his original negatives, he had to make a copy negative and on that carefully scrape away the emulsion surrounding the snow crystal. When the prints were made, the crystals stood out against a jet black background. But in order to get the copy negative he had to go through a two-step contact process: from the original negative he made a contact positive and from that made the copy negative. But where did he get the light to do this? It came from an oil lantern! He said it was necessary only to have the "lamp chimney clean [and a] good sized flame." To diffuse the light, he placed a piece of tissue paper between the lamp and the negative or positive, behind which was an unexposed photographic plate. The plates were placed at a distance of several "lantern door lengths" from the lantern and exposed from 30 seconds to a minute or more, depending upon conditions known only to Bentley.

Bentley used the sun to provide the light for his contact paper prints. He built a frame that could hold up to four glass negatives clamped tightly against the photographic paper. The frame was propped up against a log outdoors in the sun. Another niece, Alice, remembered helping her uncle expose these frames:

> He had a wooden frame . . . a double frame. . . . I'd watch the time. He'd tell me how long. I forget how long they had to stay there in the sun. And then I'd bring them in to him in the darkroom and he'd develop them.[5]

These methods of developing and printing, utterly primitive by today's standards, and probably so to many photographers at the turn of the century, were, in Bentley's patient hands, quite sufficient for high quality work of the first rank.

The seasons came and went in the Mill Brook Valley of Jericho, and Bentley continued with his work. He began to receive invitations to give lectures about it, but because of his mother's sickness he could not leave home. He could write letters to others, however, especially to Cleveland Abbe, whom he apparently kept informed of all that was going on in his life. In the November, 1905, issue of the *Monthly Weather Review* Abbe told his readers:

> Our esteemed correspondent, Mr. W. A. Bentley, of Jericho, Vt, whose beautiful photomicrographs of snow crystals are known the world over, devotes his whole thought to the prosecution of his work. Being unable to leave Jericho, owing to the illness of his mother, he therefore must cooperate with others by correspondence. Not long ago he wrote out an interesting lecture on snow crystals and sent it with many lantern slides to a friend at the Brooklyn Institute of Arts and Sciences, where the lecture was delivered with great success.

Continuing on with a missionary's zeal to convert the flock to this new branch of science, Abbe said:

This suggests that other instructors, lecturers, lyceums, etc., may also secure material for an interesting lecture on a new topic and thus interest the public in meteorological matters. We hope that the State superintendents of schools will take this matter up officially as a proper branch of nature study in school work.

Had Bentley wanted a public relations agent, he could have found none better than Cleveland Abbe.

By the end of 1906, Bentley had taken 1,354 photographs of snow crystals. Taking advantage of every snowstorm, he worked on Christmas Day that year just as he had five years before. Was he, like Scrooge, indifferent to Christmas? Or did he celebrate it with the family after his work was done? One would guess the latter, but his notebook entry that day gave no clue. It began "Great storm. Begin night before. Temp evening before 2 above, go up in night to 10. Snowing hard morn." By year's end, he had published eighteen articles, only five of which were technical in nature, the others appearing in popular magazines of the day. People other than scientists began to hear about him. Two articles about him and his work appeared in *St. Nicholas* and the *National Geographic*.

Honors began to come his way. He was invited to write articles on snow and frost for the *Encyclopedia Americana*. The one on snow first appeared in the 1904 edition. It was in all future editions until several years after his death. In 1906 he appeared in *Who's Who in America*. His list of accomplishments ended with one word: Republican. Like most Vermonters, Bentley was proud of his conservative heritage. It was these Republican values that his brother had ridiculed twenty years before in a letter from Florida.

Bentley's achievements by the end of 1906 were many, but they were offset by a great tragedy earlier that year. His mother died on the nineteenth of March, just four days after he obtained the last snow crystal photographs of the winter. There is no record of how Bentley took her death, but it must have affected him deeply. Fanny Bentley was the person responsible for introducing her son to the wonders of nature, and the only one in the family constantly encouraging him onward in his early struggles. Her own struggles with sickness in the final years were carried on with a quiet courage. A notice in the *Burlington Free Press* four days after her death read:

> [Mrs. Fanny E. Bentley], widow of the late Edwin Bentley ... died Monday morning of bronchitis and general debility. Mrs. Bentley has been an invalid and a great sufferer for some years, but has always borne her sickness with cheerfulness and fortitude. She was seventy-five years old and leaves two sons.

Fanny was buried alongside her husband in the village cemetery in Jericho Center.

Wilson Bentley, who seldom wrote anything personal in his notebooks, wrote in an undated entry in the spring of 1906 "Melissa McGee and children. Sunny. 4 o'clock. Taken in shade of house." Since this appeared on the page after his notes on his snow crystal work four days before his mother's death, one must assume that Melissa had returned to Jericho with her children to attend her adopted mother's funeral, and Bentley took her photograph. Since leaving the Bentley homestead to marry Edwin McGee in 1893, Melissa had been mentioned only once before in the notebooks. This was in September of 1889 when Bentley took pictures of his mother and Melissa. After 1906, Melissa never again appeared in Bentley's notebooks.

When Fanny Bentley died, the charlatans and quacks still plagued the medical profession as they had forty-one years before when Wilson was born. An ad in the *Free Press* the week of her death read:

> Dr. Williams' Pink Pills have cured the worst cases of bloodlessness, indigestion, influenza, headache, lumbago, sciatica, neuralgia, nervousness, spinal weakness, and the special ailments of girls and women whose blood supply becomes weak, scanty or irregular.

[1] Wilson A. Bentley, "Studies among the snow crystals during the winter of 1901-2, with additional data collected during previous winters," *Monthly Weather Review*, 1902, vol. 30, pp. 607-616

[2] Wilson Bentley's second notebook, 1897-1906.

[3] The memos are in the records of the Weather Bureau, Record Group 27, general correspondence file 1894-1942, File No. 6262, National Archives, College Park, Maryland.

[4] Oral communication: Amy B. Hunt to Duncan Blanchard, July 26, 1969.

[5] Oral communication: Alice B. Hamalainen to Duncan Blanchard, June 26, 1971.

Chapter 8

Raindrops and Dough Pellets

"Attend now, and I will explain how rain collects in the clouds above, and how the showers are precipitated and descend upon the earth." These words were written two thousand years ago by the Roman poet Lucretius. In his great poem, *On the Nature of Things*, he ranged over a vast number of subjects that included clouds, rain, thunder, and lightning. But, typical of the thinkers of his day, he never put his ideas to the test of experiment. Some were subsequently shown to have much merit. Others, however, were either so vague and general that they said nothing at all, or else were little more than interesting and sometimes amusing speculations. For example, he said that one of the causes of rain was the wind pressing against "swollen clouds." And the cause of lightning and thunder? Lucretius reasoned that when clouds collide they produce sparks and noise, as sometimes happens when two stones are struck together.

As the centuries passed, many an illustrious thinker pondered the mystery of the formation of raindrops. There was Aristotle with his ideas on the changing of air into water.[1] There was Descartes who thought that raindrops were formed when winds blowing from different directions pressed cloud droplets together. Closer to our own time, Benjamin Franklin speculated on the possibility of electrical effects being involved in the growth of raindrops. These men, and many others whose names are now but footnotes on the pages of history, advanced numerous hypotheses on raindrop origins. There was little agreement among them. Progress in understanding was pitifully slow and had about ground to a halt by the end of the last century. Meteorologists were spending much of their time in the collection of daily or weekly measurements of rainfall, temperature, and atmospheric pressure. They did this with such energy that page after page of the *Monthly Weather Review* spilled over with these data. Rainfall was measured with great accuracy and reported to the nearest one hundredth of an inch.

In spite of the tremendous labors that went into these measurements, no one ever took the next step to ask several important questions. What are raindrops like? How big are they? Are they all the same size? Do they vary in size from rain to rain? Could I perhaps learn something of their origin if I determine their size and how they are distributed in rainfall? Until some of these questions were answered, it was about as useless to inquire into the origin of raindrops as it was to speculate on the outcome of a horse race without knowing something about the size and speed of each of the horses.

Meteorologists may not have thought these questions important enough to ponder, or, worse, they may not have thought of them at all, but to Wilson Bentley, who by 1898 was beginning to think that some raindrops had their origins in the melting of snowflakes, these questions were most important. Since no meteorologists in the United States had ever tried to measure the sizes of raindrops, Bentley's work on rain led him into a new research frontier. He began his pioneer experiments in 1898, continued them for the next six years, and in the October, 1904, *Monthly Weather Review* published "Studies of raindrops and raindrop phenomena," an extraordinary article that sparkled with new ideas and concepts on raindrop size and formation. In the opening sentences, Bentley, with great simplicity and clarity, went straight to the fundamental problem of rain formation and outlined the areas where work must be done. He wrote:

> Our knowledge in regard to the mechanism of rain formation,
> i.e., the precise manner in which the nucleus of each raindrop is
> organized and the method by which the aqueous material is

added to the nucleus during its growth, so that eventually raindrops of considerable size are produced, has hitherto been very unsatisfactory. Equally so is our knowledge of the actual altitudes within the clouds at which various rainfalls originate, the relative quantities of rain precipitated from different clouds and storms, the dimensions of the individual raindrops, and their variation in different storms and in different segments of the same storm.

Part of Bentley's motivation to enter this new area of research was simply the "desire to add, if possible, a little to our knowledge regarding rainfall phenomena." And add he did! In an effort that must certainly qualify him as among the world's most diligent chasers of raindrops, he obtained 344 measurements of raindrop sizes from seventy different storms, including twenty-five thunderstorms. With each measurement he kept a record of the type of storm, the segment from which the raindrops came, the date and time of day, temperature, winds, cloud types and estimated heights, and the presence or absence of lightning. He was as thorough in collecting data for his raindrop work as he was for his work with the snow crystals.

The first in the country to make measurements of raindrop size, Bentley had to develop his own method for accomplishing this feat. It was simple and ingenious. He used flour, a common staple in the farmhouse kitchen used in the baking of bread. Bentley wrote:

> The method employed was to allow the raindrops to fall into a layer one inch deep of fine, uncompacted flour, with a smooth surface, contained in a shallow tin receptacle about four inches in diameter, which was generally exposed to the rain for about four seconds, although a longer time was given when the drops fell scatteringly. The raindrops were allowed to remain in the flour until the dough pellet that each drop always produces at the bottom of the cavity was dry and hard. These dough pellets . . . were found by careful experiment to correspond very closely in size with the raindrops that made them.

Bentley's "careful experiment" again showed his ingenuity.

> Drops of water of about one-twelfth of an inch [2.1 mm] and one-sixth of an inch [4.2 mm] in diameter, suspended from the end of a broom splint and a glass pipette respectively, were carefully measured and then allowed to drop into flour from heights of from twelve to thirty feet.

Although Bentley did not say, he must have realized that such heights were necessary for the drops to accelerate and reach their final or terminal speed. They would then strike the flour at about the same speed as falling raindrops. Bentley's estimate of the heights necessary to reach terminal speed for his drops was an amazingly lucky guess, for a guess was all it could be. It was not until many years after his death that the first measurements were made of the distances necessary for water drops to attain a terminal fall speed in air. Bentley had guessed correctly.[2]

Such calibration experiments, so necessary before Bentley could experiment with natural raindrops, must have been done with the enthusiasm that most scientists feel as they anticipate the experiment that lies ahead. A smile may have crossed Bentley's face when he found that his broom splint and glass pipette were working so well. It is unlikely, however, that those around him, especially his brother and nearby farmers, shared that enthusiasm. Perhaps they saw Bentley with his pipette high up on the peak of his roof dropping water drops in an effort to hit the tiny pan of flour thirty feet below. If so, they must have scratched their heads in bewilderment, thinking that this simply confirmed what they had long thought about Bentley. It was bad enough that he wasted his time in the winter fussing with snowflakes, but now he was wasting his time in the summer fussing with raindrops!

One more thing needs to be said before we look at what Bentley found in his experiments with raindrops. Initially, he had no idea whatsoever that the raindrops would form dough pellets when they fell into his pans of flour, nor was flour the first medium he tried. Since he had worked with photography for. so

102

many years, his first thought was to photograph the impressions or holes the raindrops made in the flour. It was only by serendipity, the way that most scientific discoveries are made, that he stumbled across the flour pellets buried deep in the flour. Bentley did not mention this in his article. Most scientists do not tell about the failed experiments or the tortuous dead-end trails they follow; they tell only about the final experiment that led them to their discoveries. But on the first page of a small notebook titled *Snow*, Bentley told what really happened.[3] In an entry for October 30, 1898, he wrote: "I secured first photos of raindrops, magnified 4 diameters. They were impressions made in flour. After trying various mediums I found flour to be best to secure their impressions in." The next day, in fog and drizzle, he obtained and photographed additional impressions. More than a week later he wrote:

> I secured some raindrops on evening of Nov. 10. I made an important discovery regarding them today. . . . In the bottom of each rain drop impression in the flour there could always be found a roundish granule of dough nearly exact size of rain drop. After experimenting with artificial rain drops I could measure diameter before falling into the flour, and thus tell if the dough granule corresponded in size with the measured rain drop

For all of his 344 samples of raindrops, Bentley determined the number of drops in each of five size categories: very small, small, medium, large, and very large. Each category covered a certain size range. For example, the "very small" drops were less than one-thirtieth of an inch (0.85 mm) while the "very large" drops were greater than one-fifth of an inch (5 mm) in diameter. With his numerous raindrop samples, Bentley was able to make some generalizations on how drop size varied as a function of position in the storm (east edge, west edge, center, etc.) and with cloud type. His most complete analysis was with the latter, where he recognized seven different cloud types or combinations. For example, thirty of his drop samples were obtained from cumulus clouds and fifty-three when cumulus and cirrostratus clouds were present. He found that drops of all sizes were present in most rains, but in general smaller drops vastly outnumbered the larger ones. Raindrops from low clouds were not very large, and even most of the cumulus clouds produced relatively few large drops. He found his largest drops were produced by clouds or thunderstorms that reached far upward in the atmosphere.

Bentley was the first one to observe and puzzle over the mystery of monodisperse raindrop-size distributions. Though most of his distributions showed the usual mixture of small, medium, and large drops, twenty-six (7.5 percent) were monodisperse. These curious distributions, or perhaps we should say lack of distribution, were sometimes composed entirely of small drops, sometimes of only large drops. Bentley concluded that this was due to "the melting of snow crystals or granular snow. As is well known, snowfalls often occur in which the individual crystals, or granular snow pellets, are of practically uniform dimensions." Whether he was right or wrong in this interpretation of his data we cannot say. The origin of monodisperse drop distributions is still being debated today, though it seems clear that wind shear in the atmosphere can play a role in their formation.[4]

The association of lightning with rain had been observed by many people long before Bentley appeared on the scene, but he was the first to show that the drop sizes in these rains were much larger than they were with rains when the lightning was absent or some distance away. An analysis of nearly eighty raindrop-size samples from each of these three types of rain showed that all the rains had mixtures of drops of many sizes, but the largest drops (larger than 5 mm) were nearly ten times more numerous with lightning overhead than when in the distance and nearly thirty times more than when there was no lightning at all. From these observations he concluded that the largest drops were responsible for the lightning.

How could they cause it? He said, without giving any evidence, that "snow crystals are frequently, if not invariably, highly charged with electricity." When they melt into small raindrops, their surface area is reduced. The electrical charge, which always resides on the surface, is squeezed into a smaller area and the charge density increases. As these small drops fall, many coalesce together to form the largest drops. The surface area is reduced even more. This, Bentley concluded, caused the charge density to increase to the point that electrical breakdown produced lightning.

Though Bentley would never know it, his ideas on the association of lightning with rain helped open a Pandora's Box of hypotheses on what really is happening in a thunderstorm. Are electrically charged raindrops, or other forms of precipitation, really the cause of lightning? Or is it the other way around — does lightning cause the formation of raindrops? This chicken-or-the-egg scenario is being played out in laboratories around the world today. Though most atmospheric scientists believe that precipitation causes the lightning, there are some who point to numerous anomalies or flaws in this idea and place their bets that the lightning comes first.[5]

One of the more intriguing deductions made by Bentley from his measurements of raindrop size was that most of the rain in thunderstorms came from the melting of snowflakes. He was not the first to make this suggestion. Over the centuries, two main ideas had evolved for the formation of rain. One was that raindrops evolved from the melting of snowflakes, the other that liquid processes within the cloud were all that was required. Scientists today refer to rain formed by these mechanisms as either cold or warm rain.

Bentley was, however, the first to use the relative volumes of large and small raindrops to argue that both mechanisms came into play in thunderstorm rain. He knew that the growth of large drops required long distances of travel through the clouds, probably starting their journey far above the earth near cloud top. He wrote:

> Assuming, accordingly, that the larger raindrops issue from
> the upper portions of the clouds and are due to the melting of

snow, or, conversely, that the smaller ones originate by liquid processes alone within the lower clouds, we have a means of approximately ascertaining which process produces the major part of the rainfall. We have only to group together the individual raindrops (flour pellets) within the samples secured during various rainfalls, and weigh each group separately.

Bentley did this for all the raindrop samples obtained from four thunderstorms, putting in the first group the "large" and "largest" pellets and all smaller pellets in the second group. The weight of the first group was more than twice that of the second, and Bentley concluded "that the major portion of the rainfall of thundershowers is of a snow origin."

Bentley's clever use of the volumes of the raindrops to arrive at what he called a "dual origin of rain" can be criticized on a number of grounds, including his neglect of the effects of updrafts and downdrafts in the clouds on drop growth, and no mention of what drop breakup might do. It is interesting, however, that in 1976, atmospheric scientists at the University of Toronto, knowing nothing about Bentley's work, had independently arrived at a similar conclusion for the dual origin of rain.[6] Which all goes to prove that good ideas, even though buried in the pages of a technical journal gathering dust on a library shelf for nearly three quarters of a century, can rise again to compete in the scientific arena.

By one of those curious coincidences in the annals of science, Philipp Lenard, a German scientist, began his studies of raindrops the same time as did Bentley, in the fall of 1898.[7] Again, like Bentley, he did not publish his work until six years later, in 1904. His article, *Uber Regen*, mostly about raindrop size, shape, and stability, was published in the German journal *Meteorologische Zeitschrift*. Though their research was started and published at the same time and on the same subject, there is no evidence that either of these men ever saw or heard of the article the other had published. It is hard to imagine two men whose backgrounds stood in such stark contrast. Here was Bentley, the self-educated Vermont farmer who seldom strayed far from the village of Jericho. In 1904, Lenard was a brilliant experimental physicist who had studied and taught at universities in Budapest, Vienna, Berlin, Heidelberg, Bonn, and Kiel. In the following year, he would receive the Nobel Prize in physics for his work with cathode rays.

Lenard was not the first in Europe to publish work on raindrops. Another German had done so a few years before, and Lenard used his blotter method to catch and measure raindrop size. Ordinary blotters were lightly dusted with a water soluble dye and exposed to the rain. The size of the permanent spots left on the blotter were related to the size of the raindrops by a calibration curve obtained in the laboratory by dropping drops of known size on the blotter. Since Lenard obtained only ten raindrop samples, he could not generalize as did Bentley on how cloud structure controlled drop sizes. His most important finding dealt with the shape of raindrops. To study large water drops falling at their terminal speed through the air, as raindrops do, he built a vertical wind tunnel in which the upward speed of the air was the same as the speed at which large raindrops fall (6–8 meters per second). With this apparatus he was able to get water drops to float stationary in the air before his eyes. He found that the largest water drops that could be floated without breaking were about one-quarter inch (6 mm) in diameter. These were about the largest that Bentley had found in his many raindrop samples. Lenard discovered that the shape of the large drops was much like a hamburger bun, and not at all like the tear-shaped drops so commonly drawn by artists today to represent falling raindrops.

Though Lenard's vertical wind tunnel was crude and plagued with turbulence that limited what he could do, it became the prototype for vertical wind tunnels that were built decades later. Today, sophisticated vertical wind tunnels, in which the temperature, humidity, and air speed can be varied, are used by atmospheric scientists not only to study properties of raindrops but also cloud drops, snowflakes, and hailstones.

Lenard never again published on raindrop phenomena. He returned to experimental work in basic physics where many honors came his way. In addition to the 1905 Nobel Prize, he received the Rumford Medal of the Royal Society of London and the Franklin Medal of the Franklin Institute. His later years, however, were not so honorable.[8] As early as 1924 he became an admirer and follower of Hitler, and in 1933, for his efforts on behalf of the Nazi party, was awarded the Eagle Shield of the German Reich. Hitler made him Chief of Aryan or German Physics, and in 1936 Lenard published his four-volume *Deutsche Physik*, whose pages were filled with his anti-Semitic views. These books were praised by the Nazis for making science relevant to the philosophy of the party. Lenard died in Messehausen on 20 May 1947.

❄

Bentley, like Lenard, never published another article on raindrops, though occasionally he would make a few measurements of raindrop size. His niece Alice, nine or ten years old at the time, remembers watching him. She saw him:

> . . . sifting flour into these [small tin containers], and I said, Uncle W. A., what are you making? 'Never mind, little Alice,' he said. He was busy [and would tell me later]. And then it began to rain. He ran outdoors with them. It was raining hard. . . . Then later on I saw these little pellets, dried, so I asked what they were, and then he'd explain the whole thing to me. He said he was trying to measure the size of the raindrops. In different storms they'd be different sizes. He had these little pellets all around on the table.[9]

One might have expected that Bentley's article, reporting on the first measurements of raindrop size, and so full of new ideas on the formation and distribution of the drops, would have excited the interest of other meteorologists. But it did not. No one tried to repeat his experiments or to extend his work. No one even commented on it. There was complete silence regarding his work in the pages of the *Monthly Weather Review*, not only in the year of publication but during his entire lifetime. If anyone wrote to Bentley either to praise or criticize his efforts, there is no record of it.

It is understandable why Bentley's work was neglected. It was decades ahead of its time. Most meteorologists at the turn of the century had little interest in the basic physics and chemistry of the formation of clouds and rain. That area of research, known today as cloud physics, did not attract much attention until the 1940s. The first notice of Bentley's work, nearly forty years after it was published, was in 1943 when scientists at the United States Soil Conservation Service used Bentley's flour pellet method to obtain measurements of the distribution of raindrop sizes as a function of the intensity of the rainfall.[10] In 1948, J. S. Marshall and W. McK. Palmer, cloud physicists at McGill University in Montreal, combined these measurements with some of their own, put them in mathematical form, and got what today is known as the Marshall-Palmer equation.[11] This equation, relating the raindrop-size distribution to rain intensity, is widely used by cloud physicists around the world. Bentley would have been excited and proud to know that someone finally had used his work to help advance our understanding of the age-old mysteries surrounding the formation of rain.

---

[1] W. E. Knowles Middleton, *A History of the Theories of Rain*, Franklin Watts, Inc., 1966, p. 6.

[2] J. Otis Laws, "Measurements of the fall velocity of water-drops and raindrops," *Transactions, American Geophysical Union*, 1941, vol. 22, pp. 709–721.

[3] This small notebook, now at the Buffalo Museum of Science, Buffalo, New York, contains entries dated from 1898 to 1902. In addition to his notes on the measurement of raindrop size, Bentley includes an outline of an article on snow crystals and the names of those who have requested slides or photographs.

[4] Duncan C. Blanchard, *From Raindrops to Volcanoes*, Doubleday, 1966, p. 11.

[5] Bernard Vonnegut, "The atmospheric electricity paradigm," *Bulletin of the American Meteorological Society*, 1994, vol. 75, pp. 53–61.

[6] R. List and J. R. Gillespie, "Evolution of raindrop spectra with collision-induced breakup," *Journal of the Atmospheric Sciences*, 1976, vol. 33, pp. 2007–2013.

[7] Duncan C. Blanchard, "Bentley and Lenard: Pioneers in cloud physics," *American Scientist*, 1972, vol. 60, pp. 746–749.

[8] Nobel Lectures, Physics, 1901–1921, published for the Nobel Foundation by Elsevier Publishing Company, 1967.

[9] Oral communication: Alice B. Hamalainen to Duncan Blanchard, June 26, 1971.

[10] J. Otis Laws and Donald A. Parsons, "The relation of raindrop-size to intensity," *Transactions, American Geophysical Union*, 1943, vol. 24, pp. 452–460.

[11] J. S. Marshall and W. Mck. Palmer, "The distribution of raindrops with size," *Journal of Meteorology*, 1948, vol. 5, pp. 165–166.

Chapter 9

A Prophet Without Honor

Bentley's side of the farmhouse was anything but neat and orderly. Perhaps his mother, an invalid in her later years, insisted that he spend a few hours each week keeping the rooms clean and presentable should neighbors come knocking at the door. If so, her insistence did not make a lasting impression on him. It was not long after her death in 1906 that housework was practically forgotten. The big downstairs room where Bentley ate and did much of his work became a sort of organized confusion. A kitchen stove, a huge wood box, a bureau, several chairs, two tables, a piano covered with piles of sheet music, books, manuscripts, odds and ends of experiments, photographic equipment, correspondence, and photographs of snow crystals all blurred together in one large room. But somehow, mysteriously, by methods known only to him, Bentley was able to find things when he wanted them. As the wife of his nephew Alric succinctly put it, "He was an old bach. He was more interested in his work than in housekeeping."[1]

The wood box was indeed huge, but Bentley did not use it as a wood box. "It was . . . built in . . . and as long as a fireplace," his niece Alice said:

> . . . [and when he died] it was nearly full with letters and things
> and papers of different kinds. . . . He used to throw [everything]
> into the wood box. Instead of putting wood into the wood box,
> he didn't. He had the wood piled in a [smaller] box and brought
> in from the woodshed.[2]

Bentley's casual use of the wood box as a makeshift filing system for everything sometimes nearly caused him grief. His niece Amy once found an unopened letter in the wood box. She gave it to him. "He opened it up and there was a check. . . . It was for someplace he had lectured. I don't think he had any business head on him. He said 'I don't know how I happened to throw that away.'"[3]

Bentley's bedroom was directly over the kitchen. Other than a bed, the only furniture in the room was a large table and two chairs. But, like downstairs, this Spartan simplicity was offset with a hodgepodge of photographic materials, papers, and other equipment that spilled off the table and spread across the floor like water overflowing the banks of a brook. Amy, who with her brothers and sisters were allowed in his room only when they had to go through to the attic, said "it was pretty cluttered and often would smell of developer."[4]

Bentley cooked his meals on the old wood stove used by his mother for so many years. He was no cook, nor did he desire to be. His wants were simple. By all accounts hot muffins, biscuits, and johnnycake constituted his main culinary skills. He ate little red meat, being nearly vegetarian in his selection of foods. Fruit, vegetables, berries of all kinds, and milk were staples in his diet. "He was great on fruit," Alric's wife said. "He used to can his berries two quarts at a time and eat them like soup."[5] When he had a fish, he would not fry or bake it, but cook it in cream. And he urged others to do the same. Izetta Barrett, Amy and Alice's friend who lived just down the road, said that Bentley sometimes gave her a fish or two when he returned from a successful afternoon catching trout in Mill Brook. "He'd always say, 'cook it in cream.' Don't fry it, and don't do this and don't do that. 'Cook it in cream.' And of course they were delicious."[6]

Bentley may have prepared his meals quickly, but the eating of them proceeded with glacial slowness. "Nothing was ever swallowed before thorough chewing," Amy said. "He told me he chewed his food thirty-six times before swallowing. I think I heard that he had stomach spells when younger, and that is why he had this curious form of eating."[7] Even people outside the family noticed how slowly he ate. Izetta remembered that "it took him as long to eat one little thing as the rest of us to eat the meal. Well, I guess he was healthy anyway."[8]

By now, in his early forties, Bentley's hairline was receding; by age sixty, it ran vertically over his head from ear to ear. He had little use for clothes. As Amy put it:

> He wasn't anything for fashion. He had this suit, and he always wore a white collar and tie. I don't remember his ever wearing a derby hat. He wore a straw hat in summer. . . . In the winter he always wore a black cap that came down around his ears.[9]

Alice remembered the "overcoat and hat that he wore when he went on his lectures. Every day he always wore a suit coat, even when it was quite warm. He always used to wear black."[10] One would hope that the overcoat remembered by Alice was not the same one recalled by a neighbor, Arthur Pratt, who pointed out that Bentley, though:

> . . . only about five feet tall . . . had an overcoat big enough for a six-footer. And there wasn't a button on the damn thing. It was green with age. And he'd walk around, and when he stooped over the corners would actually drag in the snow.[11]

Bentley was polite, soft-spoken, never aggressive in his speech. "I wouldn't call him shy," Alric's wife said, "but he wasn't a fellow that would push himself forward. He was kind of a quiet type." Pratt recalled a peculiar mannerism:

> He'd never look up, never look at you. I don't think he was shy. I don't know. . . . A hired man once said, 'Willie, why the hell don't you ever look at me when I talk to you? . . . Willie, I'm talking to you. Look up.' He'd look up and grin.[12]

This mannerism could not have been present all the time, because of all the many people who have talked or written about Bentley, Pratt is the only one who mentioned it.

Bentley's love of fruits took him to Burlington once or twice a year for half barrels of pears and many boxes of grapes. He would eat some and can the rest. These trips, however, weren't without their mishaps, as Alice, who occasionally went with him, recalled.

> I remember this year he got a horse, Old Tom . . . a very high faluting horse. . . . We had very few cars then, and so we went down and stayed overnight, and when we came back we got . . . about a mile from Nashville, about where Jim Berry's farm was. And we saw a car coming, a doctor, of course. Not many people, only the doctors had cars in those days. He never used a whip on a horse. He didn't have a whip, so he tried to make Old Tom go ahead, but he turned right around and he went into a barn door and the door wasn't open wide enough for the buggy to go in, so we went there with the wheels right up against the barn door. The horse went in, but he scraped his hip. . . . Grapes and pears were spilled all over.[13]

Alice doesn't say if her uncle, who was seldom known to swear, set a record for the use of cuss words that day.

On quiet evenings, Bentley often took his clarinet up on the hill behind the farmhouse and played for his own entertainment. But the neighbors below were entertained too, as they heard the soft notes of the music drifting down from above. Izetta remembered that "on a nice, warm summer's evening, perhaps with a tiny bit of breeze, it would come on the air. It was so nice."[14] Sometimes Bentley would play from his own porch. Alice said that "Uncle used to sit out evenings, nice evenings, with his clarinet, and people would come out on their porches. You could hear it all over Nashville. He'd play all kinds of music."[15] Not only did Bentley entertain people from his porch and the hillside with his clarinet, but at an evening's gathering at the schoolhouse he would with his violin and sense of humor imitate birdcalls, frogs, barnyard animals, and certain people in the village![16]

During the long, cold winter evenings the people of the Nashville region of Jericho entertained themselves with square dances, or perhaps just getting together to sing and have a few ciders. Sometimes they would gather at the Bentley home, other times at one of the neighboring farmhouses. If it was for an evening of singing, it was not complete without hearing from Balthsar Trieb and his wife, Katharina. They had emigrated from Germany to settle in Nashville and had brought their love of singing with them. Usually it took a bit of urging to get Balthsar up alongside the piano, but less so after a few ciders. "Old Balthsar had a big heavy mustache that curved around like this," said Howard Wagner, who lived a couple miles toward the Richmond Road but took in some of these parties.

> I can still see him. He never lost his German accent. He'd say 'Ah, Katharina, we shouldn't not be doing this, but we'll do it.' This was after he had a few ciders, maybe a dozen or so. They'd get him in to the piano, and he'd take his stance by the old lady with his arm on her shoulder, just like you see in the pictures in the old days, and he would sing *I'll take you home again, Kathleen*, and everybody had to be quiet. . . . She had a nice voice and he had a nice voice, and this had to happen sometime during the evening . . . and they'd always sing that song.[17]

When the gathering was at the Bentley home, it was in Charles's side rather than Wilson's, since it was the larger. And almost always it was for dancing. Amy recalled:

> [Uncle Willie] was really the organizer of those dances, square dances and waltzing and schottische. He'd play the piano, and Homer Locke from Bolton was the fiddler. . . . There was a Mrs. Nash who would play to relieve him so Uncle Willie could dance with us. He wasn't a very graceful dancer, but he always enjoyed it all. . . . We'd get that floor all waxed. . . . They had

enough room for three sets, two in the dining room and one in the living room.[18]

Whether the dances were held at the Bentley home or elsewhere, it was always Wilson Bentley who did most of the piano playing. Toward the end of one particular evening, when Bentley was playing the piano at a square dance at a neighbor's house, Arthur Pratt and a few other boys quietly left the house and went outside to where Bentley had left his horse and buggy. They had decided to play a trick on him. Quickly they reversed the wheels on the buggy, so that the larger rear wheels were on front while the smaller front wheels were on the back. This gave a strange and lopsided appearance to the body of the buggy. Pratt and his friends hid in some bushes to eagerly await Bentley's reaction when he came out and saw what had happened. And what was his reaction? There wasn't any! "He went home like that," said Pratt in amazement, "and drove that buggy several days before he noticed it. I don't know what you'd call that."[19] One might call it absentmindedness or one might just call it an example of Bentley's puckish humor. Years after his death, Alice, upon being told this story, said:

> I remember that because I rode with him out to Jericho Center with the big wheels still in front. He went out to the Jericho Center village store, but he didn't let on; course he knew about it the night he came home. . . . He let them know it didn't bother him at all.[20]

Alice asked her uncle why he was being so different from all the others in driving his buggy that way. He told her there was nothing wrong in being different from other people. That was a lesson in courage a little girl never forgot.

Being different, however, sometimes caused interesting and amusing clashes with the law. Take the time that Bentley, who in addition to his interest in the water wonders of the atmosphere was also an avid amateur geologist, was down along the river in Richmond collecting stones. He picked some up, inspected them,

116

Plate 1. Top left: Fanny Bentley, Wilson's mother, date unknown. **Top right:** Wilson Bentley as a young man, date unknown. **Bottom left:** Charles Bentley, Wilson's brother, late 1880s. **Bottom right:** Mary (Blood) Bentley, Charles Bentley's wife, late 1880s.

Plate 2. Top: An artist's conception of Bentley at age 15 drawing a snow crystal while observing it through his mother's old microscope. Courtesy of National Life of Vermont, Montpelier, Vermont. **Bottom:** The Bentley farmhouse and barn about 1890.

Plate 3. Top: The Bentley farmhouse about 1890. Wilson and his mother lived in the left side, while his brother Charles and his family lived in the right. Wilson's mother is standing on the lawn on the left. Charles is sitting on the porch on the right. His wife Mary sits on the porch steps while their young son Alric stands near the carriage holding his baby sister Agnes. **Bottom:** Dendritic snow crystals photographed by Bentley. The crystal on the left was one of his favorites and he used it many times in his articles and on postcards.

Plate 4. Wilson Bentley with his clarinet, date unknown.

 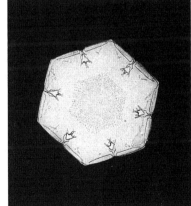

Plate 5. Top: Wilson Bentley's side of the farmhouse about 1925. Sitting on the lawn near his rock collection are Florence Durlacher (left), one of his Fresh Air Fund Children, and Mary (Brunell) Bentley, Alric's wife. Helen Shiner, dressed in white, is seated on the edge of the porch. Two of her brothers are nearby. Note the lattice shaped like snowflakes at the base of the porch. The shed at the rear of the house (left) is where Bentley took all of his pictures of snow crystals. **Bottom:** Hexagonal plate snow crystals photographed by Bentley.

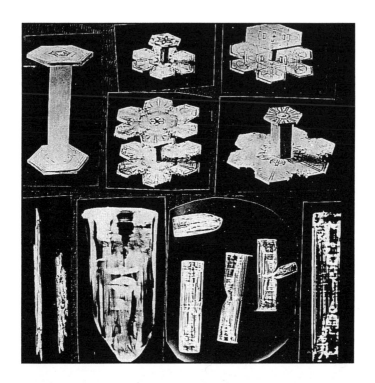

Plate 6. Top: A variety of snow crystals. The five at top are hexagonal columns of ice with hexagonal plates at both ends. At the bottom are four other types of crystals – from left to right: ice needles, bullets, combination of bullets, and what might be a hollow column. **Bottom:** Dendritic snow crystals.

Plate 7. Top: A collection of twenty snow crystals that Bentley called "among the choicest specimens of crystal architecture in a twenty-five years search." **Bottom:** One of several snow crystal montages made by Bentley. He used more than one hundred of his photographs to make this elegant arrangement.

Plate 8. Top: A postcard showing some of Bentley's photographs of different types of snow crystals. **Bottom:** A Sunday afternoon croquet party with neighbors and friends at the Bentley's, about 1910. The woman in the foreground with white stripes on her skirt is Agnes Bentley. Second to the right of her is Alric Bentley; second to the right of him, wearing a dark suit, is Wilson Bentley; and to the right of him is Clarence Shiner.

Plate 9. Top: A sugarin'-off party at the sugar house in the early spring. Fanny Bentley is kneeling and scooping up some snow, while Charles Bentley, in the derby hat and wearing a neck yoke, is returning with two buckets of maple sap. Date unknown. **Bottom:** Halloween at the Bentleys. Amy (Bentley) Hunt (right) with some of her brothers and sisters, about 1907.

Plate 10. Top: Wilson Bentley with his marching band. Bentley is at far left with his clarinet. Date unknown. **Bottom:** Haying time at the Bentleys. Wilson is at far right in the white straw hat, while his nephew, Arthur, is pushing a forkful of hay up to a neighbor on top of the hay wagon. Date unknown, but probably sometime in the 1910s.

Plate 11. Jean Thompson, author of the book *Water Wonders*. Jean went many times to Jericho to visit with Wilson Bentley.

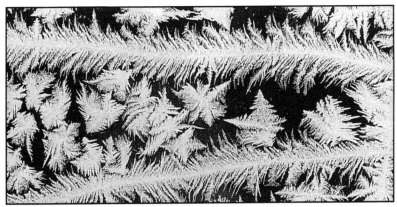

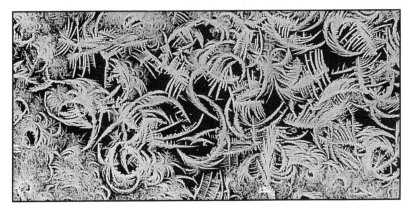

Plate 12. A selection of Bentley's photographs of frost patterns on window panes.

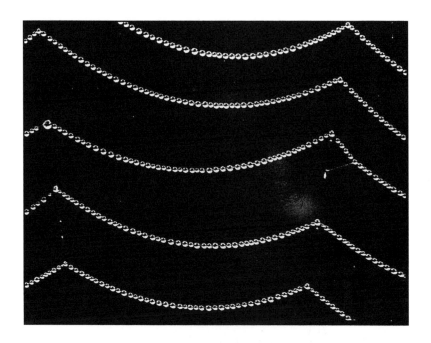

Plate 13. Top: Droplets of dew on a portion of a spider's web. **Bottom:** Dew drops on a grasshopper that had been tied down overnight atop a flower.

Plate 14. Posed photographs of Bentley, about 1917. In actuality, the work depicted here would have been done inside the shed at the back of his house, never out of doors. **Top:** Preparing his camera. **Bottom:** Transferring a snow crystal from the black board it fell upon to a glass slide under his observation microscope. The broom splint he used to pick up the crystals would never have been as large as the object he is holding here.

Plate 15. Top: Bentley with Helen Shiner (left) and Florence Durlacher (right). **Bottom:** Florence Durlacher at Mill Brook near bridge on Nashville Road just east of Bentley's house. Both photographs taken about 1925.

Plate 16. Top: Bentley at his piano, probably during the mid-1920s. The snowflake cross at far right is similar to the one he gave to Robert Hadley's parents. **Bottom:** Just about everybody, including Hagar the Horrible, is familiar with the bit of winter lore that no two snowflakes are alike, a point that Bentley was forever fond of making in his lectures and writings. (Hagar the Horrible reprinted with special permission of King Features Syndicate.)

tossed most back, but kept a few interesting specimens to take back home. "There was a young woman living alone," said Amy.

> She saw him down there wandering around. She got nervous. .
> . . His actions were peculiar, so she called the sheriff and told
> him that this man was acting kind of funny. So the sheriff, Mike
> Murphy, came down, saw uncle, and said, 'Humph, I might
> have known it was you.'[21]

Another time, in Burlington, he "saw this big cloud over the Vermont Hotel," Alric's wife recalled.

> He started on the run with his camera, came out of Lapierre's
> camera store. A cop took after him. He thought he stole the
> camera from Lapierre's. [Bentley] said, 'I'll see you later,' and
> he kept running. . . . He got the picture from the roof of the
> Vermont Hotel and then he told the cop what he was doing. He
> wanted that cloud before it got away from him.[22]

Bentley was small, wiry, agile, and could hold his own with any man when working outdoors. "He wasn't very big," said one of his neighbors, "but by Christ it took a damn good man to follow him in digging potatoes. He dug potatoes and boiled sap and everything else. Cut his own wood."[23] Arthur Pratt remembered digging potatoes with Bentley.

> We dug in the morning, and I'd go just as fast as I could go.
> He didn't seem to hurry at all, and he was doing a better job
> than I was. I stuck it out in the morning, and in the afternoon we
> came out. We were digging two rows at one time and throwing
> the potatoes in between. So this time, just for the fun of it, I
> started on just one row and he started on his two. I easily kept
> up with him. After a couple hours he says, 'Why this morning I
> could keep up with you and now I can't.' I had to tell him I was
> digging one row and he was digging two. He didn't get angry. I
> never saw him angry.[24]

Pratt was right. Bentley seldom got angry and few people got angry with him. But they never understood why he spent so much time with his studies of the snow crystals. Howard Wagner laconically summarized Bentley's neighbor's feelings about this when he said that:

> My father's opinion of him and I think perhaps a great many of the neighbors around him, farmers who worked hard for their money, their opinion was that this would never amount to anything, and that he's just an old duff messing around taking pictures of snowflakes. What the hell good are they? You can't eat them. That was their attitude, you know. You can't sell them and you can't eat them.[25]

Bentley was painfully aware of this attitude of many of his neighbors. Toward the end of his life he was asked about it. He replied:

> Oh, I guess they've always believed I was crazy, or a fool, or both. Years ago, I thought they might feel different if they understood what I was doing. I thought they might be *glad* to understand. So I announced that I would give a talk in the village and show lantern slides of my pictures. They are beautiful, you know, marvelously beautiful on the screen. But when the night came for my lecture, just *six* people were there to hear me. It was free, mind you! And it was a fine, pleasant evening too. But they weren't interested.[26]

Once again, the old biblical injunction had come true: a prophet is not without honor, except in his own country and in his own home.[27]

[1] Oral communication: Mary B. Bentley to Duncan Blanchard, October 3, 1970.

[2] Oral communication: Alice B. Hamalainen to Duncan Blanchard, June 26, 1971.

[3] Oral communication: Amy B. Hunt to Duncan Blanchard, July 26, 1969.

[4] *Ibid.*

[5] Oral communication: Mary B. Bentley to Duncan Blanchard, October 3, 1970.

[6] Oral communication: Izetta Barrett to Duncan Blanchard, June 20, 1990.

[7] Oral communication: Amy B. Hunt to Duncan Blanchard, July 26, 1969.

[8] Oral communication: Izetta Barrett to Duncan Blanchard, June 20, 1990.

[9] Oral communication: Amy B. Hunt to Duncan Blanchard, July 26, 1969.

[10] Oral communication: Alice B. Hamalainen to Duncan Blanchard, June 26, 1971.

[11] Oral communication: Arthur Pratt to Duncan Blanchard, July 27, 1969.

[12] *Ibid.*

[13] Oral communication: Alice B. Hamalainen to Duncan Blanchard, October 3, 1971.

[14] Oral communication: Izetta Barrett to Duncan Blanchard, June 20, 1990.

[15] Oral communication: Alice B. Hamalainen to Duncan Blanchard, October 3, 1971.

[16] Charles Nash, *Wilson Bentley, Vermont's Snowflake Expert*, Vermont Historical Society, Montpelier, Vermont. Misc. #82.

[17] Oral communication: Howard Wagner to Duncan Blanchard, October 2, 1970.

[18] Oral communication: Amy B. Hunt to Duncan Blanchard, July 26, 1969.

[19] Oral communication: Arthur Pratt to Duncan Blanchard, July 27, 1969.

[20] Oral communication: Alice B. Hamalainen to Duncan Blanchard, October 3, 1971.

[21] Oral communication: Amy B. Hunt to Duncan Blanchard, July 26, 1969.

[22] Oral communication: Mary B. Bentley to Duncan Blanchard, October 3, 1970.

[23] Oral communication: William Brunell to Duncan Blanchard, October 3, 1970.

[24] Oral communication: Arthur Pratt to Duncan Blanchard, July 27, 1969.

[25] Oral communication: Howard Wagner to Duncan Blanchard, October 2, 1970.

[26] Mary B. Mullet, "The Snowflake Man," *American Magazine*, February, 1925, pp. 28–31, 173–175.

[27] Matthew 13:57.

Chapter 10

The Three Women

Of the few women in Bentley's life, his mother received most of his love and devotion. Twenty years after her death he would say, "I can't remember the time I didn't love the snow more than anything in the world — except my mother. All that I am, or that I ever shall be, I owe to her."[1] There were two other women, however, whose paths crossed with his.

Jean Thompson, two years younger than Bentley and a writer of children's stories, first showed up in Jericho about 1904 or 1905. She had married Henry Thompson of New York City in 1895, but the marriage ended in divorce before his death in 1912 and possibly before she came to Jericho. Jean and her husband apparently had an income that allowed them to savor life at its fullest and to enter into the glitter of high society. She enjoyed beautiful clothes and the excitement of travel. They were friends of Charles Sanborn, the coffee man, and occasionally were guests on his yacht. It has been said that Henry loved the good life, and he may have brought about the divorce by paying too much attention to other women at social gatherings. They had no children, and Jean never married again. In later years, Jean's sister's children and grandchildren used to joke that after her divorce she hated all males, even those only three years old, for they had only one thing in mind.

When Jean Thompson arrived in Jericho, it was near the beginning of what would become a successful career as a writer. She had published only a few articles by that time, but in later years would go on write at least five books, many poems and children's plays, and nearly one hundred magazine articles. Though her income went up and down like a roller coaster, she enjoyed a steady reputation as a children's writer who told fascinating stories about animals and the beauty that nature paints in her huge canvas of the atmosphere. Jean's many articles on snow and frost became so familiar to readers that she was known as The Jack Frost Lady.[2]

It must have been her interest in the snow crystals and frost and the desire to know more about them that brought her to Jericho and to Wilson Bentley. For several summers, she was a guest at Amy Nash's boarding house on a side road that ran into Nashville Road less than half a mile west of Bentley's house and near where Mill Brook crossed the road. It was an easy walk between the two houses, and Jean Thompson must have made the walk numerous times to visit and learn about nature's atmospheric wonders from Bentley. The boarding house could not have been very large, for Amy Nash was also running a farm and taking care of her aging parents and her brother's motherless children.

Though Bentley's mother was living at the time of Jean Thompson's first visits to Bentley's home, the sight of this smartly-dressed city woman going to visit Bentley must have set tongues awagging among the neighbors, some of whom had never traveled more than a dozen miles from Jericho. Bentley, after all, had long been and was now one of the few eligible bachelors in Mill Brook Valley. On the other side of the farmhouse, Charles and Mary too must have wondered about Willie's involvement with this woman. Was it really just to exchange ideas on the water wonders of the atmosphere? How many visits does it take to do that? Their children, sensing the questions in the minds of their parents, were well aware of the presence of Jean Thompson. Amy, remembering her, said:

> Oh yes. Yes. He used to talk with her and she'd come over there and see him a whole lot. . . . And I'll tell you a little joke. He was always playing jokes on people on April Fool's Day. So one time they fixed up a joke on him. They told him she was

coming and that she would be in Essex Junction. He got all dressed up and went to Essex Junction and she wasn't there. But you know, he wasn't even mad about that. He took it all good natured. . . . Yes, he was quite interested in her.[3]

Ruth Nash, a niece who was brought up by Amy Nash, and about age twenty when Jean Thompson came to board with her aunt, had less charitable things to say about Jean.

She was quite a [man-chaser]. . . . Lots of people flirt for the fun of it. My aunt was disgusted with her. My brother and I just felt that Willie was nice to her, and he was nice to everyone. . . . Unless I size Willie up wrongly, he never would have brought a woman like her into his mother's home. Willie did not flirt. He was one of the serious-minded people. . . . Mrs. Thompson spent several summers at Aunt Amy's and one winter visit. She probably is not of this world, but if she is, she will show up and try to horn in. So watch out. Her big interest used to be money, and I do not think she has changed any. . . . Aunt Amy heard plenty about Mrs. T., and she and grandmother did not like it. When she wrote the third year, there was no room for her. She tried to keep up the correspondence, but Aunt Amy did not answer. None of the Nash's liked her. So I would just write her out of the picture.[4]

Willie Bentley may indeed have been "one of those serious-minded people," but it was clear he did not share the Nash's opinions of Jean Thompson. On February 20, 1907, in the first of only three surviving letters[5] of the many they exchanged, Bentley wrote:

Dear Mrs. Thompson,

Yours, telling of the operation you underwent, & of your continued activities in a literary way, came duly to hand. I am glad to learn you are so well as to resume literary labors, altho [sic] doubtful of its wisdom just now, untill [sic] you give those eyes a good rest. I note with pleasure that Mrs. Stuart is to come for a stay with Amy Nash, & of course I shall go over and play for her if she cares to hear my amateurish melodies. Much has happened to me since writing you. On Feb 5 I secured the largest & most beautiful & valuable set of snow crystals that I ever secured from a single storm. Many odd rare ones, which I greatly prize. On the 15th I went to Burlington & heard Prof Moore, Chief [of the] Weather Bureau, lecture on Meteorology. You can imagine my pleasure when he threw some of my snow crystals on the screen, & spoke so highly of them. His references to me & my work were very flattering indeed. He seems to be a very bright forceful man, & I was very glad to meet him. I presented him with a souvenir of Vt, & of his visit, an album containing many of the choicer snow & frost forms secured this winter. He was greatly pleased and interested in it. Well, one lecture has come to me unsolicited, & I of course will deliver it, one on snow crystals, before the "Social Club" of St. Albans, Vt. Kindly write me soon, that I may know how you are, & of your work.

With kind regards,
W. A. Bentley

Bentley's promise to go to Amy Nash's place and play the piano for Mrs. Stuart, who is never identified further in any of Bentley's writings, suggests that he must have played for Jean Thompson, either at his own home or at that of Amy Nash, and Jean liked it so much that she asked him to do the same for Mrs. Stuart. He clearly is exhilarated upon hearing that the Chief of the United States Weather Bureau spoke highly of his work with the snow crystals. But the request for a lecture from the St. Albans Social Club could not help but remind Bentley once again that in spite of the invitations he had to give lectures in other towns in Vermont, he had not yet been asked to talk about his work in Jericho.

Jean Thompson replied to Bentley's letter about a month later, and on April 8 Bentley wrote again. In this letter, even more than in the first one, it is abundantly clear that he held none of the Nash's devastatingly negative opinions toward her.

Dear Mrs. Thompson,

Your letter, so full of good news, came to hand to day, & gave me much pleasure, indeed. I am indeed enthusiastic over your prospects, they seem very bright, & I hope & trust no cloud will come to dim them. I am especially pleased at your prospects in regard to writing a new juvenile book. Hope you will succeed in securing contract for it, & will come & spend some of the beautiful summer days with us here in Nashville, while writing it. I am hammering away on the text of my own book, "Forms of Water," & making some progress thereon. Do not expect to finish it , & to secure all needed photos, data, etc for at least a year yet. I am greatly pleased at your efforts in my behalf, re the lantern slides, & appreciate it fully. Your kindly efforts may help me much in a financial way. I feel sure, however, that but few schools would go to the expense of securing the whole 160 slides. My own impression is that it is not necessary to include so many, but only a selection of the more interesting ones of each series, dew, frost, snow, etc. A lecture of great interest could be gotten up, using but 50 slides. But of course 100 would be much better. I am enclosing a list of prices of mounted slide sets, containing 50, 100 & 160 slides respectively. The prices quoted are low, yet I could do well making them here in the country (living is so cheap) at those figures, & wish your agent might procure many orders for me for such sets. I am much interested in your account regarding the book man and my autobiography. Hope I shall have the pleasure of returning the compliment some time, & of giving some of those Encyclopaedia fellows a sketch of yourself. But I have little hope, because they will surely prefer to hunt you up yourself, & to hear it from your own lips, & through the medium of that charming voice of yours. I am also much pleased & interested regarding those photographs for Magazine advertising purposes. It must be pleasing to you, & to whom would it not? to sit for a photo to be used thus. I feel sure they will be good, & only wish one of them might be reproduced within the book "Water Wonders" so that I might see it. I am exceedingly sorry to learn that your eyes are no better, & still cause you trouble. Do be careful of them. Unimpaired sight is one of our greatest blessings, & of priceless value to us. Give them all the rest possible. When writing, you should read print but little. I am awaiting with great pleasure, the arrival of your book, which you have so kindly promised me.

Very Truly yours,

W. A. Bentley

This letter is remarkable not only in revealing Bentley's warm feelings toward Jean Thompson and the imminent publication of her book, but in it we learn for the first time about the writing of Bentley's own book and his efforts as a businessman. The inclusion in the letter of a list of prices for slides suggests that Bentley's business of selling slide sets was doing reasonably well, but not so well as to prevent him from wishing "your agent might procure many orders for me for such sets." Bentley mentioned his book here and in his next letter to her but not in the rest of his surviving letters or in his published articles, though he undoubtedly did in letters to Cleveland Abbe. What happened to this 1907 attempt at a book remains shrouded in mystery; it was never published and no manuscript has ever been found.

Jean Thompson and Wilson Bentley clearly had a mutual admiration society going, for she had talked to publishers or agents about having Bentley write his autobiography, and he looked forward to returning "the compliment" by writing about her, but was certain that others would rather hear it "through the medium of that charming voice of yours." He hoped one of the pictures she sat for would appear in her book "so that I might see it." This might have been a gentle hint to send her picture to him should it not appear in the book.

Just over two weeks later, on April 26, Bentley received her book in the mail. Her picture was not in it. He read it and, later that day, sat down and penned the last of his surviving letters to Jean Thompson. Though he could not possibly have been aware of it, some of what he said in that letter suggested a reason why his own book was never published.

Dear Mrs. Thompson,

Your book "Water Wonders" which you so kindly sent me, came to hand to day, & I had to sit down at once & read it through, & to feast my eyes upon the beautiful illustrations which it contains. It is indeed a little beauty, & I am hoping that the number of copies sold will far exceed your utmost expectations, & bring you in handsome returns. You have added much, & greatly improved the text, since I have seen the same, & this gave me an added pleasure while reading it. It contains some errors, as I suppose all books do, but you have done finely in writing up subjects unfamiliar to you, ie, of which you have not made especial studies in, & have presented them in a charming way, & are to appeal to & reach the understanding of the young, & the average unscientific reader. What a beautiful book it makes, this illustrated treatment of the forms of water. I can imagine now what a thing of beauty my own book will be when issued, & it makes me almost impatient that it must wait so many months yet, before coming from the press. Yet it will be all the better for it, of that I am sure. I consider the half tone illustrations of your book, very fine indeed. Indeed, I think I recall none better, not even those used in [the] Harper's article. I have been writing an article, (which has been accepted) touching on snow, frost & ice photography for the Photo Era. It will not appear untill next Nov, when timely. Except for this, have done but little writing lately. Have been compiling data regarding window frost crystals, helping my Nephew with farm work, filling orders for slides etc, & of course eating up the sweets of the maple, which all Vermonters do, at this season of the year. I wish you could have been here, & had a share in the latter pleasure. Mrs. Stuart has doubtless wrote you of what a good sugar season we have had. The zero weather ceased at so early a date, that it left me no opportunity of finishing most interesting studies of ice crystals as formed upon water containing salt in solution. Hence this must go over untill next Winter. We are now having what must be called most diversified weather. Some beautiful summer like days, & some cold snowy ones. As I write, the snow is falling, & there is already 2 inches on the ground. Permit me in closing, to heartily congratulate you on the successful publication of your book. I can imagine what intense pleasure must have been yours, when the first copy was in your hands.

Very Truly yours,
W. A. Bentley

Water Wonders, the "little beauty" so admired by Bentley, was Jean Thompson's first book. Published by Doubleday as the eighth book in what presumably was a prestigious series on a variety of topics under the general title of "The Every Child Should Know Books," *Water Wonders* was a 233-page account of the forms of water in the atmosphere and on the ground. She wrote extensively about dew, frost, snow crystals, and the formation of raindrops. Her eloquent and graceful prose was accompanied by no less than 154 photographs, all taken by Bentley. Not only were his photographs sprinkled liberally throughout her book, but so were his ideas, especially those on the snow crystals and raindrops. Thompson's book gave abundant testimony that the several summers spent in Jericho learning from Bentley were not wasted. The master had taught his student well. At the front of the book she acknowledged her indebtedness to Bentley "for valuable assistance in the arrangement of this book, and particularly for permission to reproduce the micro-photographs," and mentions him several times throughout the pages.

Bentley had seen an earlier draft of her book but not the final one. One senses his disappointment at not seeing the final draft when, immediately after saying he had read and enjoyed the book, he writes that "It contains some errors." Undoubtedly he felt he could have caught these errors had he seen the final draft. But he does not dwell on this bit of mild, implied criticism and softens it somewhat by saying he supposes that all books contain some errors, especially if the authors, like herself, are writing about subjects of which they are unfamiliar. Bentley is correct in saying she had presented her ideas "in a charming way." He may have taught her the science in the book, but she came to him an accomplished and polished writer who was his equal at crafting elegant prose that painted vivid word pictures with metaphor and simile. She wrote that "the snow crystal is most ethereal, born in the vast spaces of the heavens, fashioned by the changing clouds and vapours, its lullaby the hoarse crooning of the mighty blizzard." To her, thunder is "Heaven's artillery," and the retreating clouds from a thunderstorm "leaden, ominous curtains . . . swept aside."

Although published as a children's book, it must have taken a highly precocious child to fully appreciate the ideas and beauty that covered its pages. Throughout the book Thompson used quotations from Shakespeare, Whittier, Lowell, and lesser known writers. Bentley observed correctly that it should appeal not only to young people but to the "average unscientific reader." The book did well, and probably attracted readers of all ages. It was still in print ten years after its publication. Editors of Jean Thompson's many magazine articles during that time were quick to remind readers that she was the author of *Water Wonders.*

The very success of her book is quite possibly the reason why Bentley's was never published. For what publisher would be willing to gamble on another similar book, especially when Bentley had contributed most of his best photographs to *Water Wonders* and many of his ideas about the forms of water in the atmosphere? His book probably was doomed the first day Jean Thompson showed up in Jericho.

After their summers of working together, can we conclude, as did Amy, her brothers and sisters, and possibly the Nash's, that there may have been a romantic involvement between Bentley and Jean Thompson? Probably not. It seems unlikely. Clearly, they shared a passion in sensing the beauty of nature's atmospheric wonders and wanting to share that with others, but that was it. Both in their early forties, they were far too set in ways that were worlds apart. He cared little for how he dressed, had no desire to travel far from Jericho, and lived only for the next winter's treasures of the snow. She, on the other hand, liked to dress well, traveled extensively, and wanted to write about many things other than the snow crystals. No one seems to know how much they interacted after the publication of *Water Wonders*, though there had to be some, because many of her magazine articles were illustrated with his photographs. In his photographic notebook, in February of 1916, Bentley included her name along with others in a list of people to whom he wanted to send reprints of his latest articles. Jean Thompson died many years after Bentley. Of the extensive correspondence that must have existed at the time of her death, little has survived. But among it were reprints of Bentley's articles, several newspaper accounts of his death, and the three letters he sent her in 1907.

❄

Schoolteachers came and went in the one-room schoolhouse down the road from the Bentley's. Though they came from other towns in Vermont, during the months of the school year they boarded with a family within walking distance of the school, and Bentley got to know them. It is said that he developed more than a passing interest in some of them, and one in particular has always been remembered by those who knew him. She was Mina Seeley, whose hometown was in Johnson, Vermont, about twenty miles northeast of Jericho. Nothing is known of her family or how she happened to come to the Nashville section of Jericho, but it is possible that Henry Seeley, who helped Bentley get started in photography, was either her father or uncle, and she was returning to the area where they grew up. One of Henry's sisters was Mina Jane and it is conceivable that Mina Seeley was named after her.

"He liked the girls when he was younger," Alric's wife said, "and then there was Mina Seeley. . . . She was teaching and boarding with the Whittemore's. . . . He kind of got liking her pretty well. . . . He did spend quite a bit on her."[6]

Amy had more to say about it:

> I imagine she was probably the only one he ever fell in love with. Of course he was a bachelor and she was an amazing lady then. . . . I think if he ever had any idea or notion of ever getting married, he would of at that time, but evidently she wasn't as interested as he was.[7]

Alice recalls "that there was a few schoolteachers that had a crush on him, and he'd get letters from them. I remember one, a Miss Seeley was one."[8] But Izetta Barrett felt differently: "I guess he kind of liked her, but he wouldn't be anything she'd bother with much. The temperaments would be not compatible at all. She was a schoolteacher, and she was kind of a sassy one."[9] Bentley's sister-in-law, Mary, without identifying the woman, said that Bentley was once briefly engaged to be married, but the engagement was broken off when the woman realized she would have to compete with the snow crystals for his love and attention.[10] If this woman was Mina Seeley, as seems likely, she had reluctantly come to the same conclusion as did Izetta Barrett that a clash of "temperaments" prevented her from spending the rest of her life with Wilson Bentley.

What did Bentley himself have to say about Mina Seeley? Nothing is known about letters that may have passed between them for they have been lost, but she is mentioned in his notebooks. On January 7, 1912, after many pages of details about his photography of frost, snow crystals, and dew, he wrote: "Mina Seeley's photo . . . taken by bay window front & side light. Black background." He took a second photograph with the same exposure time, seven seconds, "in middle room direct front light." Two weeks later he mentioned taking more photographs of Mina, this time along with photographs of his oldest niece, Agnes, who was married to Lee Whittemore, and her son Kenneth.

Three years passed. During that time the pages of Bentley's notebook were filled only with the details of his work.

But early in February, 1915, he wrote, along with a few details on exposure time and the setting of the camera bellows, "Window frost Feb 4 monogram Mina." Never again is Mina mentioned in his notebooks. What is one to make of this window frost monogram of Mina? In one of Bentley's articles on frost, he wrote about the curious patterns the frost makes on windows, often following scratches on the glass. To illustrate, he lightly scratched his initials WAB on the windowpane, let the frost form overnight, and the next morning took a photograph that showed his initials formed by elegant, feathery lines of frost. Perhaps in a similar way he had scratched Mina's name on a winter's windowpane to let the beautiful frost patterns poignantly remind him of the beauty of a woman who had left his life forever.

---

[1] Mary B. Mullet, "The Snowflake Man," The *American Magazine,* February, 1925, pp. 28–31, 173–175.

[2] Letter: Elizabeth Sansalone to Duncan Blanchard, March 30 & April 16, 1990; *Who's Who in America*, 1938–1939.

[3] Oral communication: Amy B. Hunt to Duncan Blanchard, July 26, 1969.

[4] Letter: Ruth A. Nash to Duncan Blanchard, September 18, 1969 & May 9, 1971.

[5] The three letters to Jean Thompson from Wilson Bentley were given to Duncan Blanchard by Elizabeth Sansalone, September 5, 1991.

[6] Oral communication: Mary B. Bentley to Duncan Blanchard, October 3, 1970.

[7] Oral communication: Amy B. Hunt to Duncan Blanchard, July 26, 1969.

[8] Oral communication: Alice B. Hamalainen to Duncan Blanchard, June 26, 1971.

[9] Oral communication: Izetta Barrett to Duncan Blanchard, June 20, 1990.

[10] Letter: Allene Davis to Duncan Blanchard, May 18, 1993.

Chapter 11

A Discovery Not Made

In late May of 1906, Willis Moore, Chief of the Weather Bureau, asked Cleveland Abbe to visit and evaluate the meteorology courses given at Syracuse University and St. Lawrence University in New York, and at the University of Vermont and Norwich University in Vermont. Abbe apparently spent most of June visiting these universities. On July 2, soon after his return to Washington, he wrote a long letter to the Chief reporting on his trip.[1] After several pages of detailed analysis of the courses and meteorological research at each of the universities, Abbe abruptly changed the subject and ended his letter as follows:

> As I left Washington I received a beautiful and important memoir from Mr. W. A. Bentley, who lives about sixteen miles east of Burlington. I carried this with me, drove over to see him, brought him back to Burlington, and spent two days with him, examining the details of his manuscript, which with its numerous photographs of frost and ice, I now submit to you, and recommend its publication in an early number of the Monthly Weather Review. This great paper represents twenty years of work, and will everywhere be recognized as a remarkable contribution to our knowledge. The expense involved in the preparation of this copy can scarcely be estimated at less than one hundred dollars, while the return to the Weather Bureau Library, by way of exchanges for the Monthly Weather Review, will be fully as great. I therefore request that you ask Mr. Bentley whether he will accept that sum and allow us to publish it.

Mr. Bentley is anxious to extend his researches on snow and ice to other portions of the country, and especially mountain stations. He should also have better apparatus than his own home-made instruments, but he has, by persistence, accomplished a wonderful work with crude materials.

Respectfully,
Cleveland Abbe
Professor and Editor

The Chief, who had been away from Washington visiting the Weather Bureau research observatory at Mount Weather, Virginia, replied to Abbe[2] in a memo dated July 12:

Prof. Abbe:

I herewith return Mr. Bentley's paper. I agree with you that it is a valuable piece of work. It will be impossible for us to adequately compensate him for it, but I think that we can consistently allow him an honorarium of $200.00. Please have the Accounts Division make up vouchers for him for the purchase of the manuscript and illustrations at that price.

When you write to Mr. Bentley you might tell him to make up a list of such apparatus as he may need to continue his work. If it is not too elaborate we may purchase it and lend it to him with the understanding that we have access to the results of his researches as they successively appear.

Respectfully,
Willis Moore
Chief of Bureau

The Chief clearly agreed with Abbe that Bentley had written "a beautiful and important memoir." His offer of an honorarium of $200.00 was a complete reversal of his position three years earlier when in the midst of bureaucratic entanglements he would not approve any form of financial support for Bentley. Abbe promptly had the vouchers sent to Bentley who immediately signed and returned them, probably in the next mail before the Chief had a chance to change his mind about the size of the honorarium. Though Bentley may have known he would be given an honorarium, the princely amount offered must have been far more than he ever expected. Consider this: $200 in 1906 had the purchasing power of about $4,000 today. No wonder he immediately signed and returned the vouchers!

It is only in Abbe's letter that we learn of Bentley's interest in working elsewhere in the country, especially at mountain stations. He never did go to any mountain stations, but he would leave Jericho about twenty years later to work briefly in Canada. The Chief shared Abbe's concern about Bentley working with "crude materials" when he requested that Abbe get from Bentley "a list of such apparatus" to continue his work. There is no evidence, however, that Bentley made such a list. It was never mentioned in his photographic notebooks, but it is possible that Weather Bureau money was used to buy some of his photographic plates and the other cameras that were used for the photography of clouds and dew. As for the apparatus used in his snow crystal photography, so crude and primitive in appearance to Abbe and others, it was to Bentley something he had lovingly put together by trial and error as a teenager over twenty years before. Perhaps in other hands it would not work, but in his it worked with the precision of a magnificent piece of clockwork. As long as it wasn't broke, why fix it!?

Although Bentley would in later years publish three more articles in *Monthly Weather Review*, never again would he write one that covered such a wide range of activities, that was so well researched, or as long as the one submitted to Abbe in 1906. Titled "Studies of frost and ice crystals," it was published in five consecutive monthly installments of *Monthly Weather Review* from August through December 1907. Its crowning glory was the 271 photomicrographs, with the magnification given for each one, of frost, ice crystals forming on water, hail, and other forms of ice.

Bentley had been studying the forms of frost as long as he had been studying snow crystals. In fact, he took his first photograph of frost in December, 1884, a month before he took the first successful photograph of a snow crystal. By 1906, he had studied and photographed over seven hundred frost formations, and was quick to point out, as he did with the snow crystals, that no two are alike. He was interested in hoarfrost, the frost that forms on vegetation, fences, or on the ground on clear, cold nights, and the frost so familiar to all, that seen on windowpanes on frigid winter mornings. He wrote in such detail about so many forms and subforms of hoarfrost, each accompanied by numerous photographs, that a reader who got through it all was apt to think, in paraphrasing Hamlet, that there are more forms of hoarfrost in heaven and earth than are dreamt of in any philosophy.

Depending upon the magnification required, Bentley used three different camera arrangements. If he needed no magnification, he used "an ordinary view camera." For magnifications from four to eight, he found that "a simple, rigid, inexpensive, home-made extension, containing . . . a one-fourth size portrait or rectilinear lens . . . coupled to the view camera answers admirably in most cases." For higher magnifications he attached a microscope objective to one end of a brass tube. The other end slid by rack and pinion within a larger tube and was attached to the view camera. When he used this for taking pictures of window frost, he attached the camera to slats nailed across the window casings. The camera could be moved horizontally, but once firmly secured to the slats there was no motion between the frost and the camera while the picture was being taken. He wrote that this setup could not be used in a city because of "tremors due to traffic, but in the country, where the inmates of the house can be kept quiet, it serves admirably." One can imagine that Bentley quietly but firmly told his nieces and nephews that they were not to run around their side of the house or visit him while this work was being done.

His work with the window frost was done with as much enthusiasm and attention to detail as that with the hoarfrost. He used the windowpanes in three unheated rooms of his house for these studies. One room was cold but very humid because of an open water tank, another cold but relatively dry, and the third one somewhat in between the others in humidity. With a sling psychrometer he obtained both temperature and relative humidity every time he observed or photographed a frost formation. His eleven classifications of window frost were put in familiar terms such as frost resembling serrated lines, trees, stars, and columns. He found the types of frost to depend not only on temperature and humidity but on the cleanliness of the glass and whether or not it was free of scratches. Sometimes frost appeared only after a thin layer of dew droplets fogged the glass; other times, when the humidity was not too high, the frost formed directly on the glass as water molecules streamed in toward it. One of his more curious photographs showed long pairs of frost lines meandering over the window pane that suggested an aerial view of railroad lines moving across the countryside. Bentley could not explain how these lines formed, but said that:

> The invisible, but potent, something that we blindly call crystallic impulse, or tendency, which traveled along those tiny crystallographic main lines, is perhaps just as wonderful in a way, if viewed from an atomic or molecular standpoint, as are the ponderous engines of human construction that thunder along the railroad lines represented upon actual railroad maps.

Not only did Bentley study hoarfrost and window frost, but he was fascinated by the "marvellous 'alchemy' or mechanism of ice formation, which, as if by magic, converts a fluid into a seemingly structureless solid" In other words, how does ice form on ponds, lakes, and rivers? He studied this by observing and photographing the formation and structure of ice crystals on the surface of water that was being slowly cooled in a pail or dish. He found that he could easily observe these crystals by looking at them reflected from a mirror placed on the bottom of the container. Though he found many types of ice crystals, he was puzzled that so many could form at the same time and grow in different ways in the same container of water. This caused him to think that though the environment can have some control over crystal formation, "there is a mysterious something — individuality, or whatever it may be called — inherent within the crystals themselves, that enters into the problem of form determination." Bentley need not have felt dejected in not solving these problems in ice crystal formation, for they are still being struggled with in laboratories around the world today.

Looking back at Bentley's 1907 article after a century of progress on many fronts in the atmospheric sciences, one becomes strikingly aware of how close he came to discovering in his windowpane frost formations what today is known as the Bergeron mechanism for the initiation of precipitation from supercooled clouds. But to understand Bentley's thin sliver of a miss on a great discovery, we must first turn to what Bergeron did.

Tor Bergeron, one of the great pioneers in unraveling the mysteries of the atmosphere, was a Swedish scientist whose discoveries in the first half of this century will forever be remembered.[3] In 1919, he was a member of a tiny but immensely creative group of young meteorologists whose new and revolutionary ideas on frontal theory were introduced to the world of meteorology. Their concepts of warm and cold fronts, and the development of storms along these fronts, are still being used by weather forecasters today.

Important as these ideas were to the development of dynamic and synoptic meteorology, Bergeron is perhaps even better known for a discovery in 1933 that laid one of the cornerstones of that branch of the atmospheric sciences known as cloud physics, the science dealing with the formation of clouds, rain, and snow. As the result of a serendipitous event, Bergeron was the first to realize that the rapid formation of snow from supercooled clouds would follow nature's production in the clouds of a number of tiny ice and snow crystals. These tiny bits of ice, Bergeron explained, even if initially much smaller than the cloud drops, have a lower vapor pressure than that of the cloud drops. Because of this vapor pressure difference, the ice particles grow rapidly as nearby cloud drops evaporate, their water vapor recondensing onto the particles or snow crystals. The crystals begin to fall as they grow larger, collide with and stick to other

138

crystals, and fall out of the cloud as snowflakes that may melt to raindrops before they reach the ground.

A most beautiful demonstration of the Bergeron mechanism, the rapid growth of ice crystals at the expense of the nearby cloud drops, can be made with nothing more complicated than a home freezer that opens at the top, a flashlight, and a small piece of dry ice. This most elegant of all experiments in cloud physics was first done in 1946 by Vincent Schaefer,[4] whom we met in Chapter 6. If one breathes into the freezer, the water vapor in the breath condenses to form a cloud of supercooled water droplets that can be seen as a whitish-greyish mass that undulates slowly as the air quiets down. Now hold a small piece of dry ice in the room air above the supercooled cloud. Gently scratch the dry ice with a fingernail until a tiny bit of it breaks off and falls down through the cloud. Look closely now. You will see what appears to be a tiny white thread left in the trail of the dry ice. Within seconds the thread gets fatter, and soon you'll realize it's made up of tens of thousands of tiny ice crystals that begin to grow rapidly and twinkle a rainbow of colors as the light from the flashlight is reflected and refracted in each of the crystals. But look even closer. The air around this growing vertical line of ice crystals is becoming clear as the water drops evaporate and the crystals feed on their water vapor. Within ten to twenty seconds a completely cloud-free cylinder of air perhaps a centimeter in diameter is cut in the supercooled cloud like a miniature eye in a hurricane. The release of the latent heat of fusion now creates convection and turbulence. The crystals are mixed through the rest of the cloud, which soon evaporates and is transformed into ice crystals that fall out to the bottom of the freezer. This experiment leaves no doubt about the validity of the Bergeron mechanism, and, incidentally, provides the way for cloud seeding to get the Bergeron mechanism going when nature needs some prodding.

Nearly thirty years before Bergeron, Bentley repeatedly observed and photographed this mechanism as frost formed on his farmhouse windows. Often he watched the condensation of water vapor on a cold windowpane that contained a few isolated frost crystals. He realized that the condensate was composed of "minute liquid particles or droplets of water that collect like tiny dewdrops on the glass." This was no surprise to him, but something else was. He was astonished to find that the misty, dew-like deposit did not extend right up to the frost crystals, but stopped some distance away. There was an obvious ring of clear glass surrounding each frost crystal, a veritable no-man's land containing neither frost nor dew. Bentley called this "one of the most singular, and doubtless most important, phenomenon that occurs in connection with the formation of window frost" Why did he consider this a "most important phenomenon?" Because he realized that it had significance far beyond what he saw on the windowpane. He made that great intuitive leap, so common to creative minds, from the clear area between the frost and the supercooled droplets on the windowpane to a clear space surrounding each snow crystal growing among the droplets in a supercooled cloud. Here was the Bergeron mechanism, pure and simple. Shouldn't the credit and honor for this great discovery have gone to Bentley and not to Bergeron? No, because Bentley had arrived at the wrong explanation for it.

The crucial bit of information, the one missing link needed by Bentley to understand what he saw, was that the vapor pressure of supercooled water is always slightly higher than that of ice at the same temperature. Though this was known to some scientists of Bentley's time, apparently it was not known to him. Thinking that the clear areas on his windowpane may be caused by electrostatic repulsion, he said:

> Possibly the snow and frost, and the liquid cloud or dew droplets, possess an excess of the same kind of electricity, positive or negative. If so they would naturally repel each other. . . . The repulsion operates also within the clouds while snow crystals are in process of formation, and hence has an important bearing on forms and structures of snow crystals, and in keeping them free from granular deposits of a like nature. . . It is quite possible that were it not for this repellent phenomenon, enacted

within the clouds among the snow crystals, clear, transparent, and beautiful snow crystals would rarely, or never, occur in nature, and fall to earth.

So it was that Bentley, grasping for an explanation for this "most important phenomenon," appealed to something that seemed to explain what he saw, but it was all wrong. No readers of his article, either in 1907 or in later years, came up with the correct explanation and its significance. Of course, if they had, the Bergeron mechanism would today be somebody else's mechanism.

Not long after his studies on frost were published, Bentley's interest, in addition to the snow crystals, turned to two other forms of water in the atmosphere. Both were produced by the condensation of water vapor, but one, the dew, was nearby and made of droplets that sparkled like diamonds when the morning sun found them on spiders' webs and blades of grass on lawn and meadow. The other, the clouds, seemed forever remote far above the earth, mountains of white foam churning upward into clear, blue skies. The more Bentley observed and photographed the many ways in which water appeared in the atmosphere, the more he realized it was all part of nature's grand tapestry. He said in one of his articles that:

> The deeper one enters into the study of Nature, the further one ventures into and along the by-paths that, like a mystic maze, thread Nature's realm in every direction, the broader and grander becomes the vista opened up to the view.[5]

---

[1] Records of the Weather Bureau, Record Group 27, general correspondence file 1894–1942, File No. 4331, National Archives, College Park, Maryland.

[2] *Ibid.*

[3] Duncan C. Blanchard, "Tor Bergeron and his 'Autobiographic Notes,'" *Bulletin of the American Meteorological Society*, 1978, vol. 59, pp. 389–392.

[4] Vincent J. Schaefer, "The production of ice crystals in a cloud of supercooled water droplets," *Science*, 1946, vol. 104, pp. 457–459.

[5] Wilson A. Bentley, "The latest designs in snow and frost architecture," *The American Annual of Photography*, 1906, vol. 20, pp. 166–170.

Chapter 12

The Long Silence

That incident involving Bentley running from Lapierre's camera store to the roof of the Vermont Hotel with a policeman in close pursuit, simply to get a picture of a cloud, reminds one of those hilarious chase sequences in the Keystone Cops' comedies. But to Bentley cloud photography was serious business. He felt that most people took pictures of clouds "with no definite end in view, except to perpetuate some cloud effect pleasing to the eye." He said that:

> Those with a love for nature's secrets, those with a desire to increase the sum of human knowledge, should try to go further, to picture every kind and species of cloud, and especially to secure views showing the birth and development of shower clouds. The formation and growth of a large cumulus cloud, and its passing from a simple cumulus of mountainous aspect, through the mushrooming stage and into a cumulonimbus, or rain cloud, crowned with a cirrus cloud crest, is a phenomenon of grand beauty and interest.[1]

Both "grand beauty and interest" motivated Bentley in nearly all that he did, no less here in his work with the rain clouds. His interest was trying to understand the mysteries behind the formation of the raindrops and how their sizes vary from one storm to the next. He saw the beauty in "the towering alpinelike pinnacles of our thunder clouds, stretching grandly upward in seemingly solid array toward the blue sky, and buttressed from below by mighty piles of expanding vapor."[2] Though he probably took several hundred pictures of clouds in various stages of formation, only a few appear to have survived. He never published an article devoted solely to clouds. Of the 154 photographs taken by Bentley that appeared in Jean Thompson's book, only two were of clouds.

Turning his camera downward from the clouds to the ground below, Bentley roamed the meadows near his home early on those clear summer and fall mornings when dew covered everything like a fine gauze. He was aware that dew collected differently on various plants and grasses, and since these varied widely at different locations he confessed to:

> . . . a keen wish to travel far afield, even into other lands and climes, for the purpose of observing and photographing the varied arrangements of the dew as it may occur upon the natural forms in these unknown fields.

Though there were difficulties to overcome in his photography of the dew, Bentley found them much easier than those he faced in his first attempts at snow crystal photography.[3] After some experimentation, he found that a long extension camera fitted with a quarter-size portrait or similar lens served admirably for this work. Wanting nothing to detract from the beauty of the dew drops on various objects, he provided a black background by painting the insides of a pail black and placing it behind the objects but facing the camera. As if the photography of dew on inanimate objects like blades of grass and flowers was not difficult enough, Bentley photographed tiny dew drops on the fine hairs of caterpillars and the antennae and legs of grasshoppers. But how does one get any self-respecting grasshopper or caterpillar to sit atop a flower all night collecting dew? It's easy. Tie it down! Late in the afternoon Bentley would catch, say, a grasshopper, and with a fine thread tie it to the top of a flower. Then at sunup the next morning he would be there with his camera to capture the first rays of the morning sun sparkling from the dew drops covering the antennae and legs of a most confused grasshopper. With the photography done, Bentley, like Albert Schweitzer, who did not want to bring harm to any living creature, cut the restraining thread to let the grasshopper stagger across the meadow, shaking off dew drops and wondering what strange thing had happened to him the night before.

The drops of dew that hung like miniature pearl necklaces on some spider webs fascinated Bentley. "Strings of matched pearls," he said, "imperial in their splendor, lie carelessly strung along a thread provided by an industrious spider."[4] The photography was sometimes difficult, as the slightest morning breeze stirring in the meadow caused the dew-laden web to vibrate. To minimize this, Bentley took a length of stiff wire and bent one end into a loop. He rubbed some pitch on the loop from a pine or spruce tree to make it sticky and brought it up against a small section of the spider web to capture it. He then stuck the other end of the wire in the ground, and overnight the dew necklaces once again collected on the web. Held firmly by the loop, there was no vibration of the web and photography was easy. Often he had his nieces collect pitch for him. Amy remembered that "he used to have us take a wire and go out and get pitch off the trees, and then he'd hook it under a spider's web."[5]

✳

The tension that had developed early between Bentley and his brother never went away with the passage of the years. Rather, it seemed to intensify as Bentley's wintertime passion with the snow crystals extended to a summertime passion with the dew, raindrops, and the clouds. They still continued to work together on the farm, but Charles's firm conviction that his brother's atmospheric ramblings were a senseless waste of time left him with a smoldering irritation that often erupted when they worked side by side. Amy remembered one morning when they were about to go out and work in the pasture:

> [Uncle Willie] took one look around and said to my father, 'Well, you'd better not cut any hay today because we're going to have a storm,' and my father would grumble and say 'You're not

going to tell me when to cut my hay.' And it would come out
more or less the way [uncle predicted]. You could rely on what
he had to say about the weather.[6]

Alice remembered an incident at the woodpile that
suggests perhaps Bentley was the one being obstinate.

[Father] had an awful time to make uncle do his share of the
sawing with the crosscut saw. My father used to get pretty mad
at him. They'd saw up the wood with these long crosscut saws,
one on each end, and uncle wouldn't pull when he was supposed
to. To do his share, my father had to push the saw and pull the
saw also. I used to watch them through the window, and my
father he'd stop and get so mad. Of course, I couldn't hear what
they were saying.[7]

The tension between the brothers never existed between
Bentley and his nieces and nephews. Alice recalled how kind her
uncle was a year after she got hurt.

When I was seven, we were playing in the big barn, and I
didn't like to jump off into the loft. . . . The boys pushed me off
a high beam down three levels onto a wood slab floor. . . . I hurt
my hip and I was lame for about three years. The first year I
didn't go to school. The teacher came by and heard my lessons.
In the second year I could walk a little, so uncle used to take me
to school. He always rode a girl's bicycle, and he put a seat
down low. He'd ride bowlegged and take me to school and bring
me back. . . . The school was just about a quarter mile away.[8]

Then there was the parasol incident. "He always went to
the circus every year," Alice said.

I used to go down with him to Burlington. I don't know how it
was I used to go. I suppose it was because I was quiet and didn't
bother him. . . . I had a little parasol given to me at Christmas,
and of course I had to take my little parasol whether I needed it
or not.

146

Alice and her uncle sat up in the crowded bleachers, and soon after the circus began:

I got interested and dropped my parasol, and as luck would have it, it stood upright in the ground. So uncle went down two or three rows . . . down between some people and he hung by his fingers [from the boards]. . . . People were kind of put out because he kept kicking them. [9]

Hanging down under the bleachers with the fingers of one hand, Bentley stretched and groped with the other. Finally he caught hold of a loop in the handle and pulled up the parasol. Alice must have thought that the absolutely best circus act performed that day was the one done especially for her by her uncle.

❋

In 1910, Bentley published in *Technical World* an article in which for the first time he made a serious attempt to explain why snow crystals have a hexagonal shape. "Nothing absolutely certain is known," he said:

. . . as to why they grow thus, except as it is assumed that the number and arrangement of the attractive and repellent poles possessed by the molecules of water impose this habit of growth upon them. This dividing into six is necessarily discussed and best explained in somewhat technical sounding terms.

After a long discussion in which he assumed that each water molecule had in addition to two primary positive and negative poles "three or six equidistant secondary poles arranged around what may be called the equatorial diameters of the molecules," he concluded that his theory not only explains the snow crystals' "hexagonal plan of growth, but in addition gives them two specific secondary habits." Bentley's explanation of the hexagonal structure of snow crystals was wrong. We know today that snow crystals are hexagonal because of the orientation of the two hydrogen atoms around the oxygen atom in the water molecule. But none of this was known in 1910 and would not be until two years before Bentley's death.

At the end of the article he turned from theory to the recognition by artisans and manufacturers of the practical uses of his snow crystal designs. Though to Bentley they were "exquisite works of art in themselves," manufacturers had begun to use his designs in metal work, wall paper, porcelain, china, glassware, and silk. This clearly must have pleased him, but he said "their greatest field of usefulness, however, is along other lines, as objects for nature study and for illustrating the forms of water." To emphasize this, he remarked that the University of Wisconsin alone had over one thousand lantern slides of his snow crystals. As if encouraged by this recognition, he ended the article on a note of optimism.

> It seems likely that these wonderful bits of pure beauty from the skies will soon come into their own, and receive the full appreciation and study to which their exquisite loveliness and great scientific interest entitle them.

Two years later, Bentley published the last of his many articles in the *American Annual of Photography* and a detailed technical article in *Knowledge*, a monthly magazine of science published in London. The curtain then came down on an extraordinary collection of twenty-nine articles that had been published since his first in 1898. He had published at least one article a year since 1900, and five alone in 1904. A long silence would now descend over his writing. In the nine years from 1912 to 1921, Bentley would publish only two articles, one a very short one in 1914 in *Farm and Fireside*, the other in 1918 in *Monthly Weather Review* in response to a criticism of his work.

Why the silence? One can only guess, as none of the letters to and from Bentley during that time has survived. Perhaps it was simply that he had nothing more to say for the moment, or perhaps, since he had never found two snow crystals alike, he wanted to intensify the search for the Holy Grail of snow crystals, that one uniquely beautiful crystal that dwarfed all others in elegance and charm. He had once written that he had the day dream of finding "the one, or the few preeminently beautiful snow crystals that we may be certain exists among the snows."[10] He was mesmerized with their beauty. He worked long hours in the cold in the woodshed taking snow crystal photomicrographs, "and then," he said:

> . . . after the storm is over, with what keen joy of anticipation the dark-room is sought, that we may watch the exquisitely beautiful images of these wonderful crystals emerge in the plate, out of seeming nothingness, under the effects of the magic chemical baths.[11]

Though he stopped writing, Bentley never stopped working with the snow crystals. By the end of 1912 he had photographed 2,122 snow crystals, an average of about seventy-five each winter. During the next nine years, however, in a frenzy of activity that swept over him during each snowstorm, he would increase that average nearly three times to two-hundred-ten.

In the spring of 1913, a sudden change occurred in the Bentley farmhouse. Mary and Charles moved out. Sometime before, Alric, the first born of their eight children and now twenty-six, had bought a farm in Andover, a small town in southern Vermont about eighty-five miles south of Jericho. For reasons unknown, an exchange of farms occurred. Mary and Charles moved to the Andover farm while Alric returned to Jericho to take over the west side of the farmhouse next to his Uncle Willie. While Bentley may have had few regrets about his brother leaving, he must have felt a certain sadness when Mary left. They had always gotten along well together, and Mary, despite being busy over the years with her large family, often brought special treats over to him, and from time to time helped him with his photography.

When Mary and Charles left Jericho, five of their children were old enough to be on their own, but presumably Amy, fourteen, and her younger sister, Anna, and brother, Alwyn, the baby of the family, went with them. Life on the new farm in

Andover did not go well. Whether because of tensions created by the move or by those that arose earlier in Jericho, their marriage fell apart. Mary left Charles in 1915 and three years later Charles obtained a divorce.[12] Mary soon remarried and by all accounts this second marriage was a happy one.

If Bentley had any anxieties about the departure of Mary and Charles, he had little time to dwell on them. 1913 was the one-hundred-fiftieth anniversary of the founding of Jericho. At the annual town meeting that spring the townspeople voted to celebrate this in a grand manner. Committees were formed and they formed sub-committees. It seemed that nearly everyone in Jericho was involved in preparing for the upcoming activities, including Wilson Bentley.[13] One of the themes of the celebration was to recognize the "old-fashioned goodness" as expressed in the opening lines of the poem by Edgar A. Guest: "Old-fashioned folks! God bless 'em all! The fathers and the mothers, The aunts an' uncles, fat an' tall, The sisters an' the brothers . . ." After months of planning and preparation, the great event took place on five days during the first week of August.

The first day was the most solemn of all. People gathered in their churches to hear religious music, prayers, and addresses on the history of Jericho, how it began as one of the New Hampshire grants, and how the courage and bravery of the Brown family enabled them to become Jericho's first settlers. On the following days, solemnity dispensed with, the real celebration began. There were plays and band concerts. There were dinners, baseball games, and footraces. The women of Jericho Center displayed mementos from the past in the old Universalist Church, including a sword carried in the Battle of Lexington, old landscapes done in needlework, and rare old woven blankets. Not far from Jericho Corners a bronze tablet was erected near the site of the first cabin built by the Brown family.

But the most spectacular part of the celebration, the re-enactment of the capture of the Brown family by Indians and the parade of floats, was reserved for the last day. It began at the athletic field where a cabin resembling the original one built by the

Browns had been constructed. With thousands of people looking on — one estimate placed it at 4,000 which meant, since the population of Jericho was barely more than 1,300, that most onlookers came from surrounding towns — an oxcart containing descendants of the Brown family arrived on the field and took them to their cabin. Then the big parade of floats began, all eighteen of them, each drawn by one or two horses through the village and to the athletic field. One float represented Indian life, another the spirit of the Minute Men, and still another, life in vaudeville. A great white float made by the Irish settlers in Jericho was covered with green trimmings, and in it twelve of Erin's fair daughters sang while being accompanied by a golden harp. Behind the Irish float was one that far in the distance was recognizable by a huge five- or six-foot-high snow crystal made of white strips of wood mounted high up in front for all to see. It had, of course, been made by Wilson Bentley. It was, said one who saw it:

> . . . a float covered with evergreens and for a background had huge representations of snow crystals displayed on all sides. But what's that pole on the back end of the float, rising out of a mass of ice? Why the North Pole itself, with the rival claims of Cook and Peary inscribed thereon.

When all the floats had arrived at the athletic field, and all the children had been rounded up, the band played and the final event of the five-day celebration was enacted. With whoops and hollers, Indians, with tomahawks raised high, swept onto the field, ran toward the cabin, captured the Brown family, and led them off into captivity. Thus ended the five-day celebration of the one-hundred-fiftieth anniversary of the founding of Jericho. One wonders why the organizers of the celebration did not have the Browns come back on the field once more to celebrate their triumphant return to Jericho after months in captivity? Perhaps all concerned were just too tired to do more after five days of nearly non-stop celebration. Bentley may not have been tired that night when he arrived home with his horse and wagon, but he probably found that the hot August sun had left little ice to put in his icebox.

And the North Pole? That no doubt ended up on the wood pile the next day. But the big wooden snow crystals most likely were nailed to the side of the barn and were the ones admired by the many people who visited Bentley in later years.[14]

❄

On a clear cold morning on the ninth of February, 1915, Bentley celebrated his fiftieth birthday doing what he liked to do best, photographing snow crystals out in the woodshed. Twenty-three were captured by the camera lens. He wrote in his notebook that "thin clouds broke up at 10 and from then till 1 o'clock crystals fell steadily from a practically clear sky."

The next day the editorial office of the *Monthly Weather Review* received an eighteen-page, handwritten manuscript from Bentley titled "Thirty years work among the snow crystals."[15] It was read and studied by Cleveland Abbe and perhaps others in the Weather Bureau. Abbe then rejected it and returned it to Bentley. No copy of Abbe's rejection letter has survived, but Bentley's manuscript has. A reading of it gives clues to why Abbe, though long an admirer of Bentley's work, found it unsuitable for publication. Though Bentley's handwriting was hard to read, and his sentences ran end to end for eighteen pages in one continuous paragraph, this alone would not have stopped Abbe from publishing it. After all, he had not only published earlier manuscripts of Bentley's that must have been written in the same awkward manner, but he had praised them as well. The reason for the rejection was not for the appearance of the manuscript, but for the contents. Bentley had betrayed his own title. He did not discuss his thirty years of observations and photography of the snow crystals, work done more patiently and brilliantly than anyone else in the world, but instead wandered off into a dream-like world of theory where he promptly became lost.

Fully half of his manuscript was a long theoretical argument to show that, in addition to temperature, the shape and form of snow crystals was controlled by the distribution of electrical charges on the crystals. He said he could:

. . . hardly escape the conviction that the mysterious something that causes the crystals to grow outward only at certain points and to divide into six is electromagnetic in nature, and there is a play of tiny electric charges about and upon them, whose mutual repulsions and attractions and new momentary realignments as new charges are brought to them, or older ones lost by discharge into the air, determines their lines of growth and form.

He built and expanded upon this rickety theoretical structure without a shred of experimental evidence to prop it up. He said, correctly, that the electrostatic charges on a snow crystal tend to concentrate at the tips of the six arms that often grow from the corners of a hexagonal plate. But he went on to say, quite incorrectly, that when the charges "exceed the capacity of the tips to retain them," they dribble down the sides, like water overflowing the brim of a glass, "to form growth nuclei" for the branches that grow out of the six arms to produce the beautiful stellar crystals.

The latter half of his manuscript, though somewhat repetitive of his earlier work, did contain some new ideas on the sizes of cloud droplets deduced from measurements of those he found frozen onto snow crystals. But again Bentley latched onto erroneous concepts in electrostatics when he tried to explain why cloud droplets were often still liquid at temperatures far below the freezing point. He said that "the only plausible explanation would be to assume that they are highly charged with electricity, their electrification serving to warm them or to keep them in a state of undercooled fluidity." Clearly he did not know that electrical charges at rest on cloud droplets, or on anything else, would produce no heating. Heating occurs only when charges move through a resistance.

Abbe was right in rejecting Bentley's manuscript. In a manner of speaking, he was protecting Bentley from himself, but it was a sad way to end what had been a most productive collaboration in the bringing of Bentley's ideas to the scientific world in the articles Abbe had published earlier in *Monthly*

Weather Review. It's doubtful that Bentley and Abbe ever wrote to each other again, not because of the rejection of the manuscript, but because a few months later Abbe suffered a stroke. He never regained his health and died the following year.[16]

❊

Sometime in 1917, photographers from Pathé News, an organization that before the age of television made movies of news events to be shown at movie theaters, showed up in Jericho to make a short movie of Bentley taking photomicrographs of snow crystals. They made Bentley move all his apparatus out of the woodshed and place it alongside the house near his kitchen window, possibly because there was not enough room or light in the woodshed to take movies. They had him wear his best dress-up clothes: white shirt and collar, black tie, dark overcoat, and a soft felt hat. Bentley must have fussed and fumed over this, as he never worked out of doors with his camera, and he certainly never dressed up when he did his photography. Since the thin broom splint that he used to transfer a snow crystal from his blackboard to a microscope slide would never show up in the movie, the photographers had him use a tapered piece of wood as thick as a pencil. This only served to increase his irritation. But Bentley's irritation must have reached record levels when the photographers decided it would be nice to have snow falling while their cameras were rolling. But it wasn't snowing that day, though there was some on the ground. No problem. What passed as the special effects team of Pathé News leapt into action. They scooped some snow from the ground into a basket and had Alric Bentley take it to a second floor bedroom where he tossed handfuls of it into the air from an open window.

It was a disaster. Instead of having soft white snowflakes descend slowly and uniformly over Bentley, large chunks of snow fell like hailstones, some striking his hat, others his shoulders, producing splashes of snow that dotted his hat and coat with white smears. No matter. Snow was snow. The movie camera kept rolling and captured Bentley working in his element. To finish the

154

work that day the photographers took movies of individual snow crystals drifting downward. Not being able to photograph such small crystals or to control where they fell, special effects again came to the rescue. They cut models of the crystals several inches in diameter out of heavy white paper and strung them a foot of so apart on a thin wire. Someone held the upper end of the wire above and in front of the movie camera, and slowly let it descend while at the same time twisting it to make the paper snow crystals spiral as they fell downward. This was all well and good, but the person controlling the wire must have had hiccups; the movie shows sudden starts and stops superimposed on the smooth descent of the crystals.

The movie runs only a few minutes in length, but it is the only known motion picture of Bentley in action.[17] The still photographs taken that day would be used many times by Bentley and others in later articles, and they are still being used today.

In the same year the movie was made, a translation from the German of a long article by Professor Dr. Gustav Hellmann appeared in two parts in the *Monthly Weather Review*. Hellmann, one of the first after Bentley to succeed in taking photomicrographs of snow crystals, wrote extensively on the classification of rain, dew, frost, snow, and hail. In the section on snow he said that Bentley's photomicrographs were "very numerous, but some unfortunately much retouched." That's all he had to say about Bentley's work. Cleveland Abbe, Jr., who had taken over as editor after his father's death, and who had translated the article into English, had leapt to Bentley's defense and added a footnote at the bottom of the page. It read:

> This remark probably does not apply to Bentley's photographs as published in the Monthly Weather Review May 1901; Annual Summary, 1902; Annual Summary, 1907. So far as the Weather Bureau knows, there was no retouching and certainly there was none done on the prints from which our engravings were made.

For most people that would have ended the matter. With the United States Weather Bureau vouching for your honesty, what more needs to be said? A lot more, Bentley must have thought as he read Hellmann's remark. A tide of anger rose within him. It was as if Hellman had accused him of not being a true son of Vermont or a staunch Republican! Bentley was not about to let pass what he considered an attack on his character. He sat down and wrote an article for the *Review* that was a model in social decorum.[18] But just barely. It was easy to read between the lines to get his true feelings for Hellmann. Bentley said that he:

> . . . fully appreciates Dr. Hellmann's eminent services to meteorology and to general knowledge, but has no sympathy with that perverted or ultrascientific viewpoint that insists on having a photograph presented exactly as it emerges from the chemical bath, with all the false light impressions of dust and other foreign particles glaringly in evidence and falsifying the result. A true scientist wishes above all things to have his photographs 'as true to Nature' as possible; and if retouching will help in this respect, then it is fully justified.

Hellmann had said, as if in justification of his comments about Bentley's retouching of the crystals, that "it is rarely that ideally perfect crystals occur in Nature." Not so, replied Bentley, who pointed out that one must work rapidly before the crystals seen through the microscope begin to evaporate and show rounded instead of sharp edges. He said that the grouping of several snow crystals together will produce asymmetrical evaporation with the evaporation retarded most at the points where two crystals nearly touch one another. Bentley was right. He said this was the reason that many of the snow crystals Hellmann used "to illustrate his interesting book, 'Schneekrystalle,' were deformed and robbed of much of their natural symmetry."

That was Bentley's well-reasoned reply to the world of science in defense of Professor Dr. Hellmann's criticism. But up in Jericho, when talking about Hellmann with his good friend, Frank Hartwell, manager of the Weather Bureau station at Burlington, he said laconically that "the Dutchman works so slow that the corners all evaporate or melt off his snowflakes before he gets his picture made."[19]

Throughout the 1910s Bentley had steadily increased his efforts in snow crystal photography. They reached their zenith in 1919 with an explosion of activity that saw Bentley photographing during nineteen snowstorms. In one storm alone near the end of the winter, March 29, that Bentley described as a "great blizzard, about 3 foot snowfall . . . storm raged all day today . . . best crystals fell in afternoon," he worked in the woodshed most of the day and obtained a record-breaking sixty-four photographs. Only once in later years would he obtain more photographs in a single day. During the winter of 1919 he photographed 338 snow crystals, a record never to be broken but nearly equaled with 335 in 1920.

Bentley had become so obsessed with getting more and more photographs that on some days, when it stopped snowing early in the day, he would bring into the woodshed snow that had fallen on shingles that he had laid out earlier. In the afternoon he would carefully search through this snow for perfect crystals to photograph. Hours would pass. He became oblivious to all else that happened around him. He said that "business, pleasure, grief, cold . . . all are forgotten in the search for these marvelous gems from on high."[20]

A week or two after Bentley obtained his sixty-four photographs, John Hooper, another of his friends at the Burlington Weather Bureau, died. On April 17, Bentley wrote a letter of condolence to Mrs. Hooper.[21]

Dear Mrs. Hooper,

I was deeply grieved to learn of Mr. Hooper's death, and should have attended the funeral had it been possible. Accept for yourself, the mother, and the fatherless children, my deepest sympathy. I feel I have lost a very dear friend, and shall sorely miss Mr. Hooper's genial presence whenever in Burlington. I am so glad for you that you have the bright pretty children to center your affections on. You have much to be thankful for still, much to live for. Hoping a kind providence will give you strength and fortitude to bear your great loss, till happier days come.

Sincerely,

W. A. Bentley

Years later, long after Bentley's own death, Mrs. Hooper still had fond memories of him.

I can remember his many visits to the Weather Bureau. . . . He always brought us prints of his best snowflakes. . . . He was a little man, slightly over five feet in height, soft-spoken, unassuming and timid, but with the light of enthusiasm always shining in his eyes. He came often because he and Mr. Hooper talked the same language, and I think perhaps these visits gave him an outlet, since the people of his village considered him a little 'cracked.' Photographing snowflakes indeed! A strange occupation for a farmer![22]

Perhaps the rarest of the snow crystals are those that are twelve-pointed, but Bentley photographed several of them. In a letter in 1919 to a physics professor in California, he wrote that:

. . . so far as I am able to learn, the twelve-pointed ones really consist of one crystal superimposed upon another, and never growing outward on the same plane. It would seem as if there must be a short bar or connection at the center, for the rays of the one usually project at an intermediate direction between the rays of the other. Yet they are easily detached one from the other.[23]

Bentley's explanation for these curious snow crystals is accepted by atmospheric scientists today. His "short bar or connection" has been found to be nothing more than a frozen cloud droplet.

In the years since Mary and Charles had left, and most of their children had grown up to go their own ways, the old farmhouse had been eerily quiet. Bentley had continued to occupy the east side, the only home he had ever known, and Alric lived alone in the roomy expanse of the west side. But all that changed in 1919 when another Mary came to live in the house after she and Alric were married. Mary Brunell was a local girl and had known Alric as long as she could remember. As she put it, "I was born just over the fence from their farm."[24]

Mary and Alric were not the only newly-married couple to live in the farmhouse that year. Alric's younger brother, Arthur, had married Anna Trieb, the eldest daughter of Katharina and Balthsar Trieb. "Alric and his wife lived in one part, and we lived in the middle," Anna said, "and Uncle Willie lived in the other part. . . . Since I lived in the middle part I used to hear him playing [the piano] a lot of the time."[25] Anna and Arthur moved out within a year to a nearby farm, but Mary and Alric stayed to live in the old farmhouse and were there at the time of Bentley's death.

By early 1920, Bentley's work with the snow crystals, though well-known to scientists around the world, had become but a dim and distant memory in the minds of most people. After all, since 1912 he had published only that brief article in *Farm and Fireside*, and his work was mentioned only once or twice in other magazines of the day. True, he had continued to sell lantern slides and photographs to museums and universities and anyone else who wanted them, but his apparent self-imposed silence on publishing had made many people forget all about him. That, however, was about to change in a most dramatic fashion. Before the year was out, an explosion of recognition would shower down upon him. From that time onward he would be known to tens of thousands of people, perhaps not by the name of Wilson Bentley, but as the Snowflake Man.

---

[1] Wilson A. Bentley, "Snow, cloud and frost photography," *The American Annual of Photography*, 1909, vol. 23, pp. 201–204.

[2] *Ibid.*

[3] Wilson A. Bentley, "Photographing the forms of water," *The American Annual of Photography,"* 1908, vol. 22, pp. 125–128.

[4] Wilson A. Bentley, "Glories of the dewdrops caught by the camera," *The New York Times Magazine*, 1927, July 31.

[5] Oral communication: Amy B. Hunt to Duncan Blanchard, July 26, 1969.

[6] *Ibid.*

[7] Oral communication: Alice B. Hamalainen to Duncan Blanchard, June 26, 1971.

[8] *Ibid.*

[9] Oral communication: Alice B. Hamalainen to Duncan Blanchard, October 3, 1971.

[10] Wilson A. Bentley, "Snow crystal and frost photography during the winter of 1903," *The American Annual of Photography*, 1904, vol. 18, pp. 33–39.

[11] Wilson A. Bentley "How to photograph snow crystals," *The American Annual of Photography,* 1903, vol. 17, pp. 51–59.

[12] County Court, Windsor County, Vermont, October, 1918.

[13] *The History of Jericho, Vermont,* first published in 1916 by the Free Press Printing Co., Burlington, Vermont, and reprinted in 1989 by the Queen City Printers, Inc., Burlington, Vermont.

[14] Oral communication: Helen S. Poissant to Duncan Blanchard, October 3, 1970.

[15] Manuscript sent by Alice B. Hamalainen to Duncan Blanchard, October 21, 1971.

[16] "Cleveland Abbe, 1838–1916," *Monthly Weather Review*, 1916, vol. 44, pp. 517–518.

[17] Movie loaned to Duncan Blanchard by Alice B. Hamalainen, June 26, 1971; A copy is on file at the Vermont Historical Society, Montpelier, Vermont, and at the Jericho Historical Society.

[18] Wilson A. Bentley, "Photomicrographs of snow crystals and methods of reproduction," *Monthly Weather Review*, 1918, vol. 46, pp. 359–360.

[19] Frank E. Hartwell, *Forty Years of the Weather Bureau*, Long Trail Studios, Bolton, Vermont, 1958; Copy on file in Special Collections, Wilber Library, University of Vermont, Burlington.

[20] Wilson A. Bentley, "The beauty and interests of snow crystals," *The Guide to Nature*, 1922, February, vol. 14, pp. 117–120.

[21] Letter on file at the Jericho Historical Society, Jericho, Vermont.

[22] Edith S. Hooper, *The Most Unforgettable Character I've Met*, the Bentley collection, Jericho Historical Society, Jericho, Vermont.

[23] John C. Shedd, "The evolution of the snow crystal," *Monthly Weather Review*, 1919, vol. 47, pp. 691–694.

[24] Oral communication: Mary B. Bentley to Duncan Blanchard, October 3, 1970.

[25] Oral communication: Anna Trieb Bentley to Duncan Blanchard, October 4, 1970.

Chapter 13

A Silence Broken

On September 19, 1920, Wilson Bentley sat down at a table in his farmhouse and penned a letter to Dr. Charles F. Brooks, who had taken over as editor of the *Monthly Weather Review* from Cleveland Abbe, Jr. He revealed in this letter yet another scientific interest that had tested his powers of observation since he was eighteen years old, but, curiously, had never been mentioned in any of his articles.[1]

Dear Dr. Brooks,

I am sending you under separate cover a record of all the auroras observed here by me, 1883 to 1920 inclusive, with some remarks about the character of some of them. I would be grateful if you will preserve this record, so that it will be easily accessible to investigators of auroral phenomena. Of all those I have seen, the blood red one of Feb 13th 1892 impressed me most strongly. Yet those producing the bright nebulous bands of light extending across the sky from east to west, and passing overhead near the zenith, seemed very remarkable. Auroras of this character were seen on April 4th, 1883, Feb 11, 1899, June 29, 1899, April 3, 1904, and in less degree on April 1 and 28, 1910, Jan 30, 1918, and April 6, 1918. The practical absence of auroras during the years 1901–1902, and again during 1912–1913 and 1914, is very significant and instructive. Of course, many occurrences and reoccurrences of auroras were invisible at my locality because of cloudiness, and especially during fall and

163

winter months. Hoping this record may be of some real value to students of auroral phenomena.

Sincerely

W. A. Bentley

It is incredible to think that Bentley, in addition to everything else he was doing, could find the time to pay so much attention to auroras. There are few people who have peered into the night sky for those tell-tale flashes of color for as many years as Bentley did. He made his first recorded observation on February 1, 1883, one week before his eighteenth birthday. He wrote that the aurora was "faint." His last observation would be made almost half a century later, forty-nine years to be exact. It occurred on November 26, 1931, a month before his death, and he recorded it with no comment.

The aurora, technically the aurora borealis in the Northern Hemisphere, but often simply called "the northern lights," is caused when particles emitted from the sun end their long journey by crashing into the earth's upper atmosphere and producing an ionized gas. The particles come from or near sunspots, the dark spots that can be seen on the surface of the sun. The number of spots at any given time vary year by year, and when plotted on a graph show a wave-like, up-and-down pattern. The lowest number of sunspots occurs about every eleven years. One might expect, therefore, that the frequency of occurrence of auroras over the years should also show a wave-like pattern that follows or correlates with that of the sunspots. Long ago, scientists found just such a correlation.

Why didn't Bentley notice that the number of auroras he observed each year showed a wave-like pattern with a minimum about every eleven years that coincided with the sunspot minimum?[2] It's possible he did not have the data on sunspots. It certainly was not because of a lack of data on auroras. In the record sent to Dr. Brooks he listed 398 auroras, giving the date for each and a comment about its intensity and appearance. In future years he would observe an additional 236, giving a total of 634 auroras seen over forty-nine years, an average of about thirteen each year. What a feat of observation! Few of us can lay claim to even one auroral sighting a year.

One question remains. After patiently scanning the dark skies for auroras, night after night for thirty-eight years, why did Bentley choose this particular time to send all his records to Dr. Brooks? One can only guess, but it may be no coincidence that just a week later the first newspaper story ever to be done on Bentley's lifelong work with the snow crystals appeared in the *New York Tribune*, followed a few weeks later by another major article in the *Boston Herald*. A near avalanche of other articles soon appeared in both newspapers and magazines, and Bentley himself started writing once again. There was no turning back. Bentley's work had been rediscovered. Everyone wanted to know more about him, and was it really true that no two snowflakes are alike?

It is possible that in September, 1920, Bentley, aware of the forthcoming newspaper articles, knew he would have many letters to answer and numerous requests for snow crystal photographs and lantern slides. Perhaps he sensed he would never get time to work on the auroral data, so decided to send a copy of it to Dr. Brooks with the hope that it would be "of some real value to students of auroral phenomena."

The story that appeared about Bentley on September 26, 1920, in the Sunday edition of the *New York Tribune*, included a picture of him sitting in a chair, apparently out of doors. Wearing a shirt and tie under a suitcoat that seemed buttoned in haste by only the top one of three buttons, Bentley gazed directly into the eyes of his readers from beneath a flat-brimmed straw hat pulled down securely on his head. With the mustache that he was accustomed to wearing by then, he was the picture of a proper gentleman of the 1920s ready to begin a Sunday afternoon stroll down the streets of his city.

The story was unusual in that after a brief introduction by the reporter, in which he said that Bentley was known as the "farmer-scientist . . . and is recognized as the world authority on the subject of snowflakes," the rest of the story was entirely in quotes taken directly from Bentley's own words. Whether Bentley had written this by request from the reporter or whether it was taken from some unknown article of Bentley's published earlier that year, is not known. But he told the story he had repeated so often in many articles over a decade earlier: how his mother had encouraged him from the very beginning, how he struggled before he obtained his first snow crystal photographs, and how his interests had expanded to other water wonders of the atmosphere. He ended by giving an interesting glimpse into his philosophy of life.

> The moral to be drawn from my experiences seems to be, provided one has an aptitude along any given line, is to take up a hobby and follow it through life. A seemingly unimportant study sometimes brings unexpected results. . . . I have devoted almost my whole life to the study of a very small part of nature, to a part of it which few people ever give more than a moment's consideration. Yet with that small part my life has been made industrious.

The second major newspaper story about Bentley appeared the following month on October 24 in the Sunday edition of the *Boston Herald*. Like the earlier one in the *New York Tribune*, it called him the farmer-scientist, showed the photograph of him in his suitcoat and straw hat, and used many of the same quotes. Large headlines shouted that Bentley "has never found two snowflakes alike." Not to be outdone by the newspaper articles, *Leslie's Weekly* magazine on Christmas day trumpeted that Bentley was not only a farmer-scientist but also "the Columbus of the microscope."

The sudden rush of stories about Bentley was not over. Barely a week after the one in *Leslie's Weekly*, the biggest story yet appeared on Sunday, January 2, 1921, in the *Boston Globe* with huge headlines proclaiming "Fame comes to Snowflake Bentley after 35 patient years." But this story was different in one important detail from any that had yet been written about Bentley. The reporter, James Powers, was the first writer ever to go to

Jericho to visit Bentley to see how he lived, and to hear directly from him how he did his work. In the opening paragraphs he writes that in "this scattered, snow-buried village" there lives:

> . . . one of the most remarkable men who ever grew up in the Green Mountain State. . . . He has delved into the infinite treasures of nature as truly and significantly as Henri Fabre peered into the insect world.

But the remarks of the driver of the automobile taking Powers to Bentley were not quite so generous and reflected the mixed emotions that most of the villagers still had about Bentley. "Yes, Bentley is queer . . . has lived all by himself . . . years and years . . . some say he's a genius . . . some say . . ." As the auto chugged to a stop in a snowdrift outside Bentley's home, and the sounds of a piano came from the farmhouse, he said, "They call him 'Snowflake Bentley'. . . . Used to play the organ years and years ago, at church, when he was a young fellow. He don't now. Hasn't for years. Nobody knows why."

Bentley was in his element as he excitedly showed Powers how he did his snow crystal photography. "With almost incredible haste," Powers said, "he caught a flake on the board and rushed back to us." Bentley showed how he used a fine splint to transfer the crystal from the board to a microscope slide, and then press it down ever so gently with the edge of a feather. "One has to be very careful not to crush the crystals," he said. "If your hand trembles, you cannot do it. I have never used tobacco or drink on this account." When Powers asked him how he had remained motivated for such a long time, Bentley replied:

> Thirty-five years is a long time, isn't it? And in the country . . . well, you don't get any encouragement. You have to have enthusiasm in the country to study science, and anyone who lives with that work and hopes to carry it on . . . well, all he has is his own enthusiasm.

Not long after Powers left, another group beat its way through Jericho's snows and winter winds to Bentley's door. It wanted to make a movie of Bentley's work, probably much like the one made a few years before. In an article published about a year later in *The Guide to Nature,* Bentley wasted no time in telling about the movie.[3] In the opening lines he said:

> My photographic studies of snow crystals and water forms have been pursued over a period of thirty-five years. . . . Recently, the Bray Studios, New York, have made a lovely moving picture of them — Goldwyn Bray Pictograph No. 7001, entitled 'Mysteries of the Snow,' released over the Goldwyn circuit. This will enable millions of people to enjoy them.

And then, showing that in the promotion of his beloved snow crystals he would take a back seat to no one, he added: "All those who wish to see this picture should request the managers of movie houses to get it."

Five magazines covering a wide variety of interests ran articles on Bentley in 1921. The *American Embroiderer* showed its readers how Bentley's snow crystal designs could be "executed with solid plain-stitch or drop-stitch in bonnaz, or with space-stitches in hand embroidery,"[4] while the *Scientific American* said that his work required "all the patience and forbearance of the true scientist."[5] In the *National Magazine* Bentley said that "I have tried to make of life one long university course. . . . My service is for others; to do all the good I can, rather than to get rich."[6] As if the five articles were not enough, Bentley added three of his own toward the end of the year. They were published in London in *Pearson's Magazine.*

Though Bentley had for a number of years been running the farm with the aid of his nephew, Alric, his new-found fame made it next to impossible to carry his share of the load. There were letters and articles to write, more demands for photographs and lantern slides of snow crystals, and presumably more requests to give lectures in towns around Vermont and beyond. About this time, or possibly it was two or three years before when he was spending so much time on his snow crystal photography, he turned over most of the day-to-day running of the farm to a neighbor,

Clarence Shiner, whose wife was Alric's wife's older sister. The profits from the milk and hay produced on the farm probably were split between Shiner and Bentley. This arrangement, which gave Bentley enough income to live on, worked so well that it continued until his death. "My mother would always do the bookkeeping for Mr. Bentley," Shiner's daughter Helen said. "My father did all the work. . . . I think he owned the horses while Mr. Bentley owned the cows. There was an arrangement whereby they ran the farm on halves."[7]

❄

In December, 1919, the American Meteorological Society (AMS) was formed, and within a month the first copy of the *Bulletin of the American Meteorological Society* came off the presses. Two men, whose energy and enthusiasm knew no bounds, were largely responsible for these landmarks in American meteorology. They were Dr. Charles F. Brooks, who was trained as a meteorologist, and Dr. William J. Humphreys, a physicist who had turned his attention to the physics of the atmosphere. Brooks, who studied under Abbott Rotch at Harvard, was only the second person in the United States to receive a Ph.D. in meteorology.[8] He had a prodigious appetite for work on behalf of the fledgling AMS. He became its first secretary, a position he held for the next thirty-five years! He attended all of the AMS meetings, continually took notes, was active in committees, and published numerous articles in the *Bulletin* on meteorological activities across the country. He literally was Mr. Meteorology in the United States in the 1920s. In addition to all this, he was editor of the *Bulletin* for its first nineteen years. In 1931, he became both professor of meteorology at Harvard and director of the Blue Hill Meteorological Observatory.

Humphreys received his Ph.D. in physics in 1897 from Johns Hopkins, and after teaching for several years accepted an appointment as meteorological physicist with the Weather Bureau.[9] He was the first director of the Bureau's research observatory at Mount Weather on the crest of the Blue Ridge near Bluemont,

Virginia, but soon moved to the bureau's central office in Washington. His numerous researches were published in some two-hundred-fifty articles and in his classic book *Physics of the Air*. Known not only for his research but as a raconteur with a lively sense of humor, the cordial and portly Humphreys was in great demand to help run scientific societies. Among other things he was vice-president of the newly-formed AMS, its president in 1928–1929, and general secretary of the American Association for the Advancement of Science (1925–1928). Both Humphreys and Brooks held Bentley in the highest esteem, and in the 1920s would champion him and his work every chance they could get.

In 1920, Bentley, Humphreys, and Brooks were among the first to be elected as Fellows of the American Meteorological Society in honor of their accomplishments. Only sixty of the nearly six hundred members of the AMS were so honored. And in 1924, another honor came Bentley's way. As Brooks reported it in the *Bulletin*, the AMS awarded Bentley its first research grant "in appreciation of his wonderful results in snow and frost crystal photomicrography obtained during 40 years of extremely patient work"[10] It was only for twenty-five dollars, but it was the honor of receiving the very first grant that must have delighted Bentley most.

Bentley's name came up often during discussions of scientific articles presented at meetings of the AMS. One time Brooks and Humphreys could not agree on the composition of the tiny, completely round centers that frequently can be seen in the middle of a snow crystal. Brooks thought it was a frozen cloud droplet that gave birth to the snow crystal, but Humphreys thought it might be a hollow air bubble with ice walls. Brooks said he could not understand how the snow crystal could form "around a nucleus of air." But rather than debate it further, he said he would "ask Mr. Bentley to prick the round centers of crystals when he saw them."[11]

At the end of the meeting Brooks, like Cleveland Abbe so many years before, told those present about the fine work Bentley was doing and how they could help him. He said that while the AMS did not have the money:

> . . . for the furtherance of Mr. Bentley's most valuable investigations, the members of the Society could help him, and at the same time get most beautiful pictures, by asking him for sets. He sells glossy prints of individual crystal photographs for only 5 cents apiece, and lantern slides, mounted or unmounted, at correspondingly low figures (unmounted $2 per dozen). He has an assortment of many thousand photographs comprising snow crystals, window-frost, hoar frost, various other ice forms, dew, and clouds.

Bentley could not have found a better salesman to hawk his prints to the members of the American Meteorological Society.

Nearly ten years had passed since the *Monthly Weather Review* had turned down Bentley's article on his thirty years of study among the snow crystals. It was time to try again, this time with a manuscript titled "Forty years study of snow crystals." In December, 1923, two days after Christmas, Bentley wrote to Alfred Henry, the new editor of the *Review*.[12]

> Dear Professor Henry,
>
> At last I have found time to finish writing an article on snow crystals, and am enclosing you MS and photos for illustrations. I hope you will find it of sufficient interest to justify publication. The photos should be as near natural size as possible, and as funds for reproduction permit. Hoping the article will be both interesting and instructive.
>
> Sincerely,
W. A. Bentley
>
> P.S. I should like some separates,
> if you furnish such to authors.

Henry must have found the article "both interesting and instructive," because in November, 1924, when the first snows began to fall over Jericho, it was published. It would be the last major article published by Bentley in the *Monthly Weather Review*.

In the opening paragraphs Bentley tells how his work with the snow crystals began when his mother gave him a microscope "when I was about midway in my teens." He said that over the years:

> The work has not proved remunerative financially . . . yet it has repaid me a thousand-fold in the enjoyment I and others have derived from it, and in the satisfaction of having contributed a little to the world's knowledge.

As the years passed, his list of photomicrographs grew, until by the end of 1923 "my collection numbers 4,200, no two crystals being alike." About one hundred of his photomicrographs had appeared in 1923 in *Historja Naturalna Lodu* (The Natural History of Ice). Published in Poland by Antoni Dobrowolski, its nine hundred pages gave the most authoritative scientific discussion of ice of its time.

Bentley mentioned some of the curious observations he had made over the years. He wrote:

> Among the most amazing and puzzling phenomena occurring in cloudland during the wintertime is that the tiny cloud droplets . . . often retain their fluidity during zero weather, when greatly undercooled. More remarkable still is the discovery by the writer during recent years that there are times when these tiny fluid cloud droplets have imbedded within them solid crystalline nuclei of hexagonal form. By correspondence with Prof. W. J. Humphreys and others, I have found that science as yet can offer no wholly satisfactory explanation of these phenomena.

Bentley had every right to be amazed and puzzled by the phenomenon of undercooled droplets. Even today, after hundreds of articles have appeared on the topic, many mysteries remain. As for the hexagonal nuclei he saw within some undercooled droplets, all that can be said is that they have not been reported by atmospheric scientists today. Indeed, their very existence seems ruled out by thermodynamic principles. It's a pity Bentley's correspondence with Humphreys has not survived. If we understood exactly how Bentley came to his conclusion, we might be able to judge whether he had made an exciting new discovery or, as is more likely, was observing an artifact in the experiment.

Bentley pioneered an ingenious way to understand something about the relative sizes of the bumps, ridges, and lines that he saw on his snow crystals. He watched through his microscope "the modifications the crystals undergo as a result of progressive evaporation (evaporative erosion)" brought about as the minutes went by. If a particular ridge projected up above the face of the crystal much less than another ridge, it would be the first to erode away by evaporation in much the same way that wind and rain erode a small mountain faster than they do a much larger one.

Another thing that puzzled Bentley was:

> The nature of the nuclei around which snow crystals form. . . . If such nuclei are, as some assume, dust particles, they must be exceedingly small, invisible to ordinary microscopic vision, as none are found in my photomicrographs. That many of the crystals seize upon and crystallize around frozen cloud droplets seems very probable, as the nuclei of at least one half the crystals are tiny circular figures, looking much like an encased cloud droplet. Further support is given this theory by the fact that they correspond in size, also, with the cloud droplets.

Scientists today agree with Bentley that some snow crystals form around frozen cloud droplets, but in spite of decades of research still do not have satisfactory answers to Bentley's question: What is the nature of the submicroscopic nuclei around which snow crystals form?

Bentley ended his article by saying that the never-ending search for beauty in nature had been the main motivation that kept him going for decades.

> New and beautiful designs seem to be as numerous now as when I began the work forty years ago. While many of them are

very similar one to another, I have as yet found no exact duplicates. In this inexhaustible storehouse of crystal treasures, what a delight is in store for all future lovers of snowflakes and of the beautiful in nature.

In another article he expanded on this theme with eloquence and deep feeling, echoing thoughts expressed twenty years before.

Oh for a thousand hands, a thousand cameras, to preserve more of this exquisite beauty so lavishly scattered over the earth. And yet there should be no despair, for this miracle, like unto the miracle of spring's awakening, will come and come again for all time, either here or somewhere in the universe, for beauty and life and love are eternal, the things that make the universe worth-while and justify its existence.[13]

[1] The letter and aurora records are at the National Oceanic and Atmospheric Administration's central library, Silver Spring, Maryland.

[2] Sam M. Silverman and Duncan C. Blanchard, "Wilson Bentley's auroral observations," *Planetary and Space Science*, 1983, vol. 31, pp. 1131–1135.

[3] Wilson A. Bentley, "The beauty and interests of snow crystals," *The Guide to Nature,* 1922, February, vol. 14, pp. 117–119. The motion picture described here appears to have been lost.

[4] "Snow crystals," *The American Embroiderer,* January, 1921, p. 8.

[5] "Photographing snowflakes," *Scientific American*, 1921, vol. 124, p. 253.

[6] Fred Z. Holmes, "The soul of the snowflake." A photocopy of the article was sent to D. C. Blanchard by a now-deceased friend of Wilson Bentley. It appears to have been published in 1921, reportedly in the *National Magazine,* but a search through the volumes of the magazine from 1920 to 1922 failed to find the article.

[7] Oral communication: Helen S. Poissant to Duncan Blanchard, October 3, 1970.

[8] John H. Conover, *The Blue Hill Meteorological Observatory*, American Meteorological Society, 1990, p. 161.

[9] *Dictionary of American Biography*, Supplement 4, Charles Scribner's Sons, 1974, p. 409.

[10] Charles F. Brooks, "Mr. W. A. Bentley given Society's first research award," *Bulletin of the American Meteorological Society*, 1924, vol. 5, p. 21.

[11] Charles F. Brooks, "Discussion," *Bulletin of the American Meteorological Society,*" 1923, vol. 4, pp. 52–54.

[12] Letter on file in the records of the Weather Bureau, Record Group 27, general correspondence file 1894–1942, File Class 700.01, National Archives, College Park, Maryland.

[13] Wilson A. Bentley, "The beauty and interests of snow crystals," *The Guide to Nature*, 1922, February, vol. 14, pp. 117–119.

Chapter 14

No Two Smiles Are Alike

The rediscovery of Bentley and his work in 1920 by newspapers and magazines made him widely known across the country, but his neighbors could see little change in the way he lived. The giant wooden snow crystals were still nailed up on the side of the barn, and across the road several smaller crystals about a foot in diameter and painted white decorated the lattice work under the porch of Bentley's side of the farmhouse. True, Clarence Shiner was now running the farm, but Bentley could still be seen doing some of the chores. Should any of his neighbors be invited inside the farmhouse, they would see no change there. It was still a mess, the nightmare of many a housewife, with magazines, clothing, and boots gathered like wind-blown autumn leaves in every corner of the room. Frank Hartwell, Bentley's friend at the Burlington office of the Weather Bureau, said:

> Papers and bulletins lay in a circle around the table where they had fallen off onto the floor when he pushed them back to make room for the current occupation. . . . He would not allow his nephew's wife in his wing of the house; he said he never would find anything if he once turned *her* loose in there![1]

The farmers often had to hire their neighbors to help them at haying time or when potatoes had to be dug. Though Bentley was getting along in years, he never hesitated when a neighbor needed help in the fields. After a hard morning's work, the men came in to a dinner prepared by the wives. They may have put on a light shirt before they sat down at the table, but that was not enough for Bentley. He had a curious Victorian sense of decorum in such situations. "He put on a tie, one of those old-fashioned ties that stuck into his collar, and put on a coat," said Howard Wagner, who as a teenager had worked alongside the rest of the men.

> He said that a true gentlemen doesn't eat without a tie and coat. . . . I don't think he was like that when he ate by himself. . . . In those days the farmers usually had cider. . . . They made their own home brew. . . . They'd offer cider at noontime and Wilson always refused it. I never saw him take a drink.[2]

During earlier years Bentley had always enjoyed the company of his nieces and nephews and other children from nearby farms. He had led them along the banks of Mill Brook to where the big trout were lurking under cool moss-covered rocks. He showed them how the best swimming holes could be found where the waters ran quiet but deep under the protective branches of large trees. In the meadows he pointed out the remarkable geometrical architecture of spider's webs, and from the tops of nearby hills had them look upward to behold the grandeur of the clouds, dazzling white under a bright sun, as they grew and expanded upward in their passage over Mansfield, that Olympus of Vermont mountains. But all this was years ago. By the 1920s these children had grown up and either left the Mill Brook Valley or had married to start families of their own. Bentley turned his attention to a new generation of children.

Among these, one of his favorites was Clarence Shiner's daughter, Helen. Though Helen, eight years old in 1920, had three brothers, she apparently received more than her share of attention from Bentley. Half a century later, with eyes glistening, she vividly recalled the kindness of Bentley. Her parents took in summer boarders, as did other neighbors, and during summer evenings had an ice cream stand in the front yard, while nearby the young people played games. "It was always a joy to see Mr. Bentley coming down the road," Helen said. "He would not play in the games, but he would treat us to ice cream. . . . Another time he even put a tree house up for us. . . . It had a ladder instead of stairs." Bentley soon recognized a talent for singing in Helen and gave her singing lessons similar to those he had given years earlier to two of his nieces and other neighborhood girls.

> I'd go knock on his door. He'd always welcome me graciously . . . and then he'd go over to the piano . . . get the sheet music . . . and he trained me in the high notes. My voice would never break. . . . He never let me walk back home by myself. He'd walk me right to the door, and as we went home he taught me, oh, about the stars. I could pick the Little Dipper out, the Big Dipper, the North Star. And he told about the Northern Lights.

Bentley derived much pleasure and satisfaction in sharing with Helen and the other children his unbounded enthusiasm for the snow crystals. She said:

> Sometimes I'd go in after he had his evening meal and he'd say, 'Oh, I have all these pictures to show you.' And imagine, I was just a little kid now, eight or nine years old! But he took such an interest in showing me the pictures. I was right up to snuff and told him the snowflakes I liked and the ones I didn't like. I liked the lacy ones.

Helen remembered that Bentley:

> . . . always laughed and saw the funny side of things. Every day to him seemed like a vacation. . . . He could see beauty in everything. . . . I learned from him. . . . I think some of his philosophy of life rubbed off on me. . . . He wrote this in my birthday book: 'It isn't what we have, it's what we do and enjoy that makes life worth living.'[3]

Bentley's preferential attention to the young girls of the neighborhood, like Lewis Carroll's to Alice Liddell and her childhood friends, soon had the valley buzzing with malicious gossip from those who did not know him well. But from those who really knew him, there was no concern whatsoever. Wagner remembered:

. . . hearing my mother say that some of the women thought it just wasn't right that he'd go for these little girls, but my mother said that 'if I had a daughter I'd not be a bit afraid to trust her with Wilson Bentley.' He had no motive here. He just enjoyed beautiful things. . . . He saw beauty in girls. I don't know if I express myself well, but he saw beauty in little girls too that pleased him. He used to like to be with them and talk to them as if they were adults . . . and he heard every word they had to say and tried to make conversation with them. He [liked] women in general. . . . I remember one time he told me about someone . . . whose rhythm of movements had real beauty. . . . There wasn't anything smutty attached to this.[4]

Bentley's interest in girls extended to the way they smiled. Helen said:

Oh yes, but he didn't like my smile and he let me know it! I can remember one time when he was taking my picture, and he told me to show my teeth but not smile! I couldn't figure that out. He didn't like to have anybody's mouth go up at the sides when they smiled. If I remember the way he said it, they 'go up like a half moon.' He didn't like my smile, but he still took lots of pictures of me.[5]

Bentley was something of an expert when it came to women's smiles. "It was nothing unusual for him to digress to a discussion of the relative pulchritude of the curve of the lips of Mary Miles Mintern and Mary Pickford," Hartwell said, "and he never missed an opportunity to attend a cinema in which either of these women appeared."[6] But attending a cinema was not enough. Bentley bought or borrowed a number of movie magazines and photographed the features of Hollywood stars that he most admired. At the end of his photographic notebook for 1928 he wrote a list of photographs he wanted to copy. Among them were "Esther Ralston profile, *Photoplay*, Oct 1926: Perfect mouth, Laura La Plante, *Motion Picture*, Dec 1928." Laura's smile, however, may have had just the slightest hint of that dreaded

price I remember. It was a green label, Snowflake brand syrup.
My dad took orders for people he knew here.

And every year Bentley invited the Hadleys for a weekend in Jericho, where "he'd get a lot of people in the neighborhood and we'd have a sugar-on-snow party." There was one other person Bentley never forgot. She could not come to his parties, so every year he would wrap some maple sugar in a package and send it to Mary Pickford, his favorite movie star. She'd always write back with a letter of appreciation that Bentley must have treasured as much as his best snow crystal photographs.[11]

Leon and Carrie Hadley were very religious and went to the Baptist Church every week, and sometimes on Sunday afternoons attended services at the Spiritualist Church. "My father had a curvature of the spine," Robert said. "I think he thought if he went there . . . he could get some help." One Christmas, Bentley gave them a beautiful and inspiring montage of a cross made from twelve large snow crystals and sixteen smaller ones. "He knew they were religious people and that's why he gave them the cross," said Robert. "When he was here on Sundays . . . he never went to church. We did. He'd go out and walk around wherever he wanted to go. . . . He wasn't much of a church man." Bentley's aversion to formal religion apparently extended to the playing of some hymns on the piano. Robert once asked him to play a certain hymn, but Bentley would not, saying "You'll have to get your mother to play that song."

He had no aversion, however, to buying the sheet music and playing the popular songs of the day. "Every time he came here," said Robert, "he'd go down to Bailey's and find out what the latest music was." Two of the songs that Bentley brought back one day to play on the piano were *Tiptoe Through the Tulips* and *All by Yourself in the Moonlight*. Robert enjoyed having Bentley play for him and often begged him to stay another day. But Bentley's reply was always the same: "I can't, Bob. I've got to get back to tall timber." He would often call Hartwell when he was at the Hadley's. If the forecast was for snow, he would immediately head back to "tall timber," not wanting to miss any opportunity to capture on film the treasures of the snow.

Bentley occasionally visited the Burlington Savings Bank to make a deposit or withdraw some money from a savings account. When he had opened the account, he gave his occupation as "Snowflakes." Levi Smith, president of the bank during the 1920s, said that Bentley:

> . . . dressed in this little old black suit looking like a little country minister, more or less, and it was rusty with age. I think that was *his* suit. He wasn't one to waste much on clothes. . . . He was very much of a gentleman, very polite and self-effacing. The minute you spoke to him about his work, he fished in his pocket and got out these little cards with the photographs on them. He was eager to show them to you. . . . I remember one time he was standing in line at the depositor's window, and right behind him was the president of St. Michael's College, and I introduced Mr. Bentley to him. . . . He was very much interested in what the good God had done in the way of snowflakes.[12]

When Bentley went to the movies in Burlington, especially one starring Mary Pickford, he could not imagine others not enjoying it too, so often took some of the girls with him. It wasn't always Helen Shiner and her friends but sometimes older girls like Izetta Barrett and her sister Euretta. In April, 1921, Izetta, nearly twenty-one, was visiting her aunt in Williston, a town between Jericho and Burlington. The arrangements for one trip were made on April 19 in a letter to Izetta.[13]

> Dear Miss Barrett,
>
> Now try not to faint away at getting a letter from the "Snowflake" man. When on my lecture trip to Swanton, I learned that Mary Pickford's greatest photo play "Polly Anna" was to be shown at the Majestic Theater Burlington, this week thursday and friday. So I arranged to go, and have the snowflake pictures taken at my house shown too on Friday evening. And I

thought of you girls and wished you too, could see this great Mary Pickford picture. So I called at your house last evening, got your address, and Euretta's phone number, and am enclosing you — P.O. order for $2.00 to take you into the City on the bus, friday, and return Saturday, and buy your tickets. Further arrangements will be made to Euretta by phone. You girls gave me a very pleasant afternoon by that kind visit to me in the sugar works, and now I am endeavoring to give you an enjoyable evening in return. Your folks seemed very pleased to think you are going, and your Mother wished she were going too. Hoping this will find you well, and that nothing will prevent your going friday.

Sincerely,

W. A. Bentley

This letter shows how Bentley tried to cover every possible expense the girls would encounter. His mention of "further arrangements" probably concerned their staying Friday night at the Hadleys before returning to Williston on Saturday. The showing of his snowflake pictures at the theater was an arrangement he had with the management that billed him as "an exceptional added attraction."[14] At a brief intermission between the double feature, when the piano player took a much-earned rest, he would give a slide presentation of his most beautiful snow crystals. Bentley must have been intoxicated with beauty during such evenings, first from the sight of his own pictures sparkling on the screen, then from seeing the photogenic Mary Pickford smiling her way to the always-happy ending. Bentley left no record of it, but he must have thought that no two smiles are alike!

Although Bentley had hoped that "nothing will prevent your going friday," something did. Determined to carry through on his promise of a good time for Izetta (curiously, Euretta is not mentioned in a later letter), he wrote three months later when another Mary Pickford movie was in town.

Dear Miss Barrett,

As you will see, I am still endeavoring to give you that good time you missed when Mary Pickford was last in B. She is coming to the Majestic this week Mon and tuesday in the "Love Light," one of her first plays. So I am enclosing you $1.50 in P.O. hoping nothing will prevent your going this time. Your Mother thought you would prefer to go after the play to Essex Junction to stay over night. So I am enclosing you enough to do so, and to return to B next day, if you wish, and take the Bus back to your aunts. I am hoping to have the pleasure of seeing this play with you, and will, if agreeable to you, and storms or haying do not prevent. I wish you would phone Mrs. Leon Hadley, as soon as possible after arriving in town. Of course I will not know whether you will go Mon or Tuesday, as this letter may not reach you Mon. I am planning to go to Burlington Sunday afternoon, and if haying weather does not call me home monday, to stay over in B till Wednesday morning. Of course if you preferred, and arrive in B soon enough in the afternoon, you could see Mary Pickford at the afternoon matinee, and then, if you wished, take a car ride to Queen City Park, before going to Essex. My sole wish is to give you, who have been deprived of so many of the pleasures a girl ought to have, a thoroly [sic] good time, and the rest that change of scene and freedom from work will give you. With all best wishes

Sincerely,

W. A. Bentley

After receiving such a detailed letter, with so many options to choose from, Izetta finally got to see a Mary Pickford movie and thoroughly enjoyed it.

Bentley also took Helen Shiner and her friends for good times in the Queen City. Helen said:

When he took all of us to Burlington, there would possibly be six of us going down the street. Oh, we were having a wonderful afternoon. . . . It was a big treat for me to come from the country and travel down to Burlington. . . . He paid for our board and room with . . . a lovely lady and her husband [the Hadleys] . . . and we would go to the Strong theater, and after the movie we couldn't wait! We knew what was in store for us after the afternoon matinee. We'd go up on Church Street to the Concord Candy Kitchen and have a big banana split. And he was so happy. He'd get us all around the table. We always ordered what we wanted. We had that privilege. He never told us what to do. But he, I can remember, always had plain vanilla ice cream.

Bentley often took Helen with him when he had to give a lecture in the Burlington area. They had their own little vaudeville act.

I'd have to go and sing. He believed in a little recreation in the lectures. . . . At what we might call an intermission between the showing of his slides, he'd play the piano and I'd sing. And there would be so much applause that sometimes I'd have to go back for an encore. . . . Finally it got so I was singing too much and I used to beg out once in a while. . . . I was doing this from about age twelve to eighteen.[15]

For several summers in the 1920s Bentley made overnight trips to Camp Abnaki, a YMCA summer camp on North Hero, an island about thirty miles north of Burlington and in the middle of Lake Champlain. Bridges connected North Hero to South Hero and from there to the mainland, so the camp could be reached by trains several times a day. Alfred Lawton, whose job was to meet all the trains and bring passengers and their luggage to the camp, remembered meeting Bentley.

I'd introduce myself, carry the small suitcase with his clothes, and he would carry the case with his slides. . . . From the first time that I met him to the last time, he was always dressed the same. Black suit, black hat, white shirt, black tie. Certainly not a person of sartorial splendor but one got the idea it was

sufficient for him. . . . His talk about general things was not too
much, but when it came to snowflakes he would loosen up.

Around the campfire that evening he spun a spell with his
slides and his tales of the wonders of the atmosphere. "There is
where you had to admit that he was king of the hill," Lawton said.
At the end of the evening Bentley told his audience that after
chapel the next morning he would be available to show all the
pictures he had brought with him, should anyone want to buy
some. "He was definitely not a pressure salesman, and if you
found one you liked, fine, if not he would put them back in the
case — no problem."[16]

After Bentley visited the camp in 1922, a single sentence
in the camp newspaper poignantly captured the essence of this
disciple of the snows:

> Unknown glories of the snow and frost were revealed to us by
> this simple little Vermont farmer, who went not out into the
> world to acquire fame, but instead has been content to remain
> under the shadow of Mount Mansfield and let fame and the
> world come to him.[17]

---

[1] Frank E. Hartwell, *Forty Years of the Weather Bureau*, Long Trail Studios,
Bolton, Vermont, 1958; Copy on file in Special Collections, Wilbur Library,
University of Vermont, Burlington.

[2] Oral communication: Howard Wagner to Duncan Blanchard, October 2, 1970.

[3] Oral communication: Helen S. Poissant to Duncan Blanchard, October 3, 1970.

[4] Oral communication: Howard Wagner to Duncan Blanchard, October 2, 1970.

[5] Oral communication: Helen S. Poissant to Duncan Blanchard, October 3, 1970.

[6] Frank Hartwell, *Forty Years of the Weather Bureau*, Long Trail Studios, Bolton,
Vermont, 1958; Copy on file in Special Collections, Wilbur Library, University
of Vermont, Burlington.

[7] Robert B. Michaud, *Salute to Burlington*, Lyndon State College, 1991.

[8] Letter to the editor, Madelyn A. Brewster, *Boston Globe*, January 14, 1983, p.
14.

[9] Oral communication: Howard Wagner to Duncan Blanchard, October 2, 1970.

[10] Oral communication: Robert Hadley to Duncan Blanchard, June 22, 1990.

[11] Oral communication: Mary B. Bentley to Duncan Blanchard, October 3, 1970.

[12] Oral communication: Levi Smith to Duncan Blanchard, July 25, 1969.

[13] Copies of the two Bentley letters to Izetta Barrett were given to Duncan Blanchard by Izetta Barrett, June 20, 1990.

[14] Letter: Katherine D. Brigham to Duncan Blanchard, March 22, 1977.

[15] Oral communication: Helen S. Poissant to Duncan Blanchard, October 3, 1970.

[16] Alfred Lawton's undated letter about Wilson Bentley is on file at the Jericho Historical Society.

[17] *Abnaki Herald*, August 28, 1922.

Chapter 15

Riding the Lecture Circuit

Bentley seldom left Jericho during the winter months. He was afraid he would miss that one glorious, perfect specimen of snow crystal architecture. "Last winter I was to lecture in Buffalo before the Society of Natural Sciences," he told a magazine writer who interviewed him late in 1924.

> Just before I took the train at the village it began to snow, and I can't tell you how I hated to leave! A snowstorm is always so exciting to me. I never know when I am going to find some wonderful prize. But this time, when we had gone down the line a few miles, I saw that the flakes were becoming granular. Then I settled back, quite content. I knew I wasn't missing any chances.[1]

Vrest Orton, founder of the Vermont Country Store in Weston, a town in southern Vermont about eighty miles south of Jericho, said that:

> Late one fall I had invited this remarkable man to my house for a visit and to give a talk before a local group. After his highly successful lecture, I anticipated several hours visit with him in front of my fireplace. But he didn't feel he could stay. While he had been talking in the town hall, it had begun to snow. . . . He wanted to stay, I think, but he was also eager to go. He didn't make any actual excuses then, but as he got onto the train at the depot, he said something about not wanting to miss a single storm. He couldn't afford to, was the way he put it.[2]

Bentley's fascination with and utter devotion to the snow crystals so dominated his life that only once did he leave Jericho in the winter for more than a week. Of course he took his snow crystal camera with him. Dr. H. T. Barnes, a physics professor at McGill University in Montreal, had known of Bentley's work for over twenty-five years, and invited him to work in Canada during the first two months of 1925. Barnes, about the same age as Bentley, was interested in the formation of ice in rivers and especially the engineering problems associated with ice in the intake of the turbines of hydroelectric stations on the St. Lawrence River.

The last two days of 1924 must have been busy and exciting for Bentley, so much so that he neglected what had been as natural as breathing in and out, his daily listing of temperatures and cloud conditions in his weather notebook. These entries had been marching through the pages without a break in step for many a year, so their absence was significant. But the very next day, January 1, 1925, the entries appear again, though in a different handwriting, probably Alric's. The day before, Bentley and his cameras had left Jericho by train for the one-hundred-mile journey north to Montreal. "I experienced the thrill of anticipation, such as comes to an explorer about to enter unexplored regions," Bentley said. "Would the snowflakes be better, or the reverse there? And would the Canadian designs be even more marvelous than those secured in Vermont?"[3]

Bentley was met in Montreal by Professor Barnes. That same day, as if to herald his coming, an article in a Montreal newspaper featured his work with the snow crystals. The following week was a busy one for Bentley. He gave several lectures but, like any tourist, also enjoyed the sights of Montreal. "I spent a delightful week in that picturesque city, built around one of the most ancient volcanoes known, Mount Royal." During the week he met Barnes's son, William, who, like his father, had earned his doctorate in physics and was interested in the physics of ice. Four years later, William Barnes would make history by being the first to show by careful experiment that the water molecules in a unit

192

cell of ice locked themselves together in a hexagonal structure. His X-ray crystallography experiments were done at the famed Royal Institution in London in the laboratory of Sir William Bragg, a Nobel Laureate for his work with X-rays and crystal structure. Several years earlier, Bragg had deduced on theoretical grounds the hexagonal structure and unit cell dimensions of ice, but it was William Barnes who first showed that the theory was correct.[4] Most likely the younger Barnes had been influenced in his choice of research topics by his father. It is possible, however, that Bentley's lectures that first week in January of 1925 inspired him to push onward to solve the puzzle of the crystal structure of ice and snow crystals.

About a week later, Bentley went to Morrisburg, a small Canadian town on the St. Lawrence River about eighty miles west of Montreal, where Barnes apparently was involved in some research projects on river ice. He set up his camera in anticipation of photographing snow crystals "more marvelous" than those that fell back home in Jericho. Though it snowed several times in the next two weeks, only once did Bentley find the crystals of sufficient interest to take photographs. He spent time getting to know the people of the town. "They are a fine progressive people," he said, "kind and accommodating to a degree, and possessing many fine traits." He must have found the girls' smiles to his liking, for he added that "the girls of the St. Lawrence valley are [extraordinarily] lovely." On about January 22, Bentley returned to "dear old Vermont for a lecture at Randolph." Immediately after the lecture he went home. He said that "an attack of the grip kept me at home for ten days." One suspects, however, since he had brought his camera back with him, that he was anxious to return home to photograph the snows of Jericho, illness or no illness. He did just that during two storms the following week, then packed up and returned to Morrisburg on February 7.

But the snows that came in February were no better than those in January. Bentley found the air along the river too humid and foggy for his snow crystal work. He began to photograph frost formations on windows, and he gave lectures at towns near Morrisburg and at Queens University in Kingston, Ontario. His fame seemed to precede him. While passing through one town, he noticed a magnificent frost formation on the window of a hardware store. He had to photograph it. "I hunted up a photographer," Bentley said. "He seemed uninterested until he learned the snowflake man was the one desiring his services, after which he was most zealous in securing, by my help, what I wanted, a frost masterpiece."

Bentley appeared to enjoy his stay in Morrisburg. He found that the weeks:

> . . . went happily by among its friendly people, with music and
> song, and friendly converse. Much of my time was necessarily
> spent answering the flood of letters, kindly, appreciative ones,
> that I received from all over, even China, Turkey, and England,
> after the *American Magazine* article came out.[5]

This article, published the previous month, was the best and most extensive about Bentley and his snow crystals since the *Boston Globe* article of 1921.

On March 1 he left Morrisburg to return to Jericho. He had made many friends, most of whom he would never see again. "One knowing them," he said, "would not wonder that my eyes were moist as I took the train to leave them." With his friends left far behind, he sat in quiet solitude as the train rumbled along toward Jericho. Again and again a question kept coming to his mind: "Could it be that, through some strange freak of accident or providence, the one man who loves the snowflakes most had been born at the most favorable spot on earth for the study and photographing of them?"[6] He had obtained only sixteen snow crystal photographs during his winter's stay in Morrisburg. Adding those to what he had photographed in Jericho, he had only forty-two for the entire winter, one of his poorest efforts ever. But at winter's end he wrote in his notebook that he had photographed 4,362 snow crystals since 1885.

March 30, 1926, dawned clear and cold in Jericho with a temperature of barely ten degrees. Later that day, less than two weeks after he obtained his final snow crystal photographs of the winter, Bentley boarded a train at Burlington to begin the longest lecture tour of his life. In the next four weeks he would face audiences in Philadelphia, Baltimore, Boston, and New York City. As the train snaked its way south through mountains and along the Connecticut River, the blanket of snow that had heavily covered the landscape thinned and finally disappeared at Holyoke, Massachusetts. When the train passed into Connecticut, "I noted with great interest the outcrops of the ancient lava sheet that covers a part of the Connecticut Valley," Bentley later would write in a newspaper article about his lecture tour.[7] "It is the only extensive lava field in the east, except the Palisades on the Hudson River." He spent the night in New York City, and the next day went on to Philadelphia to the Franklin Institute where he was met by Dr. Howard McClenahan, who would be his host for the next two weeks and who had scheduled most of the eleven lectures on the tour.

McClenahan, seven years younger than Bentley, had been a professor of physics and Dean of the College of Princeton University, but had resigned a year before Bentley's visit to become Secretary of the venerable Franklin Institute. Though the Institute had attained eminence since its founding as a research facility in the early nineteenth century, McClenahan had a vision of it being far more than that. In addition to research, he felt strongly that scientists should also become involved in educating students and the general public. To that end he wanted to create at the Institute a great museum of science much like the Deutsches Museum of Munich. With boundless energy he presented his views to the public and eventually raised five million dollars. The museum he had long dreamed of would become a reality in 1934. But in 1926, he had just begun his mission of introducing the public to the wonders and beauty of science.[8] It is likely he had arranged Bentley's lecture tour to help do just that.

The first three days in Philadelphia were a whirlwind of activity for Bentley. He gave a lecture at the Drexel Institute, and another on the "Marvels of snowflakes and water forms" at the Franklin Institute. He attended a banquet at the Bellevue Stratford, one of Philadelphia's most luxurious hotels, where McClenahan had reserved a room for him. Bentley does not make it clear whether or not the banquet was in his honor, but the lectures, banquet, "and sight seeing, including an inspection of Independence Hall, the Liberty Bell, the bench where Franklin worked and other relics kept me pleasantly occupied."

Toward the end of the week "there was a chill in the air worthy of far northern climes. Cold winds prevailed, and to make it seem real home-like, along came a flurry of snow." McClenahan took Bentley to the Lawrenceville School, just outside of Princeton, New Jersey, where Bentley gave his third lecture of the week. They visited Princeton University and on Sunday, April 4, returned to Philadelphia. Bentley kept busy giving four lectures the next three days, three at local schools and one at Haverford College. But on Thursday and Friday he was able to relax and wander around the city. He found the Philadelphians to be a "fine, friendly, intelligent people. A keen student of faces, I soon noticed how very many people had 'pretty mouths.' Another pleasing feature possessed by a large percent was a just right slimness of figure." It seems clear that Bentley's "people" were mainly the young girls with attractive smiles!

The two men next went south to Baltimore where Bentley talked to students at the Gilman school. He had planned to give several unscheduled lectures in Washington, DC, but at the last minute, through the efforts of McClenahan, he was invited to give a lecture at the Massachusetts Institute of Technology. Though the Washington lectures had to be canceled, Bentley found time for "a flying sight-seeing visit." He made the most of it in brief visits to the Capitol, art galleries, museums, the Library of Congress, and the magnolia trees which were in bloom. "Washington is indeed a beautiful city," he said. "No wonder its girls are noted for their beauty. They just have to be to harmonize with their surroundings."

Heading back north, they stopped at the tiny town of Port Deposit, Maryland, located on the north side of the Susquehanna River about five miles from Chesapeake Bay. Here, in the town where McClenahan was born and grew up, Bentley talked about his snow crystals to an enthusiastic audience. He was impressed with the loveliness of the rural setting.

> No wonder the poets and song writers sing of the Delaware River [Bentley's geography fails him here]. It was very lovely there. I was almost homesick; its beauty was so like that of dear old Vermont.

But casting his expert farmer's eye downward, he came to a different opinion. "Yet the soil in this whole region seems poor. The scantily stocked fields, the scattering clumps of grass speak eloquently of a lack of fertility as compared to lands further north."

On April 14, Bentley said his good-byes to McClenahan and hurriedly headed to New York City. His lecture at MIT was to be given the next afternoon. He had time for only a brief visit with Dr. R. A. Wetzel, a physics professor at the City College of New York. Wetzel was one of the academics who had visited Bentley at Jericho in winters past to see firsthand how he did the near impossible in his photomicrography of the snow crystals. After enjoying "overnight the fine, kindly hospitality" of Wetzel, Bentley took the Boston express the next morning, arriving there at 2:30 PM. With little time to spare, he headed north to Cambridge to present an hour later his lecture on the wonders of the snow to students and professors at one of the world's most prestigious centers for science and technology. Curiously, Bentley makes no mention of how his lecture was received. He seems more interested in letting his readers know that he "accepted the kind hospitality, overnight, of Mrs. Hooper and her family, the wife of Burlington's one-time weatherman."

197

He returned to New York City the day after his MIT lecture. He had only one more on his schedule, a final talk at the New York Civic Club. But since that was over a week away, he went to Brooklyn to stay with friends. He mentions only "the friendly hospitality of Mrs. Elinor Durlacher and her fine family." Bentley's life had become entwined with that of the Durlacher's quite by accident three or four years earlier when, on a summer's day, he had visited the Hadleys in Burlington to find Florence Durlacher, a cheerful, sprightly teenager and the oldest of the Durlacher children, visiting for a few weeks.[9] The Hadleys had sponsored Florence's visit through the Fresh-Air Fund, an organization that since 1877 had helped city children to escape the oppressive summer's heat and experience life in cooler locations. When Bentley learned from the Hadleys of the good work being done by the Fresh-Air Fund, he immediately became involved. For the next five or more summers he sponsored visits from children living in New York City. Not only did he arrange for Florence to spend part of her summers in Jericho, but her younger brother and sister came along too. Bentley never had them stay at his home, but arranged for their board and room with Clarence Shiner and his family. Over sixty years later, Florence, long since married and still living in Brooklyn, recalled how Bentley "taught me quite a bit about photography, and all nature and its beauty." She remembered him as a "gentle man, a truly kind and really noble soul. He loved music and played the piano for hours if he had someone who would sing."[10]

During his stay in Brooklyn, Bentley became even more convinced of the virtues of the Fresh-Air Fund. There were two or three warm days, followed by:

> . . . sultry, sweaty nights, making sleep difficult. It gave me an inkling of what an inferno New York must be in mid-summer, and made me more grateful than ever that a kind providence had enabled me to have Fresh-Air children these last few years. Were I a millionaire, I surely would endow the Fresh-Air Fund.

Bentley had time to visit several museums. He was intensely interested in the meteorites at the American Museum of Natural History, the "huge iron-nickel stones that fell from space, and that probably were once a part . . . of some other world shattered by collision with some other heavenly body." He wandered down the halls in the Metropolitan Museum of Art, gazed at both ancient and modern statues, admired the gem stones, and nodded approvingly at many of the paintings, especially those of landscapes. But he had nothing good to say about what he saw in the "portrait section," and let his readers know exactly what was wrong.

> I looked in vain for one really pretty face there. It seems such a pity, with all the wealth of material at hand here in America, that the rare beauty and glory of the American girl has not been reproduced on canvas by some master painter's hand. If art, or that part of art reproducing portraits, concerns itself only with the commonplace, the homely and the ugly, then I have no great admiration for this part of art.

As if to refute what he had seen in the portrait paintings, Bentley walked along Broadway near Times Square, and stood in Grand Central station where he saw many faces:

> . . . of rare beauty. I think many Vermonters know of the writer's interest in smiles . . . from the view point of art and beauty. On my trip I found many [girls] possessing charming smiles. When complimented and questioned if they knew why they smiled prettily, the lucky possessors answer was invariably 'no.'

One wonders what unspoken questions the girls had after such encounters! The same question to a girl on a city street today is apt to produce a look of outright suspicion, a scream of terror, and a charge of sexual harassment. Fortunately, Bentley was living in a more innocent time.

His lecture at the New York Civic Club in Greenwich Village on April 28 was a great success. When it was over,

Bentley fielded questions with ease. Many he had heard before. One was: What practical use are photographs of snow crystals? He replied:

> Use? Why, a great deal of use. The photographs are already being used, and more and more uses will be discovered. They are used . . . as models for designs in the public schools and in schools of art. They are used for designs for interior decorators, for wall paper, for silk, doilies, china, any number of things. They can be used for all kinds of jewelry and glass objects.[11]

Apparently his lecture had been widely advertised; in addition to the large audience, so many journalists and writers were present that Bentley had to spend the following day filling appointments to supply them with photographs and other materials for their articles. That done, his lecture tour was over, and he was free to return to Jericho.

On the morning of the first day of May, he left Grand Central station. He changed trains at Albany, New York, and by late afternoon was nearing Vermont.

> As Lake Champlain came into sight with its wondrous appeal of beauty, its haunting memories, tears welled into my eyes, so strong an emotion did its loveliness, its memories, inspire. Thus ended a lecture trip that had carried the message of the snowflakes to thousands over a broad region, and that had also, through the landscape views shown, earned much publicity for dear old Vermont.

Bentley finally arrived home about 7 PM. Though he had to be tired, he immediately relieved Alric of the chore of making daily entries in the weather notebook. That night, along with notes about cloud conditions, he wrote that it had been a "beautiful day" with the temperature reaching seventy-eight degrees.

---

[1] Mary B. Mullet, "The Snowflake Man," *American Magazine*, 1925, February, vol. 99, pp. 28-31, 173-175.

[2] Vrest Orton, "Snowflake Bentley," *Vermont Life*, 1948, vol. 2, pp. 11-13.

200

[3] Wilson A. Bentley, "The 1925 snowflake season," *Burlington Free Press and Times,* exact date unknown, probably in March, 1925.

[4] William H. Barnes, "The crystal structure of ice between 0 C and -183 C," *Proceedings of the Royal Society* (London), 1929, vol. A125, pp. 670–693.

[5] Mary B. Mullet, *op. cit.*

[6] Wilson A. Bentley, "Some recent treasures of the snow," *Monthly Weather Review,* 1927, vol. 55, pp. 358–359.

[7] Wilson A. Bentley, "Vermont's snowflake artist: experiences on a recent lecture tour — snowflakes and pretty smiles his hobby," *Burlington Free Press and Times*, Burlington, Vermont, date unknown but probably sometime in May, 1926.

[8] W. F. G. Swann, "Obituary of Howard McClenahan," *Science*, 1936, vol. 84, pp. 475–477.

[9] Oral communication: Robert Hadley to Duncan Blanchard, June 22, 1990.

[10] Letter: Florence D. Clemens to Duncan Blanchard, March 7, 1990.

[11] William Weer, "Discovering nature's jewelry shop," *The Brooklyn Daily Eagle*, May 23, 1926, p. 4.

Chapter 16

Do Not Go Gentle . . .

Bentley's lecture tour, the newspaper articles written about him in the cities he visited, and his own never-ending production of articles made him and his snow crystals still more widely known. Even in Jericho, where his neighbors had paid little attention to his work in years past, people had at last realized they had a self-taught genius in their midst. Well, almost. A year before his lecture tour, Bentley had said that years ago he had arranged to give a lecture in Jericho, but only six people came. "A year or two ago," he quickly added:

> I again tried the experiment of giving my lecture here in the village, and my neighbors had interest enough to come. I think they found my pictures beautiful. They couldn't help that! I doubt, though, that they have changed their opinion of *me*. They still think I'm a little cracked. I've just had to accept that opinion and try not to care. It doesn't hurt me — very much.[1]

Those last two words reveal the pain and hurt that Bentley had carried with him for decades. Though dedicated to his art and willing to punish himself physically to perfect it, there seemed nothing he could do to change the lack of understanding of his work and the indifference to it that led some neighbors to think he was "a little cracked."

Change came slowly for Bentley. In the late 1920s, he was being called "Professor Bentley" by some people in Jericho and by writers who came to interview him.[2] Surely this academic title, given as a mark of respect for what he had accomplished, must have brought a smile to his face when he remembered that his brother, Charles, over forty years before, playfully and perhaps with a bit of derision, also had referred to him as "Professor Bentley."

Though he and his snowflakes were now famous, and he had many requests for pictures and answers to questions about his work, Bentley always had time for the children in the neighborhood. A short distance down the road west of his home was the one-room schoolhouse with its gas lights that were used on dark winter days. In the fall of 1928, twenty-five students were scattered among the first six grades, all taught by Miss Edna Bartlett. Bentley came to the school many times, not always to show his snow crystals but to play the organ for the children. "We had a lovely organ at the school," Miss Bartlett remembered. "A real old-fashioned one, nice sounding. High back."[3]

Requests for his pictures of snowflakes were always eagerly and enthusiastically filled, and Bentley's accompanying letters must have revealed the zest with which he pursued the hunt for that one perfect snow crystal. Though no such letters from the late 1920s have survived, one written on January 4, 1923, to a Miss Charlotte Bean of New York City is probably typical of those he received:[4]

Dear Miss Bean,

Your kind letter, enclosing $3.00 for photos snow and dew is received. I am sending you by mail 60 photos, and hope my selection will please you. It was generous of you to tell me how much you all enjoy the snow, etc photos, for it gives me pleasure to learn so many are enjoying them. The Jan McClures Magazine, and the Jan National Geographic Magazine, feature the snow etc photos. I wrote the article for the Geographic, and it pictures about 70 photos. I wish your order had come a little later, for to day I secured 24 brand new ones, some of great beauty. As usual, when good snow flakes are falling, I did not stop for dinner, or anything else, tho [*sic*] I had callers, and became ravenously hungry. What thrills you would have had, could you have been with me while at work, and seen the snow beauties in the originals under the Microscope.

Sincerely,

W. A. Bentley

"Some recent treasures of the snow," Bentley's next-to-last article in the *Monthly Weather Review*, appeared in August, 1927. It was brief, less than two pages of text, but they were followed by eighteen superb photographs of snow crystals. Missing, however, were those brilliant scientific questions that Bentley had asked and pondered in earlier *Review* articles. What is the nature of the submicroscopic nuclei around which snow crystals form? What role do snow crystals play in the formation of raindrops? Why do some cloud droplets remain fluid even in zero weather? Perhaps Bentley had become discouraged over the lack of interest of other scientists in these questions. That may be part of the story, but not all. It seems that the artistic side of his nature had won out over the purely scientific. Both artist and scientist had been beautifully balanced within Bentley since that day in 1885 when he obtained his first successful photographs of snow crystals. But by 1927, when the general public could not get enough of his pictures, while sculptors, painters, architects, and other artisans were using them in their work, Bentley was spending most of his time fulfilling their requests and writing articles about the elegance of the snow crystals. Even without this adulation from others, Bentley seems to have been programmed to pursue the haunting, ethereal beauty of the snow crystals. Nothing could stop him. This was foretold in that article of his in 1904 where he wrote that "though the beauty of the snow is evanescent, like the beauties of the autumn, as of the evening sky, it fades but to come again."[5]

A few months before the *Weather Review* article appeared, Bentley had published two articles in the *New York Times Magazine* and was pulling thoughts together for a third one. The first, on his snow crystals, had appeared on March 6, 1927. In it he wrote once again about how he got started, the difficulties in capturing the snow crystals on film, and why no two are ever alike. Although the crystals are delicate and easily broken, Bentley, in returning to a familiar theme, reminded his readers that:

> Nature's storehouse of these fragile jewels appears to be inexhaustible. In all likelihood 10,000 years from now, snowflake collectors will still be discovering forms new to science and never before seen by mortal eye.

The second article, on dew, appeared on July 31, 1927. Bentley imagined that the drops of dew on grass and plants had:

> . . . metamorphosed into surprising jewelry. . . . The edges of [strawberry] leaves are lined in pearls. The light down of the dandelion is adorned with diamonds, giving it an unwonted magnificence — one strange to the dandelion's humble birthright. Blades of grass are sceptres crusted with stones from Ophir, or blades of Damascus with glittering hilts.

The third article that completed Bentley's triumvirate of the water wonders of the atmosphere, but which would not appear until February 19, 1928, was on the frost.

On his sixty-third birthday, just ten days before his frost article was published, it began to snow in Jericho. And it continued to snow for the next three days. Late during that first day, with temperatures dropping to twenty degrees, Bentley started photographing snow crystals. It snowed another five inches that night and all during the next day. With crystals of nearly one-half inch diameter falling silently around him, Bentley, with barely a pause to eat, continued on with his photography. He was probably getting frantic by this time. Magnificent crystals blanketed the ground in a layer soft as velvet, and he could not photograph them fast enough. He needed help in changing his plates and carrying them to and from his makeshift darkroom. He got Alric's wife, Mary, probably somewhat against her will, to help him. Later that day Irene York also helped.[6] Irene, Mary's good friend, was the young schoolteacher at the Nashville school the year before Edna

206

Bartlett. It's possible that Irene, on her way home to West Bolton after school, had dropped in to visit Mary, only to be quickly drafted by Bentley to supply him with fresh slide holders when he needed them. That may have been the last time she visited Mary when it was snowing!

By the end of the day, Bentley had photographed sixty-six snow crystals since the storm had started, the most he had ever done in a twenty-four hour period. During the following two days he obtained thirty-four more, giving him a grand total of one hundred crystals captured on film during the four-day storm. Bentley jubilantly announced that this was a record for one storm, and the *New York Times* quoted him as saying it was "a birthday gift from kind Winter."[7]

Another milestone was reached in January, 1929, when Bentley photographed his five-thousandth snow crystal. On January 23, the *Burlington Free Press* said he had accomplished this unparalleled feat during a snowstorm on January 17, but Bentley's notebook shows he was still twelve short. It was not until a storm on January 29 that he went over the five-thousand mark. On that day, with light snow falling, blustering north winds and temperatures reaching four below zero, he photographed twenty-two snow crystals, "small and rather thin with features very delicate," to set a record for patience and dedication that is unlikely ever to be equaled.

❊

A month before Bentley photographed his five-thousandth snow crystal, his friend William Humphreys gave a speech in New York City. By now Humphreys was on the Executive Committee of the American Association for the Advancement of Science and President of the American Meteorological Society. The title of his annual presidential address was "Meteorology's frozen assets." In an analogy with the business and financial world, where frozen assets are unavailable for use until they become liquid, Humphreys mentioned several meteorological frozen assets that were in danger of being lost unless something was done quickly. One of these was

Bentley's photographs of snow crystals. Though Humphreys was well aware that many had been published, he knew that several thousand had been seen only by Bentley and had never left the farmhouse in Jericho. In an eloquent and moving appeal to his listeners and readers of the address, Humphreys told how the photographs had been diligently acquired over "a generation or more among the northernmost of our New England mountains," but now "this great wealth of material lies unused in the keeping of the patient genius who accumulated it. On any day . . . so inevitable an event as the snapping of the thread of a single life may indeed destroy utterly or scatter to the winds this unique collection of a lifetime." He said that "here is a rare opportunity for some one who wishes to contribute to uplift and progress." He described his vision of an attractive book containing mostly snow crystal photographs with a brief introductory text of no more than twenty-five pages.

> Thus would be made liquid — readily available to the scientist, the artist, and the layman — the meteorological assets, now mostly frozen, and in danger of being forever lost, patiently accumulated over many years by that rare and kindly genius, W. A. Bentley, of Jericho, Vermont.[8]

Humphreys' appeal was answered. In the audience that December day was Henry S. Shaw, chairman of the board of General Radio Corporation. Shaw, like Bentley, was fascinated by the vast ocean of air and all that moved within it. In later years he would give considerable amounts of money for the support of both the Mount Washington and Blue Hills Observatory, but now he was willing to underwrite the costs of publishing the book that Bentley had dreamed of for so many years. Shaw agreed to give the American Meteorological Society (AMS) fifteen hundred dollars or more if the Society would add to it five hundred dollars from a larger sum he had contributed for other purposes several months before. The Society quickly agreed to this, and Humphreys took on the task as editor of Bentley's book. Shaw's generosity, plus that of others who came forward during the next year and a half, assured that the book would become a reality.[9] The AMS began to buy from Bentley thousands of photographs of snow crystals, from which Humphreys and others would make the final selection for the book. Bentley could not do it. He was too close to his "treasures of the snow". As Humphreys put it: "This was a thing too intimate and personal for the artist himself to undertake."[10]

Two years passed from the time Humphreys appealed for financial help, and still the book had not appeared. It was a massive job to go through the many thousands of photographs, select the better ones, and categorize them according to crystal type, and Humphreys had many other jobs to do. But finally, early in 1931, the job was done, and Humphreys sent the photographs to the publisher along with a brief text explaining how Bentley did the photography and how the crystals were classified. The McGraw-Hill Book Company had agreed to publish the book. Later that spring they set the publication date for September 1931.[11]

Up in Jericho, Bentley carried on with life on the farm. Sometimes he worked in the fields and in the barn with Alric and Clarence Shiner, but most of the time he photographed what had enchanted him for a lifetime — the billowing clouds framed by Mount Mansfield, pearls of dew on spider webs on clear summer mornings, exquisite feathery plumes of frost on his windows after cold winter nights, and the "fairy-like tracery engraved within" the snow crystals that fell outside his farmhouse.[12] On Sunday, March 1, 1931, a "lovely day" as Bentley described it, with an early morning temperature of twelve degrees rising to thirty-four later in the day, he photographed a single snow crystal. That brought his total collection of photographs to 5,381! There would be no more. After forty-seven successive winters of snow crystal photography, he had taken his last picture. His old battered camera would never be used again.[13]

In April, as he had done every year since at least 1925, Bentley wrote an article for the *Burlington Free Press* giving the highlights of his life with the snow crystals during the year. The previous winter had brought little snow and Bentley photographed only forty-two crystals, but "as has been our custom for some years, the writer hopes to show a few of these newest designs from cloudland soon at Burlington movie houses." Publishers of textbooks used his designs and a glass company purchased some for reproduction on their products. "To give the people of Burlington an opportunity to see how exquisitely beautiful these new snowflake glass designs are," Bentley wrote, "I am placing one piece on exhibit in the window of Lapierre's camera shop." He saved for last the announcement of his forthcoming book with Humphreys.

> This book will serve to preserve the cream of my collection in permanent form, and insure against loss by fire or breakage of this wonderful collection of snowflake forms. It is an old dream come true. . . . It will serve to further increase the fame of Vermont's marvelous snowflakes, and to give added millions of people the chance to see them and be thrilled by their beauty.[14]

What Bentley did during the summer is not known, but one suspects he wrote often to Humphreys inquiring about the status of his book. His weather notebook with the daily entries that marched relentlessly through the pages disclosed nothing unusual. As always, his attention to detail was revealed by what he wrote every day. In addition to the morning, noon, and night temperatures, he noted the nature of any rain, light or heavy, and any squalls that had passed by. Sometimes he recorded a thunderstorm with intense lightning. Every evening he went outside to peer upward into the blackness to see if the shimmering, ghostly curtains of color of the auroras were there. He saw only three during the summer, but two on successive nights early in August.

In September, a long essay, "Hunting stones in Vermont," appeared in the *Free Press*.[15] "Among the possible pleasures of life," he wrote, "is the adoption of hobbies," and one of his was the collection and study of stones and rocks, "the foundation of the continents upon which we live." Few people outside of Jericho knew of Bentley's fascination with the rocks, but his friends and neighbors had known about it for years. In his front yard, he had built a small pyramid composed of many varieties of tiny rocks and pebbles, and scattered around the base were numerous larger rocks. Anybody dropping by to learn about his snow crystals, especially for the first time, was likely to first get a lecture on the rocks of Jericho and Vermont. In his *Free Press* essay, Bentley told about the two main kinds of rocks, the sedimentary and the volcanic, and how the glaciers had moved and scattered them over Vermont. He wrote about the semi-precious stones, the jaspers, epidotes, and garnets, and told his readers to look for the hard, red sandstone pebbles along the shore of Lake Champlain. Stone collecting has no season, he wrote, but "spring and summer are most favorable as regards our rivers and streams. . . . Green algae collects on the stones as autumn approaches, and the falling leaves . . . clutter up the gravel as winter nears." He ended his essay by saying that:

> . . . a collection of stones is not only a thing of beauty and interest in and of itself, but . . . we may learn from them, by means of their structure and by the fossils they contain, much of the past history of the earth.

One should not be surprised to learn of Bentley's interest in rocks and stones. Little in the natural world seems to have escaped his inquisitive eye, and he wanted to learn from it.

In October, Bentley published "Conical snow" in the *Monthly Weather Review*.[16] The article was brief, barely a third of a page. He said correctly that conical snowflakes "have a granular texture and are built up mainly from countless undercooled cloud droplets that have frozen loosely together." But his explanation of how the conical shape evolved from a single snow crystal falling through and collecting undercooled cloud droplets does not agree with present day ideas and experiments.[17] Nevertheless, Bentley was the first American to try to explain those curious, conical-shaped pellets of granular ice that sometimes fall from cumulonimbus clouds which penetrate far upward into the coldest regions of the atmosphere.

"Conical snow" was Bentley's last article. With it the curtain closed on a dazzling variety of newspaper, magazine, encyclopedia, and *Monthly Weather Review* articles that had begun in 1898 with the publication of "A study of snow crystals" in *Appleton's Popular Science Monthly*. Over the years, sixty-one known articles had tumbled from his pen in his Jericho farmhouse, and others may be waiting to be discovered in old magazines and technical journals that lie under decades of accumulated dust in attics and little-used back rooms of libraries.

By the end of October, the kaleidoscope of colors that marked the final blaze of glory for his sugar maples in their preparation for the coming winter was over, and Bentley's book still had not been published. Fall was beginning to turn into winter. Bentley busied himself around the farm and attended to his correspondence, some of the letters requesting the usual snow crystal photographs. He apparently made little money on these in 1931, judging from the lack of deposits to his bank account. His last deposit, for one hundred dollars, was in December, 1929. Since then he had made only withdrawals.[18]

November was a very warm month, the temperature falling below the freezing mark on only a few days. In his daily weather entries Bentley repeated many times that it was mild, a nice day, and summer-like. But a few flakes of snow fell on three days, and Bentley set up his old microscope and camera in the back woodshed in preparation for the snow crystals that surely would come in the weeks and months ahead. He looked forward to the winter with as much enthusiasm as when he first successfully used his camera back in 1885.

And then it happened, finally. The book, his life's work, was published. It was titled *Snow Crystals,* by W. A. Bentley and W. J. Humphreys. The day after Thanksgiving, Bentley received three copies in the mail. It was a large, spacious book, ten by twelve inches. The cover was dark blue and in the center of the front, embossed in gold, as if reflecting the early morning sun while falling from a dark blue sky, was a large stylized snow crystal. The frontispiece was a picture of Bentley with his camera. The first twenty-one pages, written by Humphreys, told how Bentley did the photomicrography and discussed the various forms of snow crystals, frost, and dew. But the rest of the two-hundred-five pages, with its 2,453 photographs, was Bentley's gift to the world of art and science. All but the final fifteen pages, which were of frost and dew, contained the most elegant of his snow crystal photographs. They were mounted twelve to a page and progressed from the simplest forms to the most complex. The book was a masterpiece.

Bentley wasted no time in expressing his gratitude to those who had brought it into being. He wrote immediately to Henry Shaw, and on the first of December, wasting no words, penned the following to Humphreys:[19]

> Dear Professor Humphreys,
>
> I received three copies of our book "Snow Crystals" the day after Thanksgiving and I am delighted with it. The text seems to me perfect, and the half tones are superb.
>
> Sincerely,
> W. A. Bentley

Humphreys was delighted with the book. He said it was "one of the finest pieces of bookmaking I have ever seen . . . a fine contribution to science, art, and the study of nature"[20] While both Bentley and Humphreys might be expected to like the book, what about the reaction of others not involved in its making? One book reviewer called it "a magnificent collection of snow crystal pictures," adding that Bentley's work "has been known all over the world through newspaper, magazine, and lantern slide publicity."[21] The reviewer for the *New York Times* called it a "handsomely made book, of large quarto size. . . . The reader marvels as he turns the pages at the variety of forms and the exquisite beauty of each one."[22] But one of the most eloquent expressions of praise and appreciation came from a schoolteacher in New York City. "I think the book is one of the most beautiful I have ever seen. There could be no finer expression of the beauties of nature in crystal form." It is a book:

> . . . at once so beautiful and so scientifically important. This book will ever remain the finest monument to the genius of Bentley that human beings could produce. It is simply gripping in its conveying to the reader the marvelous beauty presented in the simplest things of nature.[23]

When Bentley received the three copies of his book, he lent one to Mary and Alric in the other part of the farmhouse. About a week later, not long after he had written to Humphreys, he made a trip to Burlington. Upon his return he walked back home, Mary said:

> . . . either from Richmond or Essex Junction. . . . It was slushy and he had no rubbers on. He had invited more trouble. He was very stubborn. He wouldn't hire someone to take him home, nor telephone somebody to come and get him. He was determined to do what he was going to himself. . . . He was sick that night. I had the snowflake book in my part, and I went to give it to him, and he said, 'Don't mind. I've got an awful cold.' So I put it back on the table in my part and asked if there was anything I could do, and he said no, he'd get his own fire and go to bed.[24]

Every morning for the next two or three days, Mary knocked on Bentley's door and asked how he was. "He said don't come in. . . . He said he was OK, but he was awful hoarse." Bentley was sick but he refused to give in to it. Feebly he moved around his kitchen and did small chores in the barn. "I'd hear him out in the woodshed," Mary said, "so of course you didn't think he was that bad. I'd hear him making his fire." On Monday, December 7, he made his daily entry in the weather notebook: "Cold west wind afternoon. Snow flying." There would be no more. After forty-seven years, his daily weather observations had come to an end. And on that very day the *Burlington Free Press* ran a long article whose headline was: "Bentley's snowflakes now appear in book form." It is possible that Bentley never got to see it.

Mary vividly remembers what happened a few mornings later.

> He went to the barn that morning and got his milk and cream. That's when Clarence [Shiner] told Alric that he was awful sick. . . . 'He's sicker than he [admits]. . . . We'd better send for the doctor.' So we called Dr. Berry. . . . He came up but [Wilson] didn't want to let him in. . . . He wasn't going to let any doctor in. . . . He was stubborn. . . . No doctors and no medicines. [Dr. Berry] hid behind the door, the outside door, and my husband went and rapped on the door and told him he wanted to give him something. When he opened the door, they hurried right in. The doctor said he was a sick man. . . . You couldn't live in his part 'cause there's no fire to speak of, so we moved him over to our part, and we got a trained nurse.

For the next week and on into a second, the nurse and Mary tried to take care of Bentley, but he was not a good patient. He never had any major illness before, and he could not see why he needed all this attention now. He would get well and back to his camera and the snow crystals. His struggle to regain his health is reminiscent of the closing lines of the Dylan Thomas poem: "Do not go gentle into that good-night. Rage, rage against the dying of the light." No amount of rage, however, was going to change the inevitable end to which his illness was now taking him. At three-thirty in the morning of December 23, Wilson Bentley, weakened by lobar pneumonia, "quietly dropped off," as Humphreys later said, "into that peaceful sleep that knows no waking."[25]

Later that day and the following day, all the leading newspapers of the country carried the news of Bentley's death. Editorials praised his accomplishments. Humphreys said that success "is not unto him who has acquired great riches from others, but to him who has made our lives more worth living. In this truest sense Wilson Alwyn Bentley was indeed a most successful man."

Of all the eulogies and tributes to Bentley, it was left to an unknown editorial writer in his own hometown newspaper to capture the essence of his greatness. Buried within a long editorial in the *Burlington Free Press* the day before Christmas were the following lines:[26]

> Longfellow said that genius is infinite painstaking. John Ruskin declared that genius is only a superior power of seeing. Wilson Bentley was a living example of this type of genius. He saw something in the snowflakes which other men failed to see, not because they could not see, but because they had not the patience and the understanding to look.
>
> Truly, greatness blooms in quiet corners and flourishes under strange circumstances. For Wilson Bentley was a greater man than many a millionaire who lives in luxury of which the "Snowflake Man" never dreamed.

The funeral was held on Saturday afternoon, the day after Christmas, in the Congregational Church on the village green in Jericho Center.[27] About seventy-five of Bentley's neighbors, friends, and relatives were there to say their last farewells. The night before, the temperature had dropped sharply, and during the early morning hours it began to snow. By noon, when the snow clouds had gone and the sun shone brightly in a clear blue sky, the ground was covered with a thin veil of white. The heavier blanket of snow on Mount Mansfield and its foothills sparkled in the afternoon sun, as if nature too were sending her final farewell to the farmer from Jericho.

Bentley was buried in the family plot in the Jericho Center cemetery alongside his parents, Edwin and Fanny, and his grandparents, Shelly and Abigail Bentley. Today a small, rectangular granite marker, not quite a foot high, marks his grave. On it, with his first name in large letters, are the words:

WILSON

SNOWFLAKE MAN

[1] Mary B. Mullet, "The Snowflake Man," *American Magazine*, 1925, February, vol. 99, pp. 28-31, 173-175.

[2] Constance L. Lyon, "Snowflakes," *Nature Magazine*, 1930, January, vol. 15, pp. 19-21, 57.

[3] Letter: Edna B. MacGibbon to Duncan Blanchard, July 25, 1990.

[4] Letter on file at the Jericho Historical Society.

[5] Wilson A. Bentley, "The wonders and beauties of the snow," *The Christian Herald*, 1904, March 2, p. 191.

[6] Wilson Bentley's last photographic notebook: 1922-1931.

[7] "Vermonter gets in storm 100 new snow crystals," *The New York Times*, 1928, February 19, Section 3, p.1.

[8] William J. Humphreys, "Meteorology's frozen assets," *Science*, 1929, vol. 69, pp. 255-259.

[9] "Washington meeting, May 3, 1930," *Bulletin of the American Meteorological Society*, 1930, vol. 11, p. 124.

[10] William J. Humphreys, "Wilson Alwyn Bentley," *Bulletin of the American Meteorological Society*, 1932, vol. 13, pp. 62-63. .

[11] "Bentley's snow crystal pictures soon to appear in book form," *Bulletin of the American Meteorological Society,* 1931, vol. 12, p. 136.

[12] Wilson A. Bentley, *op. cit.*

[13] Wilson A. Bentley's last photographic notebook: 1922-1931.

[14] Wilson A. Bentley, "The 1931 snowflake crop," *Burlington Free Press,* 1931, April 10.

[15] Wilson A. Bentley, "Hunting stones in Vermont," Burlington Free Press, 1931, September 8.

[16] Wilson A. Bentley, "Conical snow," *Monthly Weather Review*, 1931, vol. 59, p. 388.

[17] Hans R. Pruppacher and James D. Klett, *Microphysics of Clouds and Precipitation*, D. Reidel Publishing Co., 1978.

[18] Oral communication: Levi Smith to Duncan Blanchard, September 12, 1969.

[19] Letter to William J. Humphreys from Wilson A. Bentley: *Bulletin of the American Meteorological Society*, 1932, vol. 13, p. 7.

[20] Letter to Henry S. Shaw from William J. Humphreys: *Bulletin of the American Meteorological Society,* 1932, vol. 13, p. 7.

[21] *Book Review Digest,* 1932, p. 79.

[22] *Ibid.*

[23] August Klock, "Appreciation of 'Snow Crystals,'" *Bulletin of the American Meteorological Society,* 1932, vol. 13, p. 129.

[24] Oral communication: Mary B. Bentley to Duncan Blanchard, October 3, 1970.

[25] William J. Humphreys, "Wilson Alwyn Bentley," *Bulletin of the American Meteorological Society*, 1932, vol. 13, pp. 62–63.

[26] "Bentley's contribution," *Burlington Free Press*, 1931, December 24.

[27] "W. A. Bentley laid to rest at Jericho Ctr.," Burlington Free Press, 1931, December 28, p. 2.

218

Bibliography

The following list is not intended to be a complete bibliography, but it will give the reader a representative selection of books, articles, and other materials that relate either to Bentley and his work or to a general discussion of snow crystals and snowflakes. There are hundreds of papers in the scientific journals on snow and ice in the atmosphere. Anyone interested in looking at some should go to a university library and search them out in the index of the yearly volumes of, for example, the *Bulletin of the American Meteorological Society* and the *Journal of the Atmospheric Sciences*.

Bentley, Wilson A., and William J. Humphreys, *Snow Crystals,* McGraw-Hill Book Co., 1931. This is a magnificent collection of nearly 2,500 of Bentley's best photographs of snow crystals. An unaltered replication of this work was published by Dover Publications in 1962.

Blanchard, Duncan C., *From Raindrops to Volcanoes: Adventures with Sea Surface Meteorology*, Doubleday & Co., 1967. The first three chapters deal with the origin of raindrops, their size, shape, and methods to measure them. Bentley's ingenious use of flour pellets to measure raindrop size was used by many who came after him.

_____, "Wilson Bentley, The Snowflake Man," *Weatherwise*, 1970, vol. 23, December, pp. 260–269. This is a brief account of Bentley's life.

_____, "Bentley and Lenard: Pioneers in cloud physics," *American Scientist*, 1972, vol. 60, pp. 746–749. Bentley was the first American scientist to measure the sizes of raindrops and how they varied with the type of storm.

_____, "Wilson Bentley, pioneer in snowflake photography," *Photographic Applications in Science, Technology, and Medicine*, 1973, vol. 8, May, pp. 26–28, 39–41. This is a general account of Bentley's life with emphasis on his method of snowflake photography.

Borland, Hal, "A lifetime of snowflakes," *Audubon*, 1971, vol. 73, January, pp. 59–65. This article contains twenty-eight of Bentley's best photomicrographs of snow crystals.

Dodson, James, "Christmas in Jericho," 1989, *Yankee*, December, pp. 60–66, 110–113. It's about life in Jericho, Vermont, Bentley's hometown. Naturally, Bentley and his work are featured.

Hallett, John, and Charles Knight, "On the symmetry of snow dendrites," *Atmospheric Research*, 1994, vol. 32, pp. 1–11. This article contains some of the latest ideas on the growth of the branches from each of the six arms of a snow crystal.

Hapgood, Fred, "When ice crystals fall from the sky art meets science," *Smithsonian*, 1976, vol. 6, January, pp. 66–73. Bentley's work is discussed, as well as that of recent scientists.

Knight, Charles, and Nancy Knight, "Snow crystals," *Scientific American*, 1973, vol. 228, pp. 100–107. The authors discuss the growth of snow crystals and how temperature determines their shape.

LaChapelle, Edward R., *Field Guide to Snow Crystals*, University of Washington Press, 1969. This book has tables of the classification of snow crystals, and numerous photographs, many showing how crystals and snowflakes change form after being on the ground for several days.

Mullet, Mary B., "The Snowflake Man," *The American Magazine*, 1925, vol. 99, February, pp. 28–31, 173–175. Of all the magazine articles written about Bentley during his lifetime, this is probably the best.

Nakaya, Ukichiro, *Snow Crystals: Natural and Artificial,* Harvard University Press, 1954. Nakaya began his studies of snow crystals the year after Bentley's death. This book is a detailed account of all that was known about snow crystals. In the laboratory, Nakaya was able to show how crystal type varied as a function of temperature.

Powers, James H., "Fame comes to Snowflake Bentley after 35 patient years," *The Boston Sunday Globe*, January 2, 1921. Numerous newspaper articles were written about Bentley during his lifetime. This is one of the best.

Rudolph, Ron, "The Snowflake Man," *Snow Country*, December, 1995, pp. 104–109. Many articles about Bentley have appeared in recent years. This appears to be the only one that has featured an elegant snow crystal montage Bentley made from over 100 smaller snow crystals.

Schaefer, Vincent J., "A method for making snowflake replicas," *Science*, 1941, vol. 93, pp. 239–240.

_____, "Preparation of permanent replicas of snow, frost, and ice," *Weatherwise*, 1964, vol. 17, December, pp. 278–287. Schaefer's technique of capturing snow crystals in a liquid plastic that hardens in a few minutes was a big advance over Bentley's laborious and demanding snow crystal photography. Schaefer once said that one of his great regrets in life was not meeting Wilson Bentley.

_____, and John A. Day, *A Field Guide to the Atmosphere*, The Peterson Field Guide Series, Book No. 26, Houghton Mifflin, 1981. This lavishly illustrated book discusses not only snow crystals but clouds, rainbows and other optical phenomena, and the changes that take place around submicroscopic particles. The book is dedicated to a number of pioneers, including Wilson Bentley, who watched the atmosphere with "a sense of wonder, and a lifetime desire to understand what they saw."

Silverman, Sam M., and Duncan C. Blanchard, "Wilson Bentley's auroral observations," *Planetary and Space Science*, 1983, vol. 31, pp. 1131–1135. This article concerns Bentley's forty-nine years of auroral data and their correlation with the number of sunspots and other geophysical parameters.

Sisson, Robert F., "Snowflakes to keep," *National Geographic*, 1970, vol. 137, January, pp. 104–111. This is an excellent article on how to use Vincent Schaefer's method of trapping and preserving snow crystals within a thin plastic shell. Many crystal photographs are shown.

Stoddard, Gloria May, *Snowflake Bentley: Man of Science, Man of God*, The New England Press, Shelburne, Vermont, 1985. This biography was written primarily for children.

Bentley Mementos

Bentley sold hundreds of his snow crystal photographs and many boxes of 3 x 4 inch lantern slides of the crystals. Many of these photographs and lantern slides undoubtedly exist today gathering dust in attics and instrument rooms of universities and colleges. There are, however, three places where Bentley photographs, slides, and other mementos are carefully protected.

1. The Vermont Historical Society in Montpelier, Vermont, has some Bentley letters, photographs, articles about Bentley, and a copy of the only known movie that was made of him. The movie is only about two minutes in length, but it shows Bentley demonstrating how he took photomicrographs of snow crystals.

2. The Jericho Historical Society, located in the Old Red Mill in Jericho, Vermont, has a wealth of Bentley materials. In addition to numerous photographs of Bentley, members of the family, and his friends, the Society has a collection of glass plate negatives and lantern slides of Bentley's snow crystals, frost, and dew. Other photographs, Bentley's camera, and the small board he used to collect his snow crystals are in the Snowflake Bentley Room. In the Old Red Mill Gift Shop one

can purchase such items as snowflake earrings and pins, snowflake prints, and an article about Bentley. The Jericho Historical Society also has a copy of the Bentley movie.

3. After Bentley's death, the Buffalo Museum of Science in Buffalo, New York, bought most of the vast collection of Bentley's glass plate negatives. Since he took over 5,000 photographs of snow crystals, and he made duplicate copies of a great many of them, the Bentley collection at the Buffalo Museum is large indeed. They have been catalogued and compared to the nearly 2,500 snow crystal photographs in Bentley's book *Snow Crystals*.

Wilson Bentley's Published Articles

In the front pages of one of his notebooks, after a long list of the names of family members, acquaintances, and their birthdates, Bentley listed his articles. He was very casual about the listing. The articles were not in chronological order nor were titles or page numbers given. He listed only the magazine or newspaper, the month, and the year. In some cases he was not even sure of the year, listing it as "probably." A few other articles have been found, mostly with the help of historical societies and libraries. The following list, therefore, may not be complete, but it probably contains most of Bentley's articles.

Bentley's General Interest Articles

1. "A study of snow crystals," *Appleton's Popular Science Monthly*, 1898, vol. 53, May, pp. 75–82. This, Bentley's first article, is the only one in which he was not the sole author. The second author was George H. Perkins of the University of Vermont.

2. "A study of snow crystals," *Popular Science*, 1900, vol. 34, March, pp. 52–53.

3. "Studies of frost crystals," *Popular Science*, 1900, vol. 34, April, p. 67.

4. "Studies of rain drops," *Popular Science*, 1900, vol. 34, May, p 92.

5. "The story of the snow crystals," *Harper's Monthly Magazine*, 1901, December, pp. 111–114. He gives some detail on crystal growth.

6. "How to photograph snow crystals," *The American Annual of Photography*, 1903, vol. 17, pp. 51–59.

7. "The wonders and beauties of the snow," *The Christian Herald*, 1904, March 2. p. 191,

8. "Midsummer rain and hailstorms," *The Christian Herald,* 1904, September 7, p. 762. Other than his detailed article on raindrops in the 1904 *Monthly Weather Review,* this is his only other article on raindrops.

9. "Snow crystal and frost photography during the winter of 1903," *The American Annual of Photography,* 1904, vol. 18, pp. 33–39.

10. "Snow crystals," *St. Nicholas,* 1905, vol. 32, March, p. 459.

11. "The beauties of the frost," *The Christian Herald*, 1905, March 8, p. 214.

12. "Glimpses of snow and frost photography — winter of 1904," *The American Annual of Photography*, 1905, vol. 19, pp. 59–66.

13. "The latest designs in snow and frost architecture," *The American Annual of Photography,* 1906, vol. 20, pp. 166–170.

14. *Photo-Era Magazine*, April, 1907. This article could not be found. Bentley apparently made a mistake in listing either the month or the year.

15. "Snow and ice crystal photography," *The American Annual of Photography*, 1907, vol. 21, pp. 20–25.

16. "Photographing the forms of water," *The American Annual of Photography,* 1908, vol. 22, pp. 125–128.

17. "Snow, cloud and frost photography," *The American Annual of Photography*, 1909, vol. 23, pp. 201–204.

18. "Cover design," *Everybody's Magazine,* 1909, vol. 21, December. In his long list of articles Bentley said it appeared "probably September 1909." Yet in his notebook titled *Rain,* in the draft of an article for *Technical World,* he says that

"the charming snow crystal cover design" is on the December 1909 *Everybody's Magazine*.

19. "Marvel of the snow gems," *Technical World Magazine*, 1910, vol. 13, March, pp. 24–27.

20. "Photographing water wonders," *The American Annual of Photography,* 1910, vol. 24, pp. 84–86.

21. "Retrospection," *The American Annual of Photography*, 1911, vol. 25, pp. 110–114.

22. "The many uses of a low power lens," *The American Annual of Photography*, 1912, vol. 26, pp. 259–261.

23. "Snowflakes under the microscope," *Farm and Fireside Magazine,* 1914, December 19, p. 12. This is a short article of only three brief paragraphs, but it's accompanied with 10 photographs.

24. "Liquid jewels," *Pearson's Magazine, (London).* 1921, vol. 52, pp. 289–291. No author is listed and there is no text. This is a collection of twelve Bentley photomicrographs of dew. Bentley may have supplied the captions. He said that the photographs were part of a Goldwyn-Bray Pictograph.

25. "The marvels of a snowflake," *Pearson's Magazine, (London),* 1921, vol. 52, pp. 552–553. No author is listed and there is no text. This is a collection of about fifteen photomicrographs of Bentley's snow crystals. He must have supplied the captions. The photographs are part of the Goldwyn-Bray Pictograph.

26. "Jack Frost — artist," *Pearson's Magazine, (London).* 1922, vol. 53, pp. 152–153. No author is listed and there is no text. This is a collection of ten of Bentley's photomicrographs of frost. He probably supplied the captions. No mention is made of the Goldwyn-Bray Pictograph.

27. "The beauty and interests of snow crystals," *The Guide to Nature*, 1922, vol. 14, February, pp. 117–120. Bentley mentioned the Goldwyn-Bray Pictograph and says that "those

who wish to see this picture should request the managers of movie houses to get it."

28. "Photographing snowflakes," *Popular Mechanics Magazine,* 1922, vol. 37, pp. 309–312. The same article also appeared in *The Boy Mechanic,* Book 4, Popular Mechanics Press.

29. "Photographing snow crystals," *American Photography*, 1922, vol. 16, pp. 10–12.

30. "The magic beauty of snow and dew," *National Geographic Magazine*, 1923, January, pp. 103–112.

31. *Pathfinder Magazine,* 1923. This article has not been found. Did Bentley again make a mistake in listing the year of publication?

32. "Snow marvels," *Tycos,* 1924, vol. 14, January, pp. 16–17.

33. "Every snowflake a master design," *Popular Science Monthly,* 1924, vol. 104, January, pp. 44–45.

34. "Snow crystals," *The North American Almanac*, 1924, pp. 52–54. The North American Almanac Co., Chicago, Illinois.

35. "Hunting snow gems," *The Keystone*, 1924, April, pp. 161–169.

36. "The 1925 snowflake season," *The Burlington Free Press,* date unknown but probably in the spring of 1925. Bentley wrote about his trip to Canada, where he spent most of the winter.

37. "Los copos de nieve," *La Hacienda Magazine,* 1925, September, p. 270–271.

38. "Marvels of snowflakes and water forms," *Journal of the Franklin Institute*, 1926, vol. 202, pp. 99–101. Though Bentley is listed as the author, the article consists only of a paragraph by the editor plus sixteen of Bentley's photomicrographs of ice crystals. Bentley had read a paper of that title before the Franklin Institute on April 1, 1926.

39. "Vermont's snowflake artist," *The Burlington Free Press,* date unknown but probably May or June, 1926. Bentley wrote

about his lecture tour in April that took him to Philadelphia, New York City, and other places.

40. "Photographing snowflakes," *The Commercial Photographer,* 1926, September, pp. 428–431.

41. "Jewels of winter storms caught by the camera," *The New York Times Magazine,* 1927, March 6, pp. 14, 20.

42. "Glories of the dewdrops caught by the camera," *The New York Times Magazine,* 1927, July 31. The page number was not obtained, but the article was on a single page.

43. "Jack Frost designs jewels of his own," *The New York Times Magazine,* 1928, February 19, p. 8.

44. "Icy jewels of the winter storms," *Popular Mechanics Magazine,* 1928, vol. 49, pp. 116–118.

45. "Snowflakes, nature's wonder gems," *Hobbies,* 1929, vol. 9, pp. 147–150, 176. *Hobbies* was published by the Buffalo Museum of Science.

46. "The 1928 snowflake season," *The Burlington Free Press,* 1929, April 4. Bentley wrote about the one-hundred-forty new snowflakes he photographed the past winter. The title of the article is "The 1928 snowflake season," but it should be 1929.

47. "The 1930 snowflake crop," *The Burlington Free Press,* 1930, March 31. Bentley said he got two-hundred-thirty new snowflake pictures to bring his total to 5,340.

48. "The 1931 snowflake crop," *The Burlington Free Press,* 1931, April 10. A poor season, Bentley said. He got less than fifty new snowflakes to bring his total to 5,381. He had taken his last picture of a snowflake.

49. "Hunting stones in Vermont," *The Burlington Free Press,* 1931, September 8.

50. Wilson A. Bentley and William J. Humphreys, *Snow Crystals*, McGraw-Hill, 1931. The book contained only about ten pages of text, but about two-hundred pages of superb photomicrographs. Nearly 2,500 are shown, most of snow

crystals but some of dew, frost, and hail. An unabridged and unaltered replication of Bentley's masterpiece was published in paperback by Dover Publications in 1962.

Bentley's Technical Articles

1. "Twenty years' study of snow crystals," *Monthly Weather Review,* 1901, vol. 29, pp. 212–214. This was his first paper in the *Monthly Weather Review*, but on page 541 of the December, 1900, issue the editor mentioned Bentley's collection of snow crystal photomicrographs, and on page 118 of the *Review* for March, 1901, several paragraphs were reprinted from Bentley's 1898 *Popular Science Monthly* article.

2. "Studies among the snow crystals during the winter of 1901–2, with additional data collected during previous winters," *Monthly Weather Re*view, 1902, vol. 30, pp. 607–616. Here, among other things, Bentley attempted to classify the crystals as a function of temperature. This was the major contribution in this paper.

3. "Snow," *Encyclopedia Americana*, 1904, vol. 14, (There were no page numbers, but it has nearly two pages of text and two of photomicrographs). This is a fine article that shows that Bentley was well read in the subject. The same article appeared eight years after his death in the 1939 edition.

4. "Studies of raindrops and raindrop phenomena," *Monthly Weather Review,* 1904, vol. 32, pp. 450–456. This was the first study of raindrops in the United States and one of the best ever carried out. Bentley sampled from seventy storms and made deductions concerning the segment of the storm that gave drops of certain sizes. He commented on the relation between lightning and drop size. He discussed the evaporation of drops. His greatest insight, however, was the recognition of the dual origin of rain. It can evolve either from melting snow or from the coalescence of liquid drops. Here Bentley was many years ahead of his time. All the raindrop samples were obtained with his flour method.

5. "Snow rollers," *Monthly Weather Review,* 1906, vol. 34, pp. 325–326. Some photographs illustrated the article.

6. "Studies of frost and ice crystals," *Monthly Weather Review,* 1907, vol. 35, pp. 348–352, 397–403, 439–444, 512–516, 584–585. This was a long, detailed account that appeared in five consecutive issues of the *Review.* Bentley described the location of his farm in detail. Along with the text, he included thirty-one plates (nine photos to a plate) of frost pictures and some of hail. He discussed the nuclei and origin of frost crystals and their classification. He also treated the formation of hail, presented some cross-sections, and gave a theory of hail formation.

7. "Snow crystals," *Knowledge,* 1912, vol. 35, pp. 9–12.

8. "Photomicrographs of snow crystals, and methods of reproduction," *Monthly Weather Review,* 1918, vol. 46, pp. 359–360. In this article Bentley refuted the charge of Prof. Dr. Gustav Hellmann that he "greatly retouched" the crystals or "mutilated their outlines."

9. "Forty years' study of snow crystals," *Monthly Weather Review,* 1924, vol. 52, pp. 530–532. Bentley showed photographs of a number of crystals containing what he believed were numerous, tiny air bubbles arranged in a symmetrical manner in the crystals. He told his readers how he got started in this work. There is some fine writing regarding the beauty of the snow. By this time his collection of snow crystal photographs numbered 4,200.

10. "Some recent treasures of the snow, " *Monthly Weather Review,* 1927, vol. 55, pp. 358–359. He now has over 4,700 photographs. Bentley wrote about past years; 1921–1926 were poor. He told about his work with Barnes at McGill. The location there was poor for his work. He concluded that Jericho was the best location. He said, "Could it be that through some strange freak of accident or providence, that the one man who loves the snowflakes most had been born at the one most favorable spot on earth for the study and

photographing of them?" He used many terms like "magnificent, exquisite, marvelous." Among the eighteen photographs in the article was his "clock" photograph. On one day he got fifty-three photographs, the record for a single storm. He told of increased interest the world over in snow crystals. His text alternated from scientific talk to exclamations of beauty. He ended with "Perhaps it is not too much to say that the results of [my] studies form one of the 'little romances of science.'"

11. "Conical snow," *Monthly Weather Review,* 1931, vol. 59, p. 388. This is a short article of only two paragraphs. The same article, with an added first sentence saying he had seen "recent articles in *Science* treating of conical snowflakes," appeared in *Science*, 1932, vol. 75, p. 383, four months after his death.

Index

Bentley, Wilson *(continued)*

Bentley, Wilson *(continued)*